D1313443

EVERY OTHER INCH A LADY

AN AUTOBIOGRAPHY BY

Beatrice Lillie

Aided and abetted by John Philip
Written with James Brough

A DELL BOOK

Published by
DELL PUBLISHING CO., INC.
1 Dag Hammarskjold Plaza
New York, New York 10017
Reprinted by arrangement with
Doubleday & Company, Inc.
New York, New York 10017
Printed in the United States of America
First Dell printing—August 1973
Second Dell printing—January 1974

To all those who have ever helped me in life;
To all those who haven't helped and might even
   have hindered;
To my loving family, friends, colleagues and
   audience.
BLESS THEM ALL!

My special thanks to my loving sister, Muriel
(*Sister Ann*), for all her loving encouragement—
both musical and personal—over the long years.

To John Philip, who possesses a beautiful baritone voice, fine talent, looks and an excellent executive ability, and is blessed with the knowledge
that professional success isn't all there is to a satisfying life. His countless sacrifices for myself, my
mother, my sister and others, over the long
years, are clearly rare and are very much ap-
preciated. I am proud to inform one and all that
John Philip is a very special love; many splen-
dored and something else.

Beatrice Lillie

Of the many people whose reminiscences of Bea made a major contribution toward the writing of this book, special thanks are due to William Brice, John Brooks, Sir Noël Coward, Billy DeWolfe, Mary Lynn Gordon, Mary Martin and Muriel Lillie Weigall; a word of gratitude, too, to the staff of the City of Toronto Public Library.

J. B.

Unlike most autobiographers I have not attempted to achieve a record listing of Appendix- or Index-worthy names—from thousands available to me—since I have never felt that these "prestige listings" had ever made a book either better or more interesting.

I prefer merely to tell my life story—as a story— with a minimum of name dropping (for instance, Joan Ward; my gratitude for her loving editorial assistance). Something, however, must be sacred, if only out of respect for others; thus I have not quite "told all," though frequently nearly so.

If you know what I mean; and I *think* you do. . . .

B. L.

CHAPTER ONE

IN THE BEGINNING,
OR CONSIDER THE LILLIES

From time to time, I have been asked whether, in fact, I was *born* balmy. The question usually comes from friends, and I don't hold it against them. But sometimes it's posed by the merest acquaintances, when it has to be regarded as treacherous. What are they getting at?

Balmy as in "Tired nature's sweet restorer, balmy sleep"? (Thank *you, Familiar Quotations.*) Or as in "Now spring brings back balmy warmth"? Or in a ditty sung in my youth that had to do with "Ginger, you're balmy, You ought to join the army"?

Born "soothing, soft, fragrant, mild," or perhaps "mildly crazy, idiotic, foolish"? (It's *my* pleasure, Mr. Webster.) I decline to answer on the grounds that I might incriminate myself, and you wouldn't want that to happen, would you now? I'll simply say here that I was born Beatrice Gladys Lillie at an extremely tender age because my mother needed a fourth at meals.

9

When I arrived, there were already three of them sitting at the table, with the soup plates clean and the fish almost finished. The company was composed of the lady mentioned a moment ago, Lucy Lillie, later to be known as Mumsie; her spouse and my father, John Lillie; and sister Muriel, who had turned up twenty-one months and one week ahead of me. Our parents evidently concluded that four Lillies were enough for any bouquet, for no additional blossoms ever bloomed in our garden.

If you really must know, I was born in a year when Grover Cleveland was in the full throb of his second term in the White House, when Marconi was fiddling with the wireless, and Count von Zeppelin was discovering his what's-it. When the battleship *Maine* has been long since forgotten, I hope they'll remember me.

If memory is serving this set (it's my ball, Maud), the day I came from the everywhere into the here was May 29, and it was probably snowing. Imagination paints the scene crystal sharp.

"Another little baby Gemini!" cries the *accoucheur*, swinging me by the heels and taking even further liberties with me, who was to become a lady. Little did I know at that moment that the astrological company I was falling in with would include John F. Kennedy, Bob Hope, Rosalind Russell and Johnny Weissmuller. Oh, yes, and Bernard Shaw. Mother used to say we were distantly related, though she never mentioned the mileage.

"My branch of the Shaw family didn't think too much of Bernard when he was a child," she used to tell, darkly.

Surveying his squalling handiwork, Dr. Silverthorne sagely nods. "Gemini, the twin soul. The intellectual.

10

The quick learner with keen powers of observation."

Enter the nurse. She, too, is as familiar with horoscopes as with stethoscopes, and rather familiar with me. She puts in her two bits. "Her life will be romantic and picturesque. A fondness for dress and finery is indicated."

The man in white is unwilling to be outdone; after all, it was *his* party. "Great success is also shown in social circles," he snaps.

"A little jewel," answers the nurse.

"An emerald, no less," concludes the good doctor, restoring me right side up. Fade-in, fade-out.

I was brought up on cod-liver oil, oatmeal, rice pudding and church three times on Sundays. Perhaps the diet was too rich in hymns or short on protein. I don't know. But I was a rather *petite* child, knee-high to a hiccup. I fancy that only my nose went on growing after my twelfth birthday.

Not that there's anything remarkable, spectacular or offensive about my nose, if you want my opinion. Maybe the tip does turn up a *soupçon*, but no more than a *soupçon*. It's bigger than a button, but, dear me, who wants a button to blow? I venture to say that it's simply a good Irish nose inherited from the Lillies, who were Ulster Irish from Lillie Corners, Hillsborough, which is near Lisburn, which is near Belfast, in County Down. The family name was originally "Lille," which is Huguenot, from guess where.

My father was a fey and somewhat fancy-free Orangeman who, in later years, looked quite like Teddy Roosevelt, or, perhaps more accurately, like Theodore as played with mustache and eyeglasses in a road-company production of *Arsenic and Old Lace*. There was also a sort of Dickensian flavor about him,

11

which wasn't surprising, because of all the books he was forever reading, his favorites were written by the great Charles himself.

"Pa" made something of a habit of running away from home. His first departure was from the thatched, whitewashed cottage on the farm where he was born. As the saying goes, when he was in knee pants, he took off to enlist as a soldier of the Queen, me lad, and found himself with a shilling in his hand and a red coat on his back, whisked off to India to serve with Kitchener. Lord Horatio H. Kitchener, if you want to be formal; *the* Kitchener.

A fighting Irishman Pa never was. He got himself promoted as a non-commissioned officer to the general's staff. "Only once was I called upon to pick up my rifle, and then, thank God, it was a false alarm," he used to tell us, stuttering a bit, as he did when he was excited.

He came back from India and the army roaring drunk, singing at the top of his lungs and stumbling up the plowed fields round the cottage of his birth in Hillsborough. He carried a souvenir of his days of imperial glory—a marmoset clinging to his collar.

The monkey traveled with him on his second take-off, when he left home again to emigrate to Canada. But the creature vanished from all the tales he used to tell about what happened after that. There was no marmoset in view when he met the girl he determined to marry. That might be called his good luck. Mumsie *never* could have been one to suffer monkeys gladly.

She was an immigrant, too, but not, if you please, to be classed among any of your poor and starving masses yearning to be free. Mumsie was always a model of deportment. She was born in Salford, which was one of the more refined suburbs of Manchester,

England, when Lancashire stood for cotton and hot pot instead of skinheads and hot pants. She was christened Lucy Ann Shaw, but she changed her name, and billing, to Lucie Anne Lillie.

Her father, let it be whispered, was a draper, and there was some Spanish-Portuguese blood somewhere on my grandmother's side. You can still find "Lillie" and "Beatriz" sardines from Portugal in the fancy food shops, so the Portuguese bit must be true. The Shaws only stayed temporarily in Canada. Then my grandfather returned to settle down in drapery in Nottingham, England.

In my mother's unstated view, she stepped a few rungs down the ladder when she married John Lillie, who was a few years older than she. I don't see how she could have refused him. When he went a-courting, he'd bring her little bouquets that he carried hidden under his hat on top of his head and which he presented to her with a deep bow as he lifted his Pickwickian top hat, which he sported in the style of those days.

A little bit of heaven had fallen down from the skies one day onto the shores of Lake Ontario. So they sprinkled it with stardust, and it became Irish Toronto. There were a lot of us among the city's then 200,000 people. Mr. and Mrs. John Lillie hadn't far to walk to find other members of the clan, flourishing to the north, east and west, mostly bearing names, such as Uncle Isaac, from the Old Testament. There weren't any relatives to the south of us, because that was the lake, where the ferryboats hootle'd and tootle'd.

The choice wee blossom that arrived on May 29 was to be found exercising her lungs and various other odds and ends of her anatomy at No. 68 Dovercourt

Road, a red-brick house with a garden as big as a handkerchief in front and a yard the size of a postal card to the rear. It was—still is—one of several dozen such houses on the street that managed to squeeze eight narrow rooms within their skinny frontage.

What we came to regard as *our* bit of Dovercourt Road ran gently down from Queen Street, where the trolley cars of the Toronto Street Railway Company clanged their merry way. At the foot of the hill, Dovercourt Road ended at the point where it was crossed by a spur of the Toronto, Hamilton & Buffalo Railway. Freight trains whistled their way across the tracks, running to and from the factories and warehouses that lined the lakeshore.

As far back as I can remember, I wanted to be slightly grand, and Dovercourt Road wasn't quite the place for that. I've enjoyed my fair share of vanity, here, which when it's matched to a notoriously erratic memory has led to a certain amount of deliberate confusion, until now, about just where I first saw the light of day, and the light of day saw me.

The confusion was worse confounded on a return visit I made to Toronto after fame and I had exchanged a nod and I could have treated myself to an analyst and an ulcer, had I been so inclined.

After a good run on Broadway, the show I was in was booked to play in the old hometown. To celebrate my return, it had been arranged, so I was told, that I'd be given a royal reception as soon as I stepped off the train, then whisked off to be presented with the keys to the city.

"How wonderful!" I thought. "I'm absolutely panic-stricken."

I could see it all. Banners strung across the street: "Welcome home, Beatrice Lillie." Thousands of people gathered at the railroad station. A brass band blaring. Children let out of school for the day— Well, maybe that *was* stretching it a bit.

On the prescribed day, long before the train pulled into Toronto, I swathed myself in pearls and mink and rehearsed the repertoire of smiles. We arrived at the station in pouring rain. Banners? No. Crowds? Couldn't see a soul. Brass band? Well, you get the idea. There was nobody and nothing in sight.

Finally, after the sad truth had dawned—and set —my dresser and I caught a taxi to a hotel. We were in the middle of consoling ourselves and I was just testing the water in my tub when the keys of the city caught up with us. The mayor—Sam McBride, as Irish as Paddy's immortal porker—arrived, full of apologies. The train had been early and he had missed us in the rain, and would we please come on down to City Hall for the ceremony? Of course. Delighted. Ha! Hee-Ho!

At City Hall, I was ushered in through a side door, thank you very much! In a little room, an assistant of Mayor McBride was waiting with what appeared to be three stunted roses. No real keys to the city, but a typewritten scroll, tied with a dark blue ribbon. The mayor insisted on reading aloud every word. It turned out to be a perilous undertaking.

"The citizens of your native city give you a welcome as thrilling as any daughter of Toronto has ever had," he said, and the brogue was as thick as Irish coffee. He said I was a "genie"—the text, I noted, read "genius." He lost the place for a second, then resumed. "Your singable beauty and poise have endangered you to the hearts of thousands . . . for no one can waylay the fact that when Irish eyes are smilin', shure it steals your heart away."

Thanking him from the bottom of my galoshes, I made to leave. There were reporters waiting. Perhaps I'd care for a bite of lunch before I departed? I thought not.

"Then what do you say to a little ride round the city so we can shoot some pictures for a Sunday feature? You know, Bea Lillie revisits the scenes of her childhood and stuff like that."

Fool that I was, I agreed. We drove from hither to thither, covering the town from the bathing beach to the country clubs and taking in two cemeteries and the zoo in the course of our wanderings. Hunger pangs now nibbled at my stomach.

"Just one more shot," said a reporter. "The house where you were born. Then we can stop for a sandwich. Okay?"

"Roast beef on rye," I murmured.

Where was I born? I didn't care at that point. We'd made all kinds of moves in my childhood, and it was a long time since I'd mulled over my birth certificate data.

"Drive on," I said. "We'll come to it."

Down a leafy street in one of Toronto's more resplendent suburbs, I was satisfied. "Here we are," I cried. "This is it. That lawn. The tall white pillars by the front door. It all comes back to me."

Determined to put a finish to such nonsense for all time, I nipped out of the car, draped myself rather briskly round one of the pillars and smiled sweetly, a graceful hand outstretched. The camera clicked. We were back in the car and away before the front door opened and I caught a glimpse of the master of the house, emerging cautiously, with the look of a man who suspects that he may be missing something, possibly a screw between the ears.

The drive back to the hotel took us past another section of the city that I'd forgotten. If Chicago was once hog butcher to the world, Toronto didn't lag too far behind in the ham and beef business. The stockyards were steaming, and the whiff of slaughterhouses was strong in the afternoon air.

"We'll have that sandwich for you in a minute now, Miss Lillie," said one of my ink-stained companions.

"Skip it," said Miss-all-you-don't-catch Lillie.

As I was saying, I always wanted to be slightly grand.

Now then, if you haven't tried playing house under a freight car, take my word that it's *fun*. Canadian Roulette, I now label it. You have to crawl under with your dolls, you know, then squinch down between the wheels. Careful, now—don't get splinters from the wood ties in your bare hands or knees or anywhere else. All a mite greasy, perhaps, but it offers all necessary conveniences on a hot, humid day. You don't notice the train whistles blowing or the bells clanging because you hear them every day in the house.

So down the road went Muriel and I, to play house under a freight car parked near the lower end of the street—we decided it would make a change from running after fire engines, which was another game we played.

Muriel was the studious one, the one that Mumsie had real hopes for. I was the tomboy, the knockabout, the one who got blamed, no matter what, even when we were both no bigger than sprats and up to our you-know-whats in mischief.

We crawled under the freight car, and that became our house. Sister sits inside, I tap on one of the enormous steel wheels.

"Who is it?"

"It's me."

"How nice of you to call!"

"May I come in for a moment?"

"Oh, please do."

"Are all these your children?"

"Oh, yes, indeed, and they'll be the death of me. Won't you stay for a cup of tea?"

Pa saw us, though we didn't see Pa. He went off to fetch a friend of his on the police force who lived a step or two away. The two of them must have spent a minute concocting their act before they turned up on our imagined doorstep.

"What in the name of God are you two girls doing under there?" the policeman bellowed, his magnificently Irish face peering down into our parlor.

"We're just playing—"

"You can come out of there this second or I'll be in after you."

"But we're just going to make the tea—"

"Out!"

He had Muriel by the back of the neck in his right hand and a matching hold on me with his left. "These . . . two . . . little . . . girls . . . ought . . . to . . . be . . . in . . . prison," said the officer, giving us a shake with every word by way of emphasis. "Have I your permission to take them off with me, Mr. Lillie?"

Pa appeared to be fighting with his conscience. "Well, if you think it's the place for them, you'd better lock them up," he said, his face as straight as a poker.

I tore myself free and ran like a hare for No. 68,

straight up the narrow stairs and into my bedroom; a fugitive from justice, and me still in kneepads!

Worse was yet to come in my career of crime. Beyond the railroad tracks, further west, on the shore of Lake Ontario, lay paradise, known otherwise as the Canadian National Exhibition, a permanent feature of our city that opened up every summer with fresh attractions added year by year. I'd have been happy to spend every day of my life there, twirling on the rides, wandering in and out of the echoing halls, admiring the ladies in their cartwheel hats and the gents in their boaters, picking up the free samples, inspecting the Crystal Palace, which was a genuine replica of the one that Queen Victoria, God bless her, had opened in London some years earlier.

Make that "many years earlier." *Our* Crystal Palace burned to the ground in 1906, if anyone's trying to put a date on all this. Call this age clue number two!

Every summer, when the Exhibition was open, that's where you'd find me, early and late, lingering by the gates if I was short of the price of admission, risking family fire and brimstone and not giving a hootle. . . .

To my way of thinking, only one thing could be better than visiting the Exhibition and that would be to work there. The job I coveted was that of attendant at one of the booths, *any* booth where free samples were given away. I could see it all clear as day. I'd wear a beautiful little black dress and over that, a little white starched apron. On my hair there'd perch a lovely little linen cap. Oh, I'd look so *good*, and as the crowning touch, everyone would adore me on this pinnacle of glory because I'd be handing out the samples.

19

"Have a sample. They're free, you know. Nothing to pay. You don't have to buy. Just take a sample. They're for *free*."

One steaming August day, I couldn't stand the thought of *not* being a sample queen any longer. I just had to hurry on out to the Exhibition and get myself a job. Trouble was I didn't have the price of admission, pocket money being chronically tight and all other sources of income dried up for the time being.

My mother had a small sinking fund, a dollar or so in change that she kept well sunk under a corner of the rug in the living room close to the upright piano. When she wasn't looking, I swiped the lot (meaning to return it soon, of course, with my first earnings).

Scurry down Dufferin Street, in through the turnstile to see a man about a job. "Please, I'd like to have a uniform and give out samples."

I suppose one word for the look he gave me is "quizzical." He said, "How old are you?" A very suspicious man.

I claim it to be every woman's right to lie about her age. "Fourteen," I said.

"Not very tall, are you?"

"I've been very sick."

Ah, the pity of it! He gave me a job, right enough. But I wasn't handed any beautiful little black dress or a starched linen cap. I was too small, he said, for the sample trade. His ice-cold stare told me I was also too plain and gawky. The only uniform I got was a big coarse apron. I was put to work in the kitchen at the back of a booth; washing dishes!

It was a long, long way home that night, dragging aching feet and wringing my dishpan hands. My mother's money had all been spent, and I hadn't yet had my wages for washing all those dishes. She had gone to check her pot of gold and found it missing. There was only one suspect.

Pa was pressed into service as judge, jury and executioner. He put down his pipe, laid aside his book and escorted me upstairs. He unbuttoned the suspenders from his trousers and gave one of the bedroom chairs a whack fit to break the back off it.

"Now why the devil did you steal?" he stormed. I joined in the performance with a heart-rending sob, to give my mother her money's worth as she listened below.

"What's to become of you?" Wham on the chair again. "You ought to be ashamed." Perhaps I was, but I couldn't admit it.

I'd told another lie to the man at the Exhibition. I hadn't really been sick. I only pretended to be. It was necessary for the purpose I'd had in mind, and I tried to make a point of always getting what I really and truly wanted. Sooner or later, one always gets that, I think, regret it or not in the end, depending how things work out.

In the window of the drugstore on the corner of King Street there was a watch displayed that I was determined would be mine. It was the first and only prize in a contest which the druggist had devised to drum up business during the slow summer months, when sales were off in cold tablets, cough mixture and suchlike. Every time you bought something at the store, you were handed a ticket, a chance to win the watch, which seemed to me to be a thing of diamonds, gold and everlasting beauty.

I vowed that the only way any other girl would win that prize to pin on her blouse would be to kill me first. The day it appeared in the window was the day I decided exactly how I'd wear it.

The contest lasted a month, which was a month of nightmare for my family and for all adults who shopped at that pharmacy. The Exhibition hadn't yet opened for the season, so I had plenty of time to loiter outside the store. Everybody who passed by was subjected to a sales talk to persuade him to go inside and buy something. Everybody who came out was asked for the precious ticket that would give me another chance at the watch.

There was no school to attend, so I was out first thing in the morning to help the pharmacist open up. Last thing at night, I was still there to see whether I could drum up one more customer before he closed.

At home, I discovered that I was suffering from everything I looked up in the medical encyclopedia that stood on the bookshelf, bursting with bloodthirsty diagrams of tripe and onions. I had spasms, shivering spells, burns, cuts, nocturnal emissions and "that tired feeling." I had headaches, toothaches, stomach aches, arthritis, neuritis and inflammation of the mucous membrane.

Mostly, I was sent running to my favorite store to buy whatever my poor mother thought the malady of the day demanded. Sometimes, I went too far and lost a day's lingering because she'd put me to bed and send Muriel out for the medicine.

Malingering was rewarded. To the surprise of nobody whatsoever, I won the watch. By then, the bathroom cabinet overflowed with pills, lozenges, tinctures and lotions. With the watch came a complimentary case of real influenza, contracted on one of the closing days of the contest, when I hung around in the rain, finding customers for the druggist.

I considered it a moral victory. Fame was complete when my picture, watch dangling in full view on my blouse, appeared in one of the newspapers. After I'd stopped the sneezing and wheezing spells, I returned to the drugstore with Mumsie.

"I'd have given her the watch, anyway," said the proprietor, "if only to get rid of her."

By this time, the first of the 'precious stones' had already fallen out of it, and the 'pure-gold' case was starting to tarnish.

You might have called the Lillies lace-curtain Irish. If you called in the evenings, you'd usually find somebody home. We were middle class, reasonably contented and, I think, quite respectable until I came along.

We were located, I'd say, about halfway up the social ladder, or halfway down, depending on which way you're looking. At the bottom were the wretched, ragged families who survived somehow in broken-down shacks on the fringes of the city, or the immigrants, from Bulgaria and God alone knows where else, who crowded into the Front Street lodging houses. Pa was the only one of us who ever saw them; early on, he had a job as guard in the city prison.

At the top of the ladder, a long way off, were the elegant people who were making their fortunes as Toronto grew and prospered. Many of them lived in the section known as Hyde Park, in brand-new mansions, all gingerbread woodwork and ornamental railings, that were shooting up all round us. We didn't know much about the ways of the rich either, until Mumsie and her music started opening doors.

Music, if you could go as far as to call it that, opened up a few doors for me, too. Or, to be more ac-

23

curate, I opened a few doors and hopped inside to sing. I was always short of money, and it irked me. I never wanted to be poor. (Who does?) I needed a certain amount of money to keep up my style of life. Not a fortune, mind you, but a nickel now and then for a ride on the trolley that ran round the Belt Line loop with the conductor perched on the running board to collect the fares.

Or, as often as possible, a dime for the movies, which afforded me every conceivable joy. It was my only true vice. I couldn't have cared less about the plots or the scenery. But I bled and died over the characters. Every little heroine was *me*. It was best of all if she was shamefully treated and wept a lot. Then I really felt that my feet were in her poor shoes and all her sorrows were mine. Such delicious torture. I invariably came away convinced that I could have done a better job—a million times better—but it did cost a dime to get in, and dimes weren't always easy to come by.

More than anything else in the world, I wanted to be a movie star. I had the name all chosen to go up in lights. *Gladys Montell.* For a year and more, in school and out, I was lost in dreams of myself as the beautiful, bewitching Gladys.

I'd do almost anything to earn the price of a ticket. I ran errands for anybody who wanted errands run. I collected old clothes to sell to the rag-and-bone man. I begged, borrowed and on rare occasions just plain stole. (But I *had* to, officer; my children were starving.) *And* I sang selections from my repertoire to the shopkeepers.

There was the grocer. I'd skip in on my way home from school to give him a noonday concert. The bell *ping*ed when you opened his door. The shop smelled

24

of soap, bacon sliced on the cutting machine and biscuits, kept in big tin boxes on the floor in front of the blackened wood counter.

"Hello. What would you like me to sing for you to-day?"

I almost always knew what he'd ask for. "Well, now, what about 'I'm Daddy's Little Girlie, I Love Him Tenderly'?"

"Will you give me a nickel if I sing all the verses?"

"You sing them all through nicely, and I'll give you a dime."

There was the Chinese laundryman, small and pale —memory names him Ah Sooo. He seemed forever bent over his ironing board in an atmosphere of steam, starch and hot linen. He knew just about as much English as I did Chinese. We depended on smiles and nods for communication. He had a favorite song, too.

> Oh, for the wings,
> For the Wings of a dove!
> Far away,
> Far away,
> Far away would I roam,
> Would I roam . . .

One day he had waiting for me what he obviously thought would be a special reward. He gravely held out a handful of lichee nuts. Frustration. How could I tell him that I'd much prefer the usual nickel? *No likee lichee?* That might offend him. *Aw, nuts?* Mother would have considered that much too common. Ah, well! I dropped him a quick curtsy and departed sadly.

It seemed to me that I'd been going to school ever

since I was born, or maybe rather longer. Reading, writing and 'rithmetic weren't made for me. The only things I was ever halfway good at were botany, drawing and, believe it or not, knitting.

Going to school meant beetling along with Muriel, up Dovercourt, then a left turn on to Queen Street and a right turn up Gladstone. There stood the red-brick establishment that I loathed with all thirty-two pounds of my person, being rather dainty at that time. En route, we passed the end of another street, at that time not much more than a glorified alley, really, that bore the grand name of Peel Avenue, named for a certain British Prime Minister, who, along with many other achievements, set up his country's police force. I read about it after I'd become one of the family, but that, of course, was much later along in life. Little did I know then. After all, *honi soit qui Lily Pons*.

The only good reason I could see for going to school was that I could see my true love there. I dawdled away the hours at an inky desk, with hardwood seat attached by iron bars, waiting for the moment I would set eyes on him. His curly hair was turning gray, and there were those who would have said he was too old for me, but I would have laughed in their silly faces. His name was Alexander Muir, and he was the headmaster of Gladstone Avenue School.

In his study, there was a Union Jack, a Canadian standard and a portrait of Queen Victoria, who looked as if she'd been carved out of soapstone. He spent most of his time not there but talking to us children, whom he addressed as "young ladies and gentlemen."

He was a shaggy-headed St. Bernard of a man, who

used to play quoits with the older boys in the school-yard on Friday afternoons. I remember him wandering into the classrooms with something gentle about his eyes.

"What can you tell me about the moon?"

"It is opaque, sir."

"Am I opaque?"

"Yes, sir."

"Why?"

"Because you are not transparent."

Peels of laughter. Young ladies giggling and young gentlemen threatening fits.

He was my love, my hero, and he wrote "The Maple Leaf Forever," which we used to sing *con gusto* at frequent intervals, along with "Holy, holy, holy! Lord God Almighty."

I was one of the lucky ones who waited after school for him so that we could walk together down Gladstone Avenue on our way home. We listened to him sing and talk about his Scottish heroes, Bruce, Wallace and the rest. He could make us forget the tribulations of school like cake after spinach.

I'd tell my mother, "Mr. Muir must be a *millionaire*, the way he throws his money around."

He did that literally as we strolled along the street, flipping pennies in the air when we weren't noticing and showing more amazement than any of us at the sudden bounty tinkling at our feet.

He came to a peculiar and undeserved end. He'd taken citrate of magnesium to relieve a touch of indigestion. He followed that up by drinking a bottle of ginger pop. The combination, so the newspapers said, produced so much gas that it killed him within minutes. We believed it, whatever doctors might have to say today. Beyond the gold in his heart, he left very little worldly wealth.

Another memory belongs to those school days. If you'll only stop sharpening your fountain pen, doctor, I'll make myself comfortable on the couch and tell you all about it.

It was there, at Gladstone Avenue School, that sex first reared its ugly. The kindergarten class, which included me, had all trooped out for midmorning recess in the playground behind the school building. The playground was bordered by a wooden fence perhaps five feet high. On this morning, when we looked toward the fence, all we little girls noticed a man's face peering at us over the top and something sticking through a knothole immediately below.

It was, in Noël Coward's immortal word, his "nasty."

We young ladies were not exactly blushing Violettas. Nobody thought of running to find our teacher. When a teacher finally happened by, to shoo us all inside and raise the alarm, she found us busy, picking up bits of sticks and pebbles to throw at the target in the knothole, in an impromptu contest to see who could hit it first.

Guess who won?

CHAPTER TWO

TORONTO, 'TIS OF THEE

Not so long ago, a good friend of mine whose name need not concern us here—but since it must concern *her*, I'll tell you that it was Mary Lynn Gordon—said to me, "If you won't write a letter these days, how the hell will you ever write a book?"

I wasn't exactly hurt to the quick, only barely *past moderato*, but I was given cause for thought and reflection about how often she writes to me (often) and the number of replies she's received lately (very few; I send Polaroid snapshots with spicy comments on the back.)

I considered her point to be well taken when Chapter One existed only in the mists of an Irish memory. However, now that we've gotten this far down Memory Lane, I suppose we might just as well continue. But before we press on again, there's just one more thing to be said about the Gladstone Avenue School while I think of it: Mary Pickford went there.

That was long before my time, of course, and she was registered as Mary Smith. She left our hotbed of talent and knotholes to embark, ringlets and all, on a theatrical career with her mother. I met her later in Hollywood and latest in London when I had become Auntie Mame. Isn't it *super cool* that "America's sweetheart" was a Canadian. . . .

She is evidence, if evidence were ever needed, that a mother is usually helpful in a theatrical career, if not for other purposes. Dear Noël, for at least one, is always quick to acknowledge all kinds of debts to *his* mother, so who am I to lag behind?

Mumsie stood about five and a half feet tall. She was a little bit terrifying, majestically poised with a will of iron. She also had visions of improving all of us, which is the only imaginable reason that I can think of why she changed her name from Lucy Ann to Lucie Anne. Subtle? But little things like that counted with my mother. I'm not altogether sure that *I* did in our Dovercourt Road days.

She was convinced that one of her daughters was destined, or doomed, to succeed. That would be Muriel, of course. My sister had the talents, and I've had the luck. She's been the clever one, and I the one who made the money. That type of thing, if you know what I mean—and I still think you do!

Even as a very young girl, Muriel was something of a prodigy as a pianist. Mumsie required her to practice two hours—three times a day. I used to wonder why Pa found it necessary to keep some social engagements two or three nights a week down at the Masonic Lodge—he was a Grand Master, no less—at the Lodge, anyway.

My mother saw to it that I served time on the piano stool, too. Occasionally, I'd take over and spell Muriel when Mother was in the kitchen, in all ignorance of which one of us was pounding the ivories on the concert-tuned upright that stood against the wall on the parquet floor of the parlor. "None But the Lonely Heart," "Hold Thou My Hand, O Lord," "Fleurette" —these were the gems in my repertoire. I was bored to tears, but some benefit from the drudgery may have rubbed off. Anyone for "Kitten on the Keys" or possibly one of my own, early compositions entitled "Quinine, and How It Is Made"?

My sister and I had a lot in common, including the thick leather belts Mumsie had us wear high up over our midsections to encourage correct breathing at vocal lessons, for proper voice production. Muriel overshadowed me in everybody's estimation, including one schoolteacher we shared, Miss Abbott.

"Both are *exceptionally* bright girls," she once noted, "but Muriel is *brilliant*." The best she could find to report about me was that "Beatrice has a sweet disposition, gives little trouble; no signs of precociousness." Get her!

Mumsie could turn her hand to almost anything. Like Grandpa Shaw, who combined drapery with professional portraiture, she could put oils on canvas like an expert, or paint a kitchen ceiling, come to that. *And* she could sing, sing, sing. She even answered the telephone with a little practiced trill: "Lucie *Lillie*." I fancy the reason we moved so often from one address to another was that the neighbors got tired of hearing scales running up and down the house all day.

It would have taken a deputation of them to present their objections to her, because Mumsie was rather vague. She'd have brushed aside any single complaint like a moth on the wing. She was at her best at a party that Fanny Brice once gave on Fire Island. Moss Hart, the playwright, was there. Mumsie somehow thought

31

he was Buddy Rogers, that cuddly young man who had married Mary Pickford—remember?—and visited England with her some months earlier.

Mother to Moss Hart: "You're that lovely boy all the girls were crazy about in London."

Moss Hart (bewildered): "Yes? And I guess they still are."

Mother (con brio): "Oh, really? Whatever for?"

Of all the songs my mother taught me, and "Songs My Mother Taught Me" was one of them, it was an encore that she and everybody else used to do that became something of a hit of mine. The credit, or blame if you like, belonged to Ethel Barrymore, who said to me one day, "Now, Bea, here's a wonderful number for you," handing me the sheet music of "There Are Fairies at the Bottom of Our Garden."

I had by this time acquired a certain reputation for being slightly wild and witty, away from Miss Abbott, and I felt sure that she was fooling. I didn't quite know whether to scream with laughter or to keep quiet about it, since Miss Barrymore was not only a great actress but also decidedly grand in her own ways.

There'd been no doubt about that point ever since the morning she and I shared a London taxi on a ride which took us around Trafalgar Square, under the Admiralty Arch and up the Mall to Buckingham Palace. At the flagstaff on top of that edifice the Royal Standard was fluttering in the breeze, the traditional sign that the King and Queen were in residence. I hasten to add that the King in those days was George V and his Queen was Mary, known before their marriage as Princess May of Teck. Ethel was aware of that bit of English history, just as she knew almost everything else.

So as our taxi trundled past the tall iron railings and the Guardsmen on "sentry go" in their bearskins and smart red tunics, Ethel observed the flag and then observed in her classic droll manner, "Oh, yes, May Teck is at home." May Teck . . . my eye and Betty Martin.

How dare I inform Miss "B," then, that I couldn't and wouldn't dream of singing "There Are Fairies at the Bottom of Our Garden"? I simpered, "Oh, I don't think it's really a song for me."

"Sing it," she commanded. "It's just your style."

I disagreed violently, but in silence. Sam Walsh, who was my accompanist, joined in the Barrymore plot to add "Fairies" to the repertoire. He kept the sheet music on the piano for a year and more, propped up in the stack on his music rack. Whenever I rehearsed, "Fairies" always turned up somehow, played over and over by Sam until I couldn't help but know the song by heart.

"Why not try it?" Sam was continually coaxing, nudged by Ethel, who hated to see any idea of hers go to waste. I still said No.

Eventually, of course, they won. They trapped me when I was appearing at a New York club. The audience that night was especially responsive, liking everything I was doing. Then in the middle of the act, Sam started to play the introduction to "Fairies." No choice but to rise to the occasion as a trout rises to the fly. I raised a hand for silence and hurried into a few impromptu words of introduction.

"Here we have a famous classic written many years ago by Liza Lehmann and Rose Fyleman, and sung by many a great singer. Such as Galli-Curci—well, it says so on the music—Tetrazzini, Gladys Swarthout, Lily Pons, Lily Gish, Lily Putians (really!). All joking apart, I'm very well known in musical circles as Be-a-tri-ce *(Italian accent)*, Be-a-tri-ce, the mezzanine soprano. And the name of the song is . . ."

I still didn't think the song was all that funny, but the audience did, and have ever since. I always take direction from the audience, you see.

> Oh, the butterflies and bees
> Make a lovely little breeze
> And the rabbits sit about and hold the
> lights . . .

"Isn't that sweet?" I interrupted. Mumsie would not have been amused.

> The King is very proud and very handsome,
> And the *Queen*—well, can you guess who
> that may be?

I broke off again for a moment. "Sssh, now this'll *kill* you." It appeared that everyone in the crowded room was about to fall off his chair.

> She's a little girl all day,
> But at night she steals away.
> Well, it's *me (in a mezzanine-type shriek)*,
> Yes, it's me!*

With a nonchalant *Whee!* I whirled the long string of pearls I was wearing so that they swung out in a revolving loop around my neck. They continued whirling until they reached my feet. Fortune had

---

* "There Are Fairies at the Bottom of Our Garden." Copyright © 1917 by Chappell & Co., Ltd. Copyright renewed. Used by permission of Chappell & Co., Inc.

smiled again. A genuine, spontaneous, refuse-all-imi-
tations "Lillieism" had been born. (Always was lucky.)

My dear, it brought the house down and I hadn't
changed so much as a word of the lyric. On my right,
Ethel and Sam, the winners and still champeens.
"Fairies" had been ruined henceforth for every other
singer. It was sad in a way. Now—forever more—if
anyone stood up at an audition or on a concert stage
and launched into "There are fairies . . ." anyone listening would have to stuff a handkerchief into his
mouth.

Mumsie was a handsome and energetic soul whose
ambitions overflowed the walls of whatever nest we
were living in. She had her sights set with equal reso-
lution on the church, music, the concert world and,
if absolutely necessary, the theatre. In one if not all
of those spheres she would win acclaim. Or if not
Lucie Lillie herself, then her girls. While what *we*
wanted most was to go out to play, Mother kept us
hard at it, singing, playing the piano, learning to be
little ladies.

Muriel was obviously going to make a name for
herself as a *pianiste*, but what to make of me? I'm not
sure that either of my parents knew. My father used
to look at me sometimes and say, "Poor little perwerse
wee Bea." Yes, he said it with a "wee," just like Sam
Weller, and he *might* have spelled it per*worse*!

I took it to be some wonderful compliment, and I'd
answer, "Oh, thank you, Pa. That's the nicest thing you
ever say about me."

Years went by before I turned to Mr. Webster to
look up the meaning. Well, I really mean I'm not
like that at *all*, and never was, except maybe on festive
occasions. Muriel didn't fare quite so well here since

Father called her "Little Plain Muriel."

Mother was a pillar of a number of churches, more for social reasons than from any burning conviction. She was mostly an Episcopalian, though she ended up a Christian Scientist. It was as a Presbyterian that she cut the broadest swathe when Muriel and I were girls.

Three times every Sunday, the two of us went with Mumsie to a monstrous red-brick building that still stands on King Street, Toronto, not far from the St. Lawrence Market. Cooke's Presbyterian Church was almost new then and highly regarded by its congregation as something of an architectural masterpiece in the style known as Romanesque, with double banks of stained-glass windows roaming all over its front and twin towers covered in Spanish tile.

According to one issue of the parish magazine that Mumsie brought home, the church had been named for an Orangeman—was Pa impressed, I wonder—"who was singularly distinguished by his adherence to sound doctrine and stern opposition to the inroads of error and superstition." I'm afraid that dear Dr. Henry Cooke of Belfast would have classed me as an inroad of error. My passion for the limelight got the better of me within those hallowed walls.

To the twelve hundred people who packed the pews and the enormous upstairs rear and side galleries it may have been a house of worship, but to me, as I scrambled up the long flight of steps to the double entrance doors, it was a theatre, and the congregation was my audience.

The very first stage I ever appeared on was the small one (still there!) in the vast Sunday school basement area, deep down long flights of stairs directly beneath the church proper, where I first performed my child-hood repertoire for an audience at various Sunday school concerts and holiday shows.

The Sunday clothes I wore—button-through boots, straw sailor hat and God knows what else—were all a kind of costume for the show, not forgetting the white kid gloves that always smelled of cleaning fluid, as kid gloves still do.

"Take care not to dirty them, girls," Mumsie used to tell us. "Keep them in your pockets until we get into church." She took great pains over our clothes, most of which she sewed herself; dressmaking was yet an-other of Lucie Lillie's skills.

She led the choir, of course, and Muriel played the organ. What was there for me to do but add my rather small soprano to the choir? It seemed that I was fated to spend a hundred years of my life in the darkly polished choir stalls that stretched up on either side of the altar. While the Reverend W. Hardy Andrews preached redemption to the faithful, little perwerse wee Bea dreamed of other things.

Such as the matinee seen the previous day with my best friend, Madeline Small, whose father managed local theatres and gave us free seats sometimes to such extravaganzas as *Nellie, the Beautiful Cloak Model* or *Strongheart* or even *Bertha, the Sewing Ma-chine Girl.*

Or my mind would turn to our next summer's va-cation, when we'd be off on the train to Muskoka, eighty miles or so to the north, where our grandpar-ents then kept a summer home. Once we arrived, I'd be up and out of the house at dawn, breathing the cool, clear air, picking blueberries to carry back to the bed-room and give to lazy plain Muriel, still in bed.

And inevitably I daydreamed about my special, personal paradise, the Exhibition, and its candy floss, popcorn and the roller coaster. While the congregation was concentrating on saints and sinners, I could hear the barker at the toss-the-ring booth crying, "You toss 'em high and drop 'em low, and over the cane they're bound to go."

It will not come as too great a shock, I trust, if I tell you that I was thrown out of the choir often. Once, temporarily, for pulling faces during sermons and making bored little boys break out in giggles. The second time was more serious. I fancied that I had been permanently banished, and because I really thought I could sing in those days, it nearly broke my heart.

The cavernous interior of Cooke's Presbyterian had (and still has) a special odor of sanctity composed in part of floor wax, furniture polish and hymnbooks, but on Sundays the smell of dry-cleaning fluid conquered all. In the summers, when the days got hot and muggy, the overall effect was quite overwhelming, and the ladies of the congregation tried to keep the air moving by generous use of big palm fans, waved to and fro before their faces.

Muriel, busily bent over the organ keyboard, had no time for fanning, but I fanned enough for both of us, in full view of my audience as I queened it in the soprano section. My neighbor in the choir pew to the left was a large, flatulent lady whose best friends should have told her. I had to be careful to make every breath of mine match every one of hers, because I had serious doubts whether I should survive if I breathed in as she breathed out.

The root of her problem could be delicately diagnosed as indigestion. A soft *hic* and a quiet *hup* regularly punctuated the service. From time to time, her stomach rumbled inside her corset like a water bubbler. I tell you, we made all *kinds* of music in that choir.

The morning of my eviction dawned hot and humid. It was obviously going to be a great day for fanning at Cooke's Presbyterian. My musical neighbor must have breakfasted high on the hog. We had provided "Hold Thou My Hand, O Lord" while the collection was being taken up and settled down to listen to the Reverend Andrews' thoughts for the Sabbath when her digestive tract roused itself. Never had there been such *hics* and *hups* and *bubbalubbalubs.* Pretending not to notice, I maintained a steady rhythm with my fan.

And then, frankly, she belched. It was the sort of sound one imagines an oil well makes before it starts to spout. My, it was a *gas*—wind round her heart, you know. Without missing a beat, I lowered my fan and froze her with a glare. The one word I spoke could be heard loud and clear.

"Really!"

The congregation broke out into coughs, stifled laughter and broad smiles. But I was drummed out. Expelled. Dishonored. A disgrace to Mrs. Lillie. A brand doomed for burning.

The next Sunday, I was demoted to pumping the organ that Muriel played. Out of sight and shamed, I was determined to atone for my sin and win back my place as a soprano. But I pumped too hard and broke off the long wooden handle. For the following two Sundays, there was no organ music in Cooke's Presbyterian, only a tinkling piano, in the wings, if you'll pardon the expression.

My mother's taste in music ran to the secular as well as the sacred, just the way her ambitions combined financial with social advancement. The announcements of the Rich Concert and Entertainment Bureau at 706 Crawford Street, which she had selected to manage her career, said, "In her varied and choice repertoire of English, Irish, Scottish, Operatic or Sacred Selections, this *artiste* can be engaged for Concerts, etc." The significance of that "etc." was entirely innocent in those unsophisticated days when the Bureau could declare without a tremor, "For terms of Mrs. Lillie, call, write, wire or phone day or evening."

In its prospectus, next to an oval-framed picture of her in a lace-collared dress and cartwheel hat, the Bureau waxed lyrical about her abilities. "This charming Vocalist has won golden opinions as to her vocal powers and is considered an *artiste* of rare talent. On the Toronto Concert Platform, as city Church Soloist, or in backwoods Oratorio, her pure, flute-like soprano voice of great range and power—sweet, clear and of distinct enunciation, void of all affectation, but artistic and intelligent interpretation, accompanied by an imposing personality—has placed her without a doubt as one of Canada's most capable and foremost sopranos."

The Bureau even offered a "litho Window Hanger FREE" to stir up the customers.

The soprano voice of great range and power had led us to move far out of earshot of Dovercourt Road to a much better address on Sherbourne Street, where Mumsie conducted what she called her "vocal studio," teaching singing and voice production. Somehow connected with this ascent of the social ladder and not too many moons after the move, though he had progressed to the status of an official in the Toronto city hall, Pa pulled out temporarily for a little peace and quiet among his friends and relations in County Down.

My mother's tears as he left the house prompted one of my earliest efforts at comedy. It proved to be a fearful flop. I hadn't seen Mumsie weep before, and I didn't really know what to do to help her. But I told myself, "This is a golden opportunity to entertain her. I'll make her laugh and cheer her up."

I raced upstairs, covered my face with black ink, took the top sheet from her bed, liberally sprinkled it with what was left in the ink bottle, and draped myself artistically in the ruined bed linen. I wasn't quite sure what I was supposed to be, but I knew it was going to be hilarious.

I tripped gaily downstairs, humming to myself as I went, "La, la, la, da, da, da, she'll love this. She loves *everything* I do." I started to sing and dance.

It did dry her tears, that's for sure. And for another thing, it gave me what-for on my you-know-what. At the sight of my face and her sheet, grief turned into fury. Off to bed! No supper! I'd never been so simultaneously amazed, pained and upset. Somehow I understood. She held me close. All forgiven.

I was enrolled now at the George Street School, a block or two from our new home. A competition was under way there to elect the most popular girl, with a wrist watch waiting for the winner. My drugstore timepiece having long since given up the ghost, I burned with eagerness to win this latest trophy. My election campaign was plotted with the utmost care. I'd appeal to the voters' humanitarian instincts. I'd make myself a Worthy Cause.

On the morning of voting day, I got out of bed early to prepare a mixture of flour from the pantry and face powder from Mumsie's dressing table. Before I left for school, I slipped into the bathroom to apply this dead-white make-up to my healthy-looking cheeks.

I turned in through the school gates, coughing piteously. Without actually coming out and saying so, I managed to convince my school friends and classmates that my days on earth were numbered, and the number probably wouldn't run into double figures.

"Please, won't you vote for me?" I'd wheeze, seized with a fit of coughing that Camille couldn't hope to match. We were each allowed one vote. Need I go any farther? Another watch was mine.

As Mumsie was always drumming into us, "Be natural. Be yourself. If you have talent, it will be discovered."

She decided to take a hand in discovering whatever talent I may have had by enrolling me for polishing at the hands of the founder, proprietor and impresario of the Rich Bureau, Mr. Harry W. Rich in person, purveyor of "private tuition in dramatic gesture, elocution and mime."

He had been a concert comedian of local repute until an accident of some kind left him a cripple, confined to a wheelchair, nursing a walking stick. He also had a song or twelve of his own writing to his credit, so most of his pupils, including me, found themselves rehearsing amongst others "The Strawberry Girl," which he had composed twenty years earlier.

His principal instrument of instruction was his walking stick. He beat out time with it, and once he used it to beat me, to the extent of a clout over the head which I can't think was accidental. And I'd been imagining I was his favorite.

"Miss Beatrice," he'd say, rapping on the floor for attention, "you are not supposed to be flagging down a trolley car. Your hands must be *graceful*. Take it

42

from the beginning again." And again and again.

"Stop!" he'd shout, beating a tattoo with the cane. "Do you think you come here to learn how to swim? Every gesture must have *meaning*. You must express *ev-er-y sin-gle word*." The cane underlined every syllable.

What were the masterworks over which we labored together? Not, to be sure, *Hedda Gabler* or *She Stoops to Conquer* or *The Merchant of Venice*. By the week, the month, the year, we toiled over such novelties as "Who Are You Getting At, Eh?" sung in an English Cockney accent. We poured out *my* blood, sweat and tears over "The Strawberry Girl," complete with yodeling, and "Daddy's Sweetheart" with its quaint little Freudian refrain:

> I don't love anyone 'cept my Daddy,
> But he's already married, don't you see?
> Oh, if Daddy hadn't married Mommie,
> Daddy might have married me.*

We risked simultaneous heart seizures, pupil and coach, matching words and gestures in a ditty to which Frank Sinatra would probably take exception today:

> Niccolini, he play da hand organ,
> He have-a da monk on da string.
> He catcha da coin from da window,
> When songs of Napoli he sing. . . .

For each ethnic ballad, I had a different costume,

---

* "Daddy's Sweetheart." Copyright © 1911 by Chappell & Co., Ltd. Copyright renewed. Used by permission of Chappell & Co., Inc.

handsewn by Mumsie. One of my favorites was the geisha outfit in which I rendered "Mimosa San." Another was the Indian maid who tackled "My Pretty Kickapoo." But costumes or no, at that time I detested Harry Rich and his Bureau, too.

Yet what he taught me at such grueling cost to both of us has stuck with me. I ask myself sometimes today, "Why this particular hand movement you're making? Where did you learn the trick of turning your head in just this way?" I know the answer. It's a Rich Gesture, drilled into me by Harry W., the unforgotten man. I was brought up to do things his way, and now I confess I am grateful.

After what seemed to be a lifetime of lessons, he rated me good enough to become a Bureau *artiste* on my own account. I was billed on page thirteen of his catalogue—was this an omen?—as "Character Costume Vocalist and Impersonator." Mumsie was resplendent on page thirty-one.

My first professional photograph showed me with hair hanging halfway down my back—it did, too!—from under a hat almost as big as my mother's, clutching an extremely artificial rose to the middle button of my home-tailored tweed suit.

Mr. Rich's prose was as lush as a chocolate malted. "This exceedingly clever *artiste* has proved herself a bright particular star in her novel and highly pleasing impersonations and latest popular songs. A winsome, captivating presence, enhanced by a really sweet musical and trained voice, remarkable for its power, most graceful poses, expressions and gestures, and attired in numerous appropriate costumes, make this charming lassie a valuable acquisition on any concert program."

I had graduated, not lacking in caps and gowns

sewn by Mumsie. She had no need to spend time on letting out seams or similar future alterations. I was still the shrimp of the family except, dear God, for the nose. I was so disappointed with *that,* that I tried to avoid looking in mirrors.

However, the sedate, serene little *artiste* on page thirteen was wearing a disguise. Beneath the tweed jacket beat the heart of the Sherbourne Street cutup, who thought she was not only very funny, but somehow very sad.

My mother had begun holding what she rather grandly described as *soirées musicales* at the house every Wednesday. We were at home to musicians of all kinds, professional, amateur, aspiring and perspiring, and to music lovers and concert patrons, too. Mumsie enjoyed entertaining and being entertained. The joy of her daughters was more restrained, because we had to perform our pieces for the guests, and then we were sent up to bed before the evening was over.

Into the parlor, in their Sunday best, would troop Mr. Hartwell de Mille, Mr. Earl Reinholt, Mr. Eugene Lockwood with his dear mother and sister, and the rest of them. Muriel was the inevitable star of the show, head and shoulders better than anybody else in the company any evening. Selections from Gounod's *Faust* loomed large on her program, while Mother would burst into "The Lass with the Delicate Air" at the twirl of a mustache.

The house was heated by hot air registers, which had removable grilles over them, through which you could look down from the upstairs rooms to see what was going on in the room immediately below. On Wednesday nights, Muriel and I were in the habit of lifting off the grille from a register over the parlor, so that when we were packed off to bed, we could enjoy a gallery view of the gathering that continued below.

We'd been doing this for years, only temporarily deterred when Mumsie caught us at it. One time we thought we'd dangle our feet through the remarkably convenient opening in the ceiling, but we were spotted by one of her artistic disciples.

"Look up there, Lucie," he beamed. "Like two little heavenly cherubs."

Two pairs of angelic feet were quickly withdrawn, but not quick enough to save two pink *derrières* from being turned a trifle pinker. Discipline was rampant.

My sister and I were caustic critics of the artistic achievements of the guests. A promising young tenor once attacked the ever-popular "Wings of a Dove," which I regarded as the private property of myself and the Chinese laundryman. When we could stand no more, I helped myself to a handful of feathers from my pillow, and Muriel and I pushed them through the open register.

The singer was in the middle of pleading that he might fly to his home far above when goose down settled gently on his pomaded hair. One feather caught on his chin, another fluttered at his lips, and for a moment we hoped he'd swallow it. We thought the whole effect was highly satisfactory. Mumsie disagreed. But it was a victory for the younger generation. That was one tenor who never came back. And he came off lightly compared with the patrons who attended another soirée.

Over the front door there was a porch, whose flat roof served as an upstairs veranda. On this winter's night, the veranda was covered in snow. Dismissed too early to bed, I gathered the snow in a wastebasket, which I brought inside for the snow to melt.

As our guests were saying their farewells, they were treated to a sudden, unexpected drenching, and the temperature was drooping near zero. You know just how long that romp lasted and how many repeat performances were allowed.

In light of the hazards to which visitors were exposed, it's surprising that they came back for more. Some of them, looking to get up concerts and the like, went so far as to engage us through the Bureau for performances "as a whole, single or double," as Harry Rich advertised.

Mumsie, Muriel and I made up "The Lillie Trio," with Lucie Lillie as the shining star, Muriel as the piano soloist and I, in the words of the catalogue, "a serio-comic singer with a refined repertoire." The Bureau kept us busy. We appeared at everything from City Hall luncheons to one-night stands in remote communities a million miles from nowhere, bearing such names as Iroquois, Sturgeon Falls and Elk Lake to conjure with. (*Never* try conjuring with an elk.)

Mother didn't believe in compromising her standards, no matter where we ventured. The audience got Tosti's "Farewell" or "The Holy City" or excerpts from *Carmen* whether they were miners, Masons or madmen, and we'll get to the madmen in a minute.

I remember trying to hurry her on through the final bars of "Farewell" one night by creeping along behind the curtain out of sight and fetching her a whack with a broom. She exhibited remarkable evidence of her system of breath control; didn't miss a note. But by the time she'd finished lecturing me later on How to Behave Like a Lady, I was much more serio than comic and a lot more tender.

We had our ups and we had our downs. Down as far as Niagara Falls, up as far as North Bay, not too far from the Arctic Circle among oceans of pine and fir. We were booked into Cobalt, which is a mining community, and I hugged myself with joy at the news, because I wanted a gold nugget, and I had the idea that you could pick them up in the streets. Instead, I lost most of my possessions I was traveling with, except my toothbrush.

We were appearing with the Orpheum Stock Company in a bill that offered a dazzling array of divertissements, opening with "a rip roaring musical comedy by Will J. Stewart" entitled *Money Mad.* The cast of characters ranged from Patsy Tripp played by the author in person ("Too fresh," explained the program in true Cobalt style) to Jimmy Valentine ("Real safe blower"), taking in along the way Rose Rosedale ("Needs the money"), portrayed by a young lady identified as "Beattie Francis." That was *me.*

Mumsie drew a sharp line between the sacred and secular. "Lillie" was fit and proper for respectable church and concert work. For livelier engagements farther afield, we all became "Francis." Lucy Francis it was who starred in the olio, in full tone, fine feather and operatic selections. Muriel Francis was the musical director for the whole company. After the intermission ("Theatre bell rings in Colonial Café three minutes before curtain rises") Beattie Francis returned to the boards in a laughable burletta by Fred G. Brown, in which Fred played Buffalo Bill ("An Indian fighter") and Beattie was a young squaw, Rain in the Face ("Always dry"). Get that!

A letter a while ago from a companion of those faraway times did a bit of reminiscing: "I always remember Bea Lillie when she showed her first signs of having comedy talent. I remember telling you to slap my face, but you doubled your fist, nearly knocking me to the stage floor. I remember the song we sang together." Ah, yes!

> Run home and tell your mother,
> Your sister and your brother,
> That they'd better keep their eye on you.*

One night during the Cobalt engagement, when the "Grand Finale with twenty trained voices" had been concluded and the Francis Trio, née Lillie, was tucked up in bed, the hotel we were staying in caught fire. It was built of wood, and it made a pretty sight, blazing like a candle, surrounded by half the inhabitants of Cobalt and a bevy of sweating volunteer firemen. We were ordered out onto the muddy street with all the other guests, chilled to the marrow in spite of the heat. The upright piano from the main lounge was also evacuated, but that was about all.

After steering one coughing matron through the billows of smoke that poured from every doorway and window, I galloped back to our room. It was a waste of time and breath. I could scarcely see a thing for the smoke, but on the dressing table close to the door lay my toothbrush. I grabbed it and scurried back in double time. Mother hadn't even missed me.

I didn't care too much to watch the building burn. I felt slightly depressed about losing everything, and I wanted to cheer myself and everybody else up a bit. So while the hoses shot water onto the flames, I sat myself down at the salvaged piano in all that freezing mud and rattled through my entire repertoire, starting with "Hot Time in the Old Town Tonight."

* "Run Home And Tell Your Mother" by Irving Berlin. Copyright © 1911 by Irving Berlin. Copyright © renewed. Reprinted by permission of Irving Berlin Music Corporation.

Sometimes you had to be mad to listen to us. This happened once a month when we appeared at a Toronto asylum at the urging of one of Mumsie's soirée friends. Between the trio and the inmates, I was never entirely sure who was supposed to be entertaining whom.

One day the doctor who was serving as master of ceremonies whispered as we went into a ward, "Did you know that every place like this has its own Queen Victoria? There's ours, sitting by the window."

A plump little woman was regally occupying a creaking rocking chair. Suitably impressed by the doctor's remark, I thought it only fitting to drop her a deep curtsy as I passed. She acknowledged my homage with a slow nod.

"I should think so, too," she snapped.

One song of mine which invariably went down well within those walls was "Won't You Come to My Tea Party?" ("All your playmates will be there"). I'd finished the final chorus when one member of the audience who had been standing by the door came over to introduce me to a friend of his.

"This is Madame Nellie Melba from Australia, the wonderful, wonderful opera singer. I trust you have heard of her?"

"Oh, yes," I said. "I certainly have." Though I played along, I was sure that the real Melba was in London at the time.

"Never have I heard a voice as superb as hers. Such range. Such diction. Such quality."

I was tired after our performance. "Wouldn't you like to sit down?" I said. He ignored me.

"The world will never be privileged again to hear such a voice as Melba's," he went on, while his lady friend sat preening herself at his praise. I wasn't scared, just weary.

"Do sit down," I urged Madame Nellie's doting admirer. He turned a haughty glare in my direction.

"I cannot sit down," he said icily. "I've got a glass ass."

I should have known.

Somewhere in the wilds of northern Ontario, the Lillies crossed the fine line that divides the amateurs from the professionals. I can't pretend that we enjoyed it, not even perwerse me. The Bureau had booked us for a two-week tour that took us from one performance to another, farther and farther from home. We were part of another traveling troupe which was billed as "The Belles of New York." As I recall, it also included, for reasons beyond my understanding now, Artie Edmunds, "the pocket Hercules."

The three Lillies had undergone the usual changes of name. My sister, as before, was Muriel Francis, but Mumsie was now Lillian Withrow, and I—oh, joy!—was that scintillating star of the silver screen, Gladys Montell.

"The Belles" had a manager, who came along with us, paying the bills as we went, collecting the box-office take, keeping our money until the tour was complete. It turned out to be the old, old story. Halfway through our travels, he skipped out with all the cash.

We were *stranded*, with scarcely the price of a cup of tea between any of us. The hotel where we'd lodged the night before was holding on to our trunks. It was December, and the grisly rain that was falling promised to turn to snow. It was all too close for comfort to *Bertha the Sewing Machine Girl*.

"If only," I thought, "I were tied down on the

tracks and a train was whistling round the bend ..."

Rumors spread later that the Lillies and the rest of "The Belles" had been compelled to walk their way out of town along the railroad ties, carrying their baggage. Not so. We caught a bus, and shivered our way back. Practical as ever, Mumsie telephoned Harry Rich to tell him our troubles. He telegraphed her a hundred dollars to bring us home to Sherbourne Street. I like to think that Artie, the pocket Hercules, helped us with our bags.

"Well," chuckled Mr. Rich as Mother related her indignant story, "you're all actors now." I had just been baptized and couldn't have liked it more. ...

CHAPTER THREE

PERWERSE WEE BEA DAYS

God knows *why* I ever became an actress, and He, as they say, won't tell. Perhaps there was no choice open and I was born totally incapable of knowing the difference between acting and reality. Only You-Know-Who up there, with whom I try to talk sometimes, would know or maybe care.

Off stage or on, I'm the same inside. There aren't two of us sharing the same single, which is the design for living of quite a few people I know in my profession. It took a few years to discover that I was homogeneous, which hasn't *anything* to do with the boys in the band. (All right, look it up.)

Aspiration kept nudging me toward the stage; legislation demanded that girls of my age had to go to school. Of course, the law won, but it was a hollow victory. Whatever school I attended—and I went to three or four—I sat there with books mostly unread, the serio-comic with a refined repertoire, a value addition, as I fancied, to any program.

Madeline Small and I continued our deathless friendship, so I could count on seeing enough free

53

movies to feed my fancies. After we'd seen a professional strong man bend nails, straighten horseshoes and make his muscles dance, I thought I'd like to copy a bit of his act. Not with nails or horseshoes, but by making my biceps dance. I practiced for weeks in my bedroom, fingertips to forehead, concentrating. I did it eventually. Only the right bicep, though, so I couldn't hope for bookings as another Little Egypt. But that right bicep still remembers how to do it; nothing else moves from finger to shoulders. Show me a snake charmer and see what happens.

There was a burlesque house that we used to sneak into on Friday nights, when the management offered prizes for local talent. Amateurs weren't encouraged to take off their clothes. That was left to the girls of the chorus, who strolled around backstage wearing more make-up than underwear.

My eyes popped the first Friday I went there to try to win a piano. That was the grand prize. I hadn't figured out what I'd do with a piano of my own. Not play it, God forbid, but you might say I was naturally competitive. I loved to *win*.

I should have rather liked being a chorus girl at some stage of my life, but Mumsie would never have approved. The closest I came was when I was one of half-a-dozen music students picked as extras for a week's run in Toronto of the Bonstelle Stock Company. In all our glory, we appeared in *Captain Jinks of the Horse Marines,* in which a beautiful young actress named Ethel Barrymore had made her Broadway debut. But for that one week there was only one future star in sight at Shea's Victoria Street Hippodrome, and I still don't have to tell you who that was.

Meantime, back at the burlesque house, it came my turn to avert my eyes from the chorus and get out on the stage. I was feeling rather self-assured in a long white dress and convinced, after my success with wrist watches, that the piano was as good as mine. I'd give them an assortment of gems from my treasure trove, starting with the comic, moving on to the serio. With sparkling eyes and gestures by Rich, I launched straight into:

> Won't you come and splash me, splash me,
> In the ocean blue?
> This is not the place to mash me, mash me,
> But we oughta
> Step into the water . . .
> (*toe dips into imaginary ice-cold ocean*)
>   Ooooh!
> But when Percy said, "Oh, Lou,
> Is that the thing to do?"
> I said, "Come along and splash me
> And I'll splash you!"*

Where were the sweet sounds of applause? Sadly missing. Nobody seemed to think I was funny. I could see the piano sliding from my grasp. I had to try harder.

"Ladies and gentlemen, I should now like to sing—"

"Afraid not, dear," said the master of ceremonies. "Only one number apiece."

"But the piano—"

"Cheer up. Here's a box of chocolates."

One of the good things that came from that Friday night was a certain sympathy with the chorus—any

* "You Splash Me And I'll Splash You." Music by Alfred Solman, words by Arthur J. Lamb. Copyright 1907. Copyright renewed 1934. Reprinted by permission of the publishers, Edward B. Marks Music Corporation and Jerry Vogel Music Co., Inc.

chorus. It emerged in an encounter I had years later in Chicago, which enjoyed some notoriety among friends and gossips. We were playing in *Set to Music* at the Shubert Theatre when, one afternoon, I set off to keep an appointment to have my hair done at Elizabeth Arden's. When I arrived, I found that some girls from the company were also being processed.

In my little cubicle, the *coiffeuse* had almost finished coiffeusing me when a very uppity female voice came floating over the partition: "Oh, if I'd known there would be chorus girls here today, I never would have come."

I could hear the good lady being persuaded to wait a minute or two, and I asked who she was. I learned she was a certain Mrs. Armour, of the celebrated meat-packing brand. Now I was ready to leave, feeling certain that I looked rather well. In the waiting room, saying au revoir to the manageress, the chance came to say:

"You may tell the butcher's wife that Lady Peel has finished."

After all, when Sir Robert Peel, second baronet and twice Prime Minister of England, died falling from a horse, I had no intention of stumbling over a mere cow.

Flashing back to burlesque: Mumsie was not impressed and definitely not amused when I returned home with my box of burlesque-house chocolates. There was no hiding where they'd come from. Little perwerse wee Bea was up to her tricks again. To listen to Mother, there wasn't more than a hairsbreadth of difference between burlesque and a bordello. But nothing could stop me from going back the next Friday for another evening out with Madeline Small.

On a subsequent occasion, my mother herself

showed a preference for burlesque over Bea. *The Show Is On* opened at the Winter Garden, in New York, on a tropical Christmas Day in 1936. In this revue, I tried a little stripping myself, a kind of take-off, if you'll pardon the slip, of Gypsy Rose Lee.

I never knew precisely what one critic meant when he wrote, "It ought to be said in honest reporting that Miss Lillie does not husk herself in the wholesale manner of Miss Lee. Miss Lillie does more of a retail business." And what did he expect, when Grandpa Shaw was a draper?

In any event, Mumsie wasn't there to see it. She was across the way for the opening of a magnificent new hothouse of burlesque, the Oriental. She got carried away by the beautifully engraved invitation she received and figured that the goings-on at the Oriental might be a social cut or two above the Winter Garden première. "H. K. Minsky and Morton Minsky cordially invite you to attend ..."

Not so long after my losing the Friday-night piano, Mother was asked to be choir leader at the Presbyterian Church in Cobourg, some forty miles from Toronto. She had made friends there in the course of several summer visits. It was a well-paid job that she couldn't bring herself to refuse. So with Muriel in tow as church organist, Mumsie took off for pastures new, still with church three times a week, always on Sundays.

She always did her best to expand a booking. If anybody started off trying to engage Muriel to play the piano, as often as not Mumsie turned it into a job for the whole Lillie Trio. We made as much as fifty-five dollars a week that way, which at the time wasn't bad money at all.

But this time the serio-comic wasn't part of the engagement, and neither was my father. He stayed behind on Sherbourne Street, renting out rooms in the house which was now much too big for him, enjoying the company and the income of paying guests. *I* was diverted to boarding school.

Schooling and I still weren't made for each other. After I'd been entered for one establishment, I played hooky for a week, while my family imagined that I was enjoying the benefits of private education. That was at Loretto Academy, a day school. Now, being forty miles away, my mother wasn't taking any chances. I was enrolled in and escorted to St. Agnes College in Belleville, Ontario, a private school that was a little too private for my tastes.

It was a fifty-year-old, red-brick monstrosity, originally built for a lumber baron by a contractor who must have copied it from a patternbook. There was a Tuscan watchtower over the front doorway, whose design was lifted intact from a sixteenth-century Venetian palace. Since no Mediterranean villa is complete without a veranda to provide shade from the sun, St. Agnes had a veranda, which faced North on a busy street. And, highly important in any anxious mother's view, St. Agnes was surrounded by a sturdy iron railing.

Elegance extended to the writing on the blackboard, which we had to copy as an exercise in penmanship. It was all a shade too graceful for me. I could manage nothing better than my usual scrawl, which grew worse the harder I tried. Before very long, I was given up as lost forever to the arts of calligraphy. Perhaps if the teachers hadn't been so exacting, I shouldn't be so petrified today when I'm asked to write anything much longer than my name (and how do you spell that?). If left alone, during wartime, I write beautifully! My illegal wartime-diary attempts bear this out.

We young ladies took a walk every morning, sedately, two by two, alike as peas in a pod in our dark green blazers, straw hats and sensible brown oxfords. To the knowing onlooker, it was easy to see how each of us had been behaving, well or otherwise, by her place in the crocodile. The good girls walked at the head of the line, average, naughty types in the middle, bad ones brought up the rear.

I can't think how I achieved it, but once, just once, I was put up front as the *leader*. It was an opportunity too tempting to pass up. Our morning jaunts were supposed to follow the same, monotonous route, out through the gates, down the main street, a few turns, then circle back in through the gates.

Now, on the main street stood a bank, and in the bank there worked a handsome young teller who had caught my eye on previous excursions. So on this auspicious day, we did not follow sober habit. When we reached the bank's door, I turned inside, without missing a step, and the rest of the crocodile obediently followed.

We paced gravely across the tiled floor, brown oxfords clicking in unison, while I got a close-up look at the young man in the teller's cage. Ah, sweet mystery of life! He was beautiful.

Without daring to bring the marching column to a halt, I performed a neat left wheel and, without a word, we made our exit as smoothly as we'd entered, our blazered arms swinging as to unheard music from a brass band.

Somebody at the bank must have telephoned St. Agnes' ahead of us. When we got back to school, we went, as usual, straight into chapel. The headmistress waited for the brief services to end before she began to quiz us, one by one. What had happened? Who was to blame? Perverse not-so-wee Bea—that's who, who is it!

I suppose we all gained something from the discipline, though not perhaps in the manner intended. We all maintained our innocence. In the spirit of girlish excitement and friendship, nobody snitched on me. But I sat shivering, thinking, "Oh, God, she'll find out I'm lying. I'll be expelled. Then what will Pa say to that?" The thought was enough to make me admit my guilt. Never again did I get to lead the crocodile.

My father was a sweet, wonderful man, who wrote to me every other day. That was a great consolation when I was a new girl, occasionally bullied by the seniors, as new girls are likely to be. One of them once grabbed a letter from him out of my hands before I had the chance to open the envelope.

"Let me see that," she said. "I bet it's from one of your *boys*." But I didn't have any boy to write to, and I don't think I was capable of writing a letter to anyone but my mother or father.

At Cobourg, when I made weekend visits now and again to see Mother and Muriel, I'd met two boys, but the circumstances were rather dampening. My sister and I went in for a swim in the lake there. Muriel came out and stood on a little jetty, watching me flounder about in my usual style, until she noticed the floundering was growing more violent and I was gurgling for help. Two young men came strolling by, and she raced to enlist them in rescuing me.

"How many times has she gone down?" one of them asked, unalarmed.

"Twice already," gasped my sister.

"Oh, they always come up three times," said the cool young man, unhurriedly pulling off his shoes to go in after me. Now don't laugh! It was really a close thing.

The company of the opposite sex in Cobourg in the days before the First World War was taken a trifle more seriously than, say, in a Swedish movie in 1972. It was close to shocking to think that the prim and proper Miss Lillie who played the organ on Sundays would ever be seen walking out with a boy at her age. So I used to delight in dressing up in a shirt and a pair of trousers and insist on going for walks with my sister.

"But what are people going to say?" she'd complain.

"Never mind," I'd answer darkly. "Come *on*."

Only once a year were boys admitted through the iron gates of St. Agnes' to join the girls. For the first party, Mumsie sent a new dress she'd made for me, and I did my damnedest to make myself look— well, passable. Mirrors occupied an important place in my life now, in the usual tradition of the stage-struck. Daily practice to perfect a tilt of the head, a turn of the hand, a winsome smile. Ah, but the nose, which Kenneth Tynan once said "suggests a Steinberg cartoon of Peter Pan." From afar, I envied the two absentee Lillies their more serene profiles.

On party day, a gaggle of the strange creatures known as males gathered round in the hot, crowded assembly hall, which had been cleared for the occasion of its usual ranks of folding chairs. Among the visitors, if you please, was the beautiful bank teller, and he was talking to me.

"Would you like some ice cream?" Magic words.

"I don't think we're allowed to go out," I stammered.

"Well, I could slip out and bring some back."

"Oh, I don't know."

He let the subject drop for a while. The young ladies of St. Agnes' busied themselves with their little dance cards and their little pencils, though I seem to remember that we weren't actually allowed to *dance*, only to fill in names.

As the evening wore on, the question of ice cream came up again. This time, the beautiful teller wasn't to be deterred. He went out, and I left the hall. When the party ended, Beatrice Gladys was nowhere to be found. I was caught eventually, of course, but it was well worth the disciplining I got later. Because when they found me, I was up in the Tuscan watchtower with the young feller. We'd eaten our scoops of vanilla there, talked a bit to each other, and it was just as innocent as that. (Sorry.)

It slowly dawned on the teachers that I was not the student type. The only studies I excelled in were drawing, music and botany. On the other hand, I took part in the plays, I sang like a lark in the choral society and for some unknown reason shone briefly as an athlete, but only for a day or two.

I had a letter recently from a former classmate. "You were the most wonderful person we had in the school," she wrote, but to me that couldn't be true. It was all a waste of time somehow. Judging by the sum total of my present academic knowledge, my school days were a flop. None of it left any permanent trace. But I mustn't grumble. Oh, mustn't I?

Muriel's reputation as a musician was spreading far and wide. She had grown into quite the young lady, with long plaits of black hair and serene gray eyes. I envied her hair as much as her nose. I teased her that I knew girls with hair blacker than hers. ("But they put *oil* on theirs," she'd insist.) "Miss Prim," thought I. . . .

Muriel was the winner of a gold medal in the all-Canada Earl Grey Musical and Dramatic Competition, which was an event much more important in our family than the Coronation that year of King George V and Queen Mary, the former May Teck.

My sister came from Cobourg for weekly piano lessons at the Toronto Conservatory of Music, where she was now an advanced student. She had also come to the attention of Lady Pellatt, whose husband, Sir Harry, was making his millions and drawing his plans for building the hilltop castle called Casa Loma, which became a city landmark, with its twenty-one fireplaces and stables for I don't know how many horses, built of mahogany and Spanish tile. Sir Harry's dreams and his bank balance both collapsed later on, and the castle stood empty for years until rescued by Glen Gray and the orchestra. But at the time, we fancied that wealth and titles went together like Sears and Roebuck. All rightee—*you* on the right shore of the Atlantic—try *Swan and Edgar!* Ah, well!

Mother decided that Muriel should acquire the final touch of polish and study in Europe before embarking on a concert career. My sister set out to win the necessary scholarships and, being a Lillie, couldn't be satisfied until she had, in fact, earned one that would take her to Germany for a year or so.

The farewell soirée really was something to see. The patroness, if you please, was none other than Lady Pellatt. The setting was the Toronto Conservatory, where Muriel gave her final recital "with Mr. Frank E. Blachford, violinist, as assisting artist," as the program said.

Such flouncing of lace, such swirl of *tulle,* such an aroma of perfume and, as always, dry-cleaned white gloves. "Lady Pellatt? How do you do? May I present Mrs. Frank Welsman, the wife of dear Muriel's teacher? Ah, here comes Mrs. Alexander, and there's Mr. Nordheimer." The Lillie girls resisted the temptation to pour water or throw feathers.

As a family, we weren't to be accused even by our worst enemies—had we any?—of being gushingly sentimental except when we stood up to sing. When the time came for Mumsie and Muriel to absent themselves still farther from Toronto, and my thoughts and hopes had to stretch for three thousand miles, I don't recall any of us dissolving into tears beyond a drop or two. It seemed all part of a master plan and we obeyed the silent call.

Bon voyage. Toodle-oo. *Auf wiedersehn.* My father and I settled down again in our way of life, together but separate, and I counted the days until graduation.

The idea was that as soon as my education was complete and the requirements of the law that said everybody had to go to school had been satisfied, I could return to being an actress. I was going to join up again as a member of the Lillie Trio, to sail to be with my mother and Muriel in England.

England? You thought I just now said *Germany.* Well, I did, but all their plans had to be changed because of the Balkans, if you know what I mean, and I *doubt* that you do.

The Balkans were all over the newspapers, though I wasn't one to bother with anything like that. There was, as always, great talk among the Irish about Home Rule, but I wasn't really listening. And there were some new names to wrestle with in geography, like Montenegro and Sarajevo. Who cared?

Mumsie did. The prospect of being in Germany when the sabers were being rattled didn't appeal to her. So she and Muriel made for London, where my sister began studying with Tobias Mathay and later with Myra Hess.

My day of liberation from all forms of schooling finally dawned. My father and I took the train together from Toronto to Montreal. Packed in my luggage were some of the costumes Mother had made for me. There was the Italian outfit for "Niccolini," the Geisha's for "Mimosa San," the Indian maiden's for "My Little Kickapoo." He saw me off aboard ship, and we kept up the family tradition of stiff upper lips and dry handkerchiefs, though a moist eye or two crept in.

Years went by before I went back to Canada. By then I was married, *a Lady in my own wrong.* According to the then notable Toronto *Sunday World,* I had managed to become "just about the most talked of woman in England and America." (The things they *say!*)

Those years covered quite a gap. The *Sunday World's* reporter, Leo Sullivan, seemed to be having trouble catching his breath as he wrote:

"Her sensational success as a light-opera singer has been the talk of two continents, and, at present, she is dazzling New Yorkers after a memorable conquest of London's exclusive Strand. *(Please note that the Strand was better known for a different kind of female pursuit or calling, but he didn't mean that, I hope.)*

"By a singular shaping of circumstances, the life of Beatrice Lillie has escaped the penetrating rays of publicity. Unusual color, with an appropriate dash of romance, surrounds the story. Never before, perhaps, has a Toronto girl successfully climbed the ladder of fame and deliberately kept the news a secret. (*Oh, Toronto girls aren't all loudmouths, you know. Maybe he meant I hadn't told him.*)

"Her success abroad did not reach the ears of Torontonians in the usual way. She was an established London favorite at the Prince of Wales's Theatre long before it was known here. During the war, the news first reached Toronto by mail. (*The pigeons weren't flying; grounded by bad weather.*)

"Various reports were then circulated locally and most of them were inaccurate and misleading, and for the first time it is possible to give an intimate sketch of Beatrice Lillie, one of Toronto's fairest daughters . . ." (*My trouble always was that I was so shy and so pretty!*)

On that first return trip to the native heath, I remember feeling singularly unpretty. The city's fair daughter hadn't slept at all on the overnight train from New York. In the suite at the Royal York, I felt too far-gone to talk, but it seemed only proper to invite one early-bird reporter to stay for breakfast.

He'd been in the crowd of reporters and photographers who were waiting at the station when I clomped down the train steps, looking like something the cat dragged in. I'd pulled on my coat over the wrinkled traveling dress, but the newspapers accounts that appeared the next day didn't tell it quite like that.

"What Toronto Smart Women Are Wearing," said the caption in the *Telegram* over a picture so smudged it might have been the Countess Dracula. The story explained, "She is wearing a lovely wrap of Kolinsky over a simple chemise dress of black *crêpe de chine* with a cape-like back and row of white buttons down the front. An English sports hat of lemon completed her costume, and she was wearing black patent shoes and beige hosiery." I'd forgotten how chic I'd become.

Getting back to the correct time zone: I sailed alone that first time I crossed the Atlantic. In the somewhat breathless years ahead, I became Miss Cunard herself, with an interval or two of being Miss *Not* Wanted on the Voyage. On that first crossing, I shared a cabin with an elderly woman, who got very sick in the lower berth, while I did the same upstairs. I was fussed over very satisfactorily by everyone I met, and I was a sure-fire hit, while still a little queasy, in the ship's concert.

The applause must have gone to my head, or perhaps it was the *mal de mer* that disturbed my mind. But I had a twinge of toothache the following day, and nothing would do but to go down to the ship's doctor and have a back molar pulled. I really didn't need to, but I liked the look of the doctor with all that gold braid on his cuffs.

On another transatlantic crossing years later, there was another girl not much younger than I'd been when I first sailed from Montreal for Liverpool. I noticed her when I was busy keeping the photographers happy with "just one more" before we arrived at the Hudson River pier. I was impressed by her beauty—beautiful dark hair and double eyelashes.

Her mother, with the insistence of every stage mother, came on over to me. "Miss Lillie."

"Hello," I answered.

"Would you do me a favor and allow my daughter to have her picture taken with you? She's just made her first important movie, and you could help her get some publicity. It's called *National Velvet*."

Click. Click. Auntie Bea and young Elizabeth Taylor.

Back in sequence: As the ship from Montreal nosed its way toward the Liverpool dock, I was peering, minus one molar, through a porthole. There she stood, waving and waiting for me in a big picture hat. She'd come up by train from London to meet the ship, the star of the Lillie Trio, its inspiration and guiding light. Magnificent Mumsie.

CHAPTER FOUR

OH, THE WICKED, WICKED, STAGE!

You'll *never* guess what happened next. Well, almost next, after an up and a down or three. I became a sort of paid, professional transvestite. I learned how to knot a bow tie, wear a top hat, wrestle with dress studs, swing a cane. I could toy with a cigarette like Gerald du Maurier and ogle a girl like Gilbert the Filbert, the King of the Knuts.

I was known, in fact, as the best-dressed man in London, and thereby hangs a tail that we'll get to in a minute. But beneath the starched shirt front there beat a heart emerald green in its innocence. I scarcely knew anything about *anything*, let alone the ways of the theaytah. After all, I was a *concert* artiste.

In the very beginning, I was unaware that there was such a thing as a stage door. I fancied it would be labeled "artistes' entrance." My mother's doing, I'm sure, but then she was always an original. I was naïve, but I learned—and fast.

I was appearing in *A to Z* with Jack Buchanan, a tall, debonair Scot, who was making his London debut. He'd never had a singing or a dancing lesson, but with his smoky-gray eyes and dark brown wavy hair, with the look of wearing evening clothes as though he'd been poured into them, he went on to become a world-wide idol of the stage and cinema.

Backstage, I was still classified as a girl even if I hardly ever got into a skirt. We girls had dressing rooms on one side of the theatre—the Prince of Wales's —while the men were accommodated on the other.

Jack used to kid me about my being a girl hero, decked out in tails or flannel slacks (tennis, anyone?) or whatever costume was called for. "Tell me, Beattie," he said one day, "how do you dress, left side or right?"

I hadn't a clue to what he was talking about, not the glimmer of an idea about the meaning of the twinkle in his eyes. I still thought *flies* were something you swatted.

"Come on, Beattie. Don't be shy. On which side do you *dress?*"

Suddenly, the light dawned, or so I thought.

"Oh, yes," I answered. "In Number Five. Stage left."

Jack roared with laughter; thought I was brilliant.

The first home I knew in England was two rented rooms in a large, shabby house owned by an Italian chef at 28 Gloucester Road, London SW. There were those who considered this to be part of Pimlico, but we invariably described the address as being "on the borders of Chelsea." Pimlico hadn't the kind of *ambiance* Mother cared for. Pimlico stood for pubs on every corner and poor, unwashed children playing in the streets. Chelsea meant the arts, soirées, hopes and dreams. We lived, therefore, "on the borders of Chelsea," and I doubled up with Mother, while Muriel slept alone in a tiny room next door.

My sister had already gone to work, not as a concert pianist, as was originally planned, but playing the piano in a movie house. She had answered an advertisement in a newspaper and landed the job, which paid her a shilling a week tea money on top of her wages. What with Mumsie's savings and the allowance my father sent us, we managed to get along, though we weren't exactly on the brink of making our fortune.

As I was saying, those were the days when it seemed Muriel had the talent, and I had the luck. The times were in my favor, not hers. Kaiser Bill was acting up, and everybody's temperature was rising. Those Balkan names that I'd never bothered with were turning up in conversation every day now.

Nevertheless, the Lillie Trio went on practicing individually and as an ensemble for the day the sun would shine. None of us had the slightest doubt that our day would come. We believed Mother implicitly when she told us, "Work hard. Be charming, and always ladies. If you have talent, it will be discovered. Remember, *en avant*—ever forward."

She persevered with her singing, no matter what. She'd stand, straight-backed and dignified with one hand over her ear, presumably to hear herself that much better. Singers *always* seem to do this. I've never regarded it as anything but an affectation, still, they all do it. The telephone would ring and, hand cupped over ear, she'd go right on with her scales.

A call came one day, and she went to answer it. "Ah, ah, ah, ah, ah, ah, ah!" Just one more scale before she spoke. "Who is it speaking, please?" she turned the question into another scale. "Do you wish to speak to Miss Muriel or Miss Beatrice? Miss Beatrice *(still vocalizing it)*, you're wanted on the telephone."

It turned out that somebody was expecting me for an audition. Audition? It was the first time *that* had happened.

On the appointed morning, I made my way by bus to the theatre. I was alone. I didn't know enough to go round to the stage door, so when I found the main entrance doors open, I went in through the front of the house. The place was in darkness, with only a work light shining over the bare stage. The only people in sight were way down front, a handful of them on the stage. I couldn't see them very well or hear what they were saying.

For a full hour, I sat in the back row of the stalls, a kid from the Canadian sticks, not knowing what to do next, too shy to walk down the aisle and ask. Then someone turned out the last light. That did it.

"Excuse me, please," I called, but it was a hoarse whisper. I tried again. "Excuse me."

Someone heard me. The work light went on again. Murmuring apologies, I made my way down to the stage and introduced myself. They were all very nice about it. They brought in the pianist, and I sang a song or two, but I didn't get the job. They showed me the way out through the *stage door*, and I went home.

Auditions? After that, I grew punch-drunk on them, apparently with no prospect in sight of the work we Lillies all wanted. Mother was constantly getting us to do *something*. Sometimes Muriel auditioned with me, sometimes not. It made no difference. I didn't get the jobs. I hadn't any idea where to begin, and I hadn't the right clothes to wear. The "Niccolini" outfit and the rest were completely out of place in London, so we had to borrow dresses for me on audition days.

One day Mother fixed me up with a dress and three auditions in a row. It was a nice, respectable dress, but at the first call, another girl who was waiting to be heard showed me how to tug open the neckline a bit to show an inch or two more of myself to disguise my up-from-the-country look.

When my turn came, I went out and bowed politely to the theatre manager, as I'd been taught to do.

"I should like to sing 'Oh, For the Wings of a Dove.'" The laundryman's favorite and one of Mother's, too. The manager didn't appear to be entranced by the prospect, but he sat patiently through it.

Then came the classic phrase of dismissal that was so familiar. "Thank you." That was another one over.

At the next call I tried another staple, "I Hear You Calling Me." The same thing happened, except that I was allowed to finish only a few bars before I had my marching orders.

"Thank you," growled a voice from the darkness.

Oh, dear! But now the Irish was rising. "I'll show them this time," I decided as I toiled on to the third ordeal of the day. I waited impatiently at the side of the stage.

"You're next," cried manager number three at last.

I walked demurely to stage center and gave him a sweet smile. I paused for just a moment to get his full attention. Then I bowed to him ever so slightly. "Thank *you*," I said and made my exit.

The very first wolf I'd encountered entered my young life at about this time. By his own account—

and it couldn't have been a bank account—Harry Hart was a theatrical agent. Eyes more experienced than mine might have detected that, if this was true, his clients could expect more pints of beer than bottles of champagne.

The only office he had, so far as I knew, was in his hat, which was a straw boater. This was now summer, the last hot summer before the world first went to war. We used to meet in the Coventry Street Lyons Corner House for tea and buns, with big red double-decker buses lurching past outside and then round Piccadilly Circus, where barrel organs jangled out the popular songs that every messenger boy seemed to whistle.

> Way up the river he would row, row, row . . .
> Then he'd drop off his oars,
> Take a few more encores,
> And then he'd row, row, row.*

Even for me, it wasn't too hard to see sooner or later that Harry Hart pictured himself as an oarsman where I was concerned. But I was a non-navigable stream. I sipped the tea and nibbled on the buns he bought for us, but no romancing, if you please. He kept trying, though. Oh, the wicked stage—and me not even on it yet!

He felt he had to do something to justify the faith I didn't have in him. He arranged a booking, such as it was.

Like most music halls of the era, the Camberwell

* "Row, Row, Row." Music by William Jerome, words by James V. Monaco. Copyright 1912. Copyright renewed 1939. Reprinted by permission of the publisher, Harry Von Tilzer Music Pub. Co. (A division of Bibo Music Publishers, Inc.)

Palace put on what was called an "extra-turn night" once a week. The Palace was an ornate establishment, fragrant with dusty velvet, cigarette smoke and beer suds, that stood in Camberwell High Street and drew a faithful audience of rowdy Cockneys.

A hoarse-voiced master of ceremonies presided over the entertainment, with a gavel in one hand and a pint in the other. There, one Friday night, I made my real debut in a London theatre. Harry got me on as an 'extra turn.'

I still pictured myself as a serious singer. It was all well and good, I thought, to make people laugh in private, but put me on a stage and I wanted to have the audience appreciate my voice, just what Mother had trained me for. If anyone dared to giggle at my singing, I shriveled inside. I hated anything funny. The diet of weepy movies had left its dent. More than anything, I yearned to be *sad*. I wanted to cry, break a leg, knock my teeth out—whatever was required to win the sympathy of people watching me. But always as a lady, as Mother insisted.

In the wings of the Camberwell Palace, I stood as nervous as a kitten with a can tied to its tail. The voice of the master of ceremonies rasped out an introduction.

"And now it's my pleasure to present for your kind applause a lovely little lady who's making her first appearance on any London stage. 'Ere she is, ladies and gentlemen, Canada's own sweetheart of song . . ."

I'd chosen something my mother liked, a melody as mournful as anybody could wish for.

> Don't steal my prayer book, Mr. "Burgular,"
> Just open it and look inside.
> There's a lock of Mother's hair,

And you'll find it lying there
With a forget-me-not beside
My evening prayer . . .

Harry Hart hadn't warned me what to expect from a Cockney audience on extra-turn nights. They had the usual bawdy response ready for any newcomer. As I finished, with hands clasped together concertwise before me, there was a storm of catcalls. I was utterly crushed, but I refused to show it. I'd been given another lesson by an audience, and again I was quick to learn.

"Ladies and gentlemen," I said as soon as the noise had died down, "I should now like to sing *for your possible approval* a number written by my dear friend, Mr. Irving Berlin—'When I Lost You.' And I might add that he wrote it the night his wife died."

Oh, the pain of it! This *fib!* Of course, I'd never met Irving Berlin. Of course, the bit about his wife was a trick to win attention. At first, the audience didn't appear to give a damn. I waved a nonchalant signal to the conductor.

I lost the sunshine and roses.
I lost the heavens of blue . . .*
When I lost you.

Did my ears deceive me? No, they didn't. Were those cheers I heard when I'd reached the end of the number? Yes, they were. I'd done my thing and made my mark, but if there were any cash awards on

---

* "When I Lost You" by Irving Berlin. Copyright © 1912 by Irving Berlin. Copyright © renewed. Reprinted by permission of Irving Berlin Music Corporation.

this extra-turn night, they went to talents that left a deeper mark on Camberwell High Street. I received my particular reward with a rather pale grin. It was a flute, which was precisely what the Lillie Trio needed at that point to make ends meet.

There was one other reward to come, though. The local weekly newspaper ran an account of my trials in front of a rowdy audience and went so far as to mention my name under a headline which I thought went just a bit too far: "Pearls Before Swine." I must confess, though, that I liked it and it *did* give me encouragement and cheer just when I badly needed both.

So far as I was concerned, the Camberwell Palace spelled the end of Harry Hart. But who was to say the experience had been wasted? Sitting in Lyons Corner House, I'd spent a lot of time watching waitresses, seeing how they talked and walked and primped their hair. You never know when that kind of thing is going to come in useful.

But for the time being, nothing useful was coming along. When the managers I auditioned for heard such gems from my repertoire as "Mimosa San" ("And so I wave my fan, For hearts don't break in gay Japan . . ."), they promised to let me know, but they never did.

Recalling those days of nothing doing, an American critic has ventured, with gentlemanly chivalry, to explain why the offers didn't pour in for my services: "The truth is that her voice was not distinguished, that her style was heavy, that her appearance, with her hair in tight buns over her ears, showed no promise." Other than that, I was clearly the stuff from which stars are made.

Somewhere about this time, the two younger members of the Trio put together an act of their own, a sister act that we called, in a burst of inspiration, "Beatrice & Muriel." (Remember, I was the lucky one.) Naturally, Muriel played the piano, but not entirely in concert style, unless concert style included leaving the left hand to pick out the music, while the right hand held a cigarette. (What *was* the world coming to?)

When we appeared together, Muriel, so help me, was often the comic, the cutup, blowing smoke rings while she inched the grand piano, behind my turned back, closer and closer toward the front of the stage, and I couldn't for the life of me understand why the audience was laughing when neither Lillie was uttering a word. Probably moving the piano was funnier than anything we said, in any event, when what we said ran along the lines of:

BEATRICE: That's my sister playing the piano.
MURIEL: Don't you believe it—she's my mother.

But there came, at last, just as Mother had promised, a day when someone detected gold dust glistening in the dross, a light flickering under the bushel, and so forth, and so on. André Charlot was a name that every aspiring actress included in her prayers. He had come from France—and he never lost his Maurice Chevalier accent—to make his reputation as a producer of the best revues in London, tasteful, lively and, in the words of today, "with it." He was demanding, highly creative, and he'd also earned a name for pursuing some of the girls whose names he put in lights. He chain-smoked cigarettes, and everybody called him "Guv," except for me. I alone called him "Dada" and he called himself Uncle André, which together with my tender age may have been the reason he treated me as a—well, if you like, a lady.

When I heard that the celebrated Charlot was holding auditions for a new revue, I was off and running, still scarred, a bit scared but *en avant!* I hadn't had a real nibble from anybody so far, though I'd shoved and pushed myself into every audition I heard of, together with those Mother and Muriel cooked up for me.

"Just you wait," I kept telling them when I limped home once again after a thankless day of "Thank you's." "Wait until the London managers see what I can *really* do."

Wait they did, with little complaining, while bit by bit the confidence I'd started with began to fade. Not that any one of the three of us had a thought of packing up and running back to where we'd come from. On the contrary, there was discussion now on the borders of Chelsea about whether and when Father might join us.

Press agents have had their fling describing the famous audition with Charlot which allegedly rushed me up the stairs to stardom. According to one account, "It ended with a comic collapse on top of the suitcase which she carried. Beatrice was promptly engaged as a comedienne, for her auditor was the renowned André Charlot."

It didn't happen anything like that, as a matter of fact. In the first place, when I got to the theatre, Charlot wasn't in. He had been carried off for a week or two in the London Fever Hospital. Tom Concannon, his business manager, was supervising that day. If anyone collapsed, it was Mr. Concannon. I always think that the only reason I was given the job was that I exhausted the auditioner.

My mood was strenuously serio. Poor fellow, he hadn't much choice but to listen to half the songs Mother had taught me, with a few I'd picked up myself. This time, I'd made up my mind that we Lillies could wait no longer. The talent just *had* to be discovered.

I opened with one of the jewels in which I'd never lost faith, "Oh, For the Wings of a Dove," thinking that Mr. Concannon might admire those swooping, drooping *Ooooh's* as much as Mother and I did.

"Well, yes," he said when I'd finished swooping, "that's fine, but—"

I interrupted. "Let me try another one." He agreed. I got under way again.

> The roses each one
> Met with the sun,
> Sweetheart, when I met you.
> The sunshine had fled,
> The roses were dead,
> Sweetheart, when I lost you . . .

. . . And so on to the heartbreaking finale. "That will do," said Mr. Concannon. "We'll get in touch if—"

"Just one more," I begged. Somewhat reluctantly, it seemed to me, he gave his consent. I stunned him with "Beside the Jasmin Door."

Thus it continued. Each time he implored me to desist, I, using all the expertise achieved giving so many fruitless auditions, implored him to let me render—that's the word—one more song. But nothing was doing the trick. Mr. Concannon, I could only conclude, was a hard man to convince, but perhaps in these stirring patriotic times, when young men were dreaming about putting the kibosh on the Kaiser and being home in time for Christmas ...

"No, no, please!" I said as he started to rise from his chair. "This will be the very last. I promise." Standing straight as a poker, hands to my sides, I drew a deep breath and gave it my all:

God save our gracious King,
Long live our noble King ...

That worked the trick. Mr. Concannon didn't say "Thank you." Instead, he engaged me as a seriosinger at three pounds five shillings a week for *Not Likely*, the new Charlot revue then running at the Alhambra Theatre. For a second, I wondered whether I should have asked for a long-term contract. But as things turned out, I didn't have a contract during all the years I worked for Charlot.

I was anxious to see the great man himself as soon as he came out of the hospital. On the first day he returned to his office, I turned up there, too. He hadn't seen me perform or really heard of my name, but I wanted him to be the first to listen to me sing what I felt was one of the most tragic songs ever calculated to drive an audience to sorrow.

I had the idea that it was best to appear for auditions looking pathetic and poverty-stricken. I habitually wore my oldest, shabbiest clothes, with an extra patch or two tacked on here and there to heighten the effect. I cultivated the appearance of a girl who'd just had some teeth pulled and eaten nothing all day except maybe one little bun, and that rather stale.

The effect, I imagined, would be so tearful that nobody could fail to feel so sorry for me that I'd get the job out of pity. The fact that it hadn't worked out like that until I pulverized Mr. Concannon didn't change my way of thinking. It took me quite a while to wise up and understand that in general it helps a girl to present herself for an audition in a Rolls-Royce and a sable coat; flashing a diamond ring, even if she has to beg or borrow it.

Soon after I got started in the London theatre, two or three people had the idea that I was the darling of an unknown tycoon, when I was in all truth no more than Mother's pet. I couldn't make out why I was cold-shouldered, and I used to hurry home, complaining, "Nobody will talk to me." Green as grass, you might say.

For my encounter with Charlot, I brought along a big, battered suitcase that had traveled all over Ontario and the Atlantic, too. I thought, "It's very sad to have a suitcase. It shows that you've left home, and you're on your way to somewhere that's going to make you unhappy."

When I showed up at Charlot's office, I was lugging the suitcase and huddling inside my patched coat.

He asked, rather pointedly, "Who are *you?*" and I told him a word or two about myself.

"Why do you want to see me?"

"Because I want to do sad numbers. I'd rather sing sad songs than do anything else in the world."

"Very well, then. What are you going to sing for me?"

I felt the tears start in my eyes and said, "We're Drifting Apart."

"I beg your pardon," Charlot said crisply.

82

I sniffled and said, "That's the title of the song. I brought the music."

"All right. Go ahead."

He had no private office then. He reigned in the midst of ringing telephones and clattering typewriters pounded by girls in shirtwaists. He ordered a little piano brought in from outside. Somebody pulled up a chair and began to play the opening bars.

I wondered how Charlot would ever be able to hear me above the din. I started, anyway, sitting like Patience on a monument, smiling at grief, upon the beaten-up suitcase.

> After all that I've been to you,
> After all of these many years,
> After everything I've been through,
> After all of my smiles and tears . . .*

I'd thought that by now everyone within earshot would have been sobbing softly, if not actually dissolving in tears. But the girls in the office went on tapping away at their typewriters and answering the telephones.

"Very rude," I thought. "Not at all ladylike. Steely-hearted, too."

It was impossible to judge from the look behind his spectacles what Charlot was thinking, but he went on puffing at a cigarette. I proceeded.

> It's the old story told once more
> Of a strange love that cannot be true.

Now look at him, picking up his telephone. Who's he calling? He seems to be doing more listening than talking. I didn't learn until later that this was a pretense, devised to cover his laughter. But let's get on with it . . .

> Though we're drifting apart,
> And you're breaking my heart,
> After all that I've been to you.

With the last, plaintive note, I collapsed, sobbing on the suitcase. I strained to hear the sobs of sympathy that I was convinced would be forthcoming. But there was no sound of weeping. All I could detect were giggles turning into guffaws. Guffaw the merrier. I opened my eyes and saw that the shirtwaisted girls were abandoning their desks to hurry toward the door.

I stood up, attempting to draw myself to the full five feet and a bit in hurt dignity, but my coat caught on a broken catch of one of the suitcase locks. The suitcase itself swung off the floor for a moment, then fell over, and I fell on top of it. The whole effect was *ruined*. The girls paused on their dash for the exit to howl with laughter. You should have seen it. Very sad.

With a handkerchief taken from the breastpocket of his immaculate suit, Charlot wiped off his spectacles. "Well, now, Miss Lillie. I don't think London is quite ready yet for that kind of thing."

But did it matter, after all? What do you think? In the legends of the theatre, and the theatre is made of legends, everybody who somehow succeeds in getting her name in lights is "discovered" by someone. If I was ever "discovered," Charlot did it. The results

---

* "After All That I've Been To You." Music by Chris Smith, words by Jack Drislane. Copyright 1912. Copyright renewed 1939. Reprinted by permission of the publishers, Jerry Vogel Music Co., Inc., and Fred Fisher Music Co., Inc.

of my sad singing for him weren't sudden, dramatic, rocket-to-stardom kind of things. I continually tried from then on to persuade him to let me do more than I was called on for in every show of his in which I appeared. Yet at that first, farcical meeting, he apparently could see something that was invisible to less discerning eyes. In some strange way, I was aware of his reaction. From André Charlot I first learned that I was a natural-born fool, one of those rare birds; a comedienne.

"I think that perhaps I will let you do a comedy number in my new show," he said, and that was all I wanted to hear, really. Of all the triumphs and disasters that come your way in the theatre, nothing is so wonderful as that first chance. (That sounds rather well, doesn't it?) Fame, money, newspaper headlines, name in lights—nothing that happens later ever equals that. (It's getting better all the time.) I was lucky enough to have Charlot give me that chance, and I grabbed it. (That's for sure.)

May we now allow our temperatures to decline by a degree or two, while I explain that the opportunity granted me by Uncle André led me in a wink or perhaps a trice into discarding skirts for trousers? The press clippings noted that "Miss Lillie makes quite a nice boy." My father had started the first clipping book when I was just a slip of a girl; my mother continued where he left off.

In the judgment of one reviewer, I quickly became "one of the most dapper and accomplished of contemporary male impersonators." That reputation haunted me for years, as long as the guns boomed and young men, including actors, went tramping down the long, long trail a-winding into the land of their dreams, leaving roles open for girls to fill. Women's Lib came early in World War One-time London.

I can't pretend that I was flattered when I read that "Beatrice Lillie always appears more as a boy than as a girl." (Appears to *whom?*) And, at the same time, I considered that the absolute, final, bloody end had come when I read the following: "I thought that in skirts she would be nothing. She was not at all bad . . . All the same, she ought to be in a revue as a young gentleman."

Those last remarks were made later, when I was trying to escape from gentleman's tailoring. I thought I'd been wearing trousers long enough—that went for time as well as length of leg—and I was happy to appear as the feminine lead in a play, of all things. But the fly season lasted right through until Armistice Day.

Mother didn't take at all to the idea of my being what they called a girl hero, though she was delighted that I was working at last—and she remained in a state of semiecstasy over my working life up to the day she died, at the age of eighty-six years and three months in November 1957.

"Really, Beatrice," I remember her saying. "*Boy's* clothes. I certainly hope that no one from Toronto will see you in the theatre. What would people think?"

In point of fact, whole brigades of Canadian soldiers, on leave from the Western Front, came to see show after show. They used to take off their collar badges and toss them up to me on stage. The letters they wrote home gave the native land the first clue to what I was up to in London.

Charlot's revues brightened up London as nothing else quite did. They were produced with a great deal of taste and very little money. Even for the stars, salaries weren't sensational, and most of the scenery consisted of curtains, hung with a decorator's taste. Costumes were imaginative, artistic and thrifty. For one song, "Goodbye, Madame Fashion," in a show named *Cheep* (that's with a double "e"), the leading lady wore an outfit that cost exactly fifteen shillings and three-pence. That was fifteen shillings for the hat, and her dress was made from half-a-dozen copies of *Evening News* at a half-penny apiece.

After the second Charlot revue for which I'd been engaged had opened, I was halfway to being a star. The suitcase audition for "Dada" took me straight out of singing with a quartet into doing a solo. With that encouragement, and a little nudging from my mother, I made pestering him my hobby. But Uncle André believed in players like me tackling small things first and proving they could handle them well before he put bigger opportunities in their path.

"I want you to hold yourself in reserve for better things in the next show," he'd say. "I intend to build you up from year to year." Patience, Beatrice! Remember what Mother says.

Every wartime show had a good long run. We played month after month to houses packed with officers and men, their families and girlfriends, who first crowded into the vast Alhambra Theatre in Leicester Square and later into the little Vaudeville Theatre. The men needed a few jokes and a little music to help them blot out for an hour or so the nightmare that waited for them when their leave ended and they went back across the Channel to face mud and bully beef and the armies of Kaiser Bill.

We were all delighted to knock ourselves out for such audiences and Dada in about equal measure, and we weren't being too noble about it. Working in a Charlot revue was a laugh, a lark, a bit of a riot.

I made my first real hit in *5064 Gerrard*, which followed on the heels of *Not Likely*, the show for which the long-suffering Mr. Concannon hired me. Uncle André, who had a fancy for unlikely titles, took the stage-door telephone number of the Alhambra Theatre as the name of this revue, which opened in the spring of 1915.

He had me fitted for farmer's coveralls and a milk pail to sing Irving Berlin's "Take Me Back to Michigan," and the audience ate it up. The girl hero was well and truly launched.

On the strength of the applause, I tried once again to persuade Uncle André to give me a tragic number; not withstanding the gentleman's tailoring, my taste continued to run to sentimental songs. Run? It positively galloped. He wouldn't hear of it. He treated the request in the manner of a schoolmaster confronting a pupil who wanted to be excused from cricket to take up crewelwork. He had a habit of treating us all like kids. That's why I called him Dada.

So in an assortment of gent's natty clothing and uniforms, as one revue followed another, I chirruped my way through the war, warbling songs about my dear old home back in Alabama, Maryland, Maine or Florida, yearning for returning, aching to be packing. Every song had something to do with going back somewhere. According to the lyrics, the only place I *wasn't* pining to get back to was Toronto.

While still playing in *5064 Gerrard*, we went into rehearsal for another revue, more ambitious this time, though again in the same theatre, the Alhambra, in Leicester Square. *Now's the Time* was amazingly lavish and extravagant considering the shortage of everything under wartime rationing, which had led to strict economies and austerity everywhere, even in

Buckingham Palace, the newspapers solemnly reported, where "sago pudding is a favorite dish of the Queen, and it figures frequently on the menu." I was a rice-pudding girl myself.

The biggest names in *Now's the Time* were those of an American couple, Clay Smith and his wife, Lee White, a wonderful, husky-voiced, sleepy-eyed singer and dancer. I worshiped her, but only from afar, until she invited me to drop into her dressing room any time I wanted to, and then I worshiped her close at hand. She seemed to me to be everything I could ever dream of being as a seriostage artiste.

Phyllis Monkman, a bewitching leading dancer and a famous English revue star for years afterward, whom I admired first as an artist and then as dear "Phyllick," my friend, was also in the show. More of her will appear any second now.

One of the highlights of the show was the scenery. Uncle André had given the designers their fling, together with printed credit in the program, which was rare praise for a designer in them there days. The sets ranged from an elaborate representation of Shakespeare's Globe Theatre to an even more elaborate Egyptian scene, full of deep blue shadows and mystery.

This was the work of a many-talented man, Arthur E. P. Brome Weigall, archaeologist, Egyptologist and author of numerous definitive works on various ancient civilizations and their treasures, including Cleopatra. Arthur—I can call him that because he soon became one of the family—encouraged the elder King Farouk to found the National Egyptian Museum of Ancient and Natural History as part of a campaign that saved many treasures, not including Cleopatra, which would otherwise have been swiped from

Egypt, like most of the contents of Tutankhamen's tomb. (Arthur was there when the museum was opened, as an honored guest, and he became the Inspector General of Antiquities, Government of Egypt.)

But let's shake the sands of the desert out of our shoes and press on to say that Arthur Weigall had turned to stage designing, directing, writing novels and lyrics and altogether proving himself to be a very useful fellow to have around. He had also choreographed the ballet for the Egyptian *scena* in the revue. The chorus was made up of slowly moving figures carrying urns and palm fronds like slaves in a stone frieze (or the ladies in Cooke's Presbyterian). The principal dancer was Phyllis, decked out as Cleopatra, doing her stuff to the smile of a sphinx. This was "The Spirit of Egypt."

Opening night proved to be slightly more sensational than anyone had anticipated. Down in the orchestra pit, the drums, cymbals and flutes were pounding out pyramid-style music. The slaves were swaying under their palm branches. Phyllis was whirling and weaving all over the stage. Then one half of Cleopatra's breastplate slipped, and one half of Phyllis came out of hiding.

Audiences weren't used to such treats in 1915. There was a gasp, then a cheer, and Phyllis rushed into the wings. She never could explain what happened next. Instead of running to her dressing room, she emerged again onto the stage, holding her bare left breast in her left hand and pointing to the trophy with her right.

"This is a pretty thing, a very pretty thing!"

The curtain came rapidly down. She had finally stopped the show.

In my customary role as girl hero, I sang a duet,

"Up the River," with Lee as the River Girl and me "the nicest boy imaginable," as one reviewer wrote. After playing that scene every night, I had to scramble back into evening dress (white tie) as Lord Lionel Lyonesse for another "take me back" song.

> . . . Back to the shack where the black-eyed
> Susans grow.
> I love 'em so.
> They're all around, on the ground . . .*

It usually went down well, but at one performance, I had encore after encore. Every time I scuttled into the wings, the audience called me back.

"Take another call," Danny O'Neill, who was Charlot's long-time stage manager, kept saying with a grin. So finally I sang the chorus over, feeling rather grand that it was my turn to stop the show.

It wasn't until the curtains finally closed that I discovered what the excitement was about. In the haste of the costume change, I'd forgotten to button my fly. It wasn't so much my singing that the audience liked as the sight of my shirt sticking out. *Way* out!

I was tempted to keep the unbuttoned fly "in" as a standard item for Lord Lionel Lyonesse, but Dada said, "Not on your *vie* Bea," *the spoilsport.*

---

* "Where the Black-Eyed Susans Grow" (Whiting-Radford) Copyright © 1917 by Remick Music Corp. Copyright renewed. Used by permission of Warner Bros. Music. All Rights Reserved.

CHAPTER FIVE

MAIDENHOOD AT MAIDENHEAD
AND ELSEWHERE

I remember being rather bashful about leaving off my trousers in public and reverting to maidenhood. Would you believe that I was *very* prim and proper in those days? Following his promise of the slow build-up, Uncle André was in the process of liberating me from shirttails and fly buttons and putting me back into skirts. I was a little uneasy about what it involved.

For the new show he was doing, and he was forever doing a new show, he had me singing along with a sextet of young ladies whose costumes were high off the ground and low from the ceiling. I hadn't seen my costume until I put it on in the dressing room (girls' side) and I was, though I do say it myself, taken aback and, come to that, taken afront, too. So much *flesh* in view after the coverage provided by jackets and trousers!

In a panic of girlish modesty, I looked around until I found a shawl, which I draped over my shoulders and clutched over my collarbones. Even then, I loitered in the wings, plucking up courage to join the rehearsal.

Charlot spotted me. "Stop, everybody! Bea Lillie, what are you doing now? You're not in church, you know. Take that shawl off!"

How we tried his patience! As a result of his influence—strictly fatherly, I promise you—I was slowly weaning myself of the idea that I was destined to be a figure of tragedy like Camille or Queen Christina or Nellie, the Beautiful Model. It might be more fun to be funny and have audiences laugh intentionally.

The first conscious, fumbling attempt cost Funny Pants Lillie five shillings. To make a curtain call one night, I came out with a big false mustache wiggling under my nose and ventured a kind of giggle. The audience rather took to it, I thought. Charlot didn't. The following morning, there was a notice pinned on the board by the stage door: BEATRICE LILLIE FINED FIVE SHILLINGS FOR TRYING TO BE FUNNY.

I wasn't discouraged in the least, but it clearly wasn't time yet to put my dress suit in moth balls. As a matter of fact, I kept my last set of tails for more than a dozen years, and the waistband still fitted me the last time I tried it on.

There was something quite wonderful about working for Uncle André. The feeling grew as one show followed another, each of them with the brief, snappy title that was a kind of signature of his. We did *Samples* and *Some* and *Cheep* and *Tabs;* all at the Vaudeville Theatre. Eventually we got to a point—I'm skipping a year or two here—when a new opening night was closing in on us, with the Prince of Wales's Theatre booked but no title to put on the marquee. So Charlot decided to call the show *Bran-Pie*—everyone could have a dip. *Bran-Pie* marked a big change in my life, but we've quite a way to go before we get to that.

Life grew more frivolous with every new show I appeared in. That must have been due very largely to the contrast between the horror of the continuing, mounting war across the English Channel and the almost frantic gaiety of night life and theatre in the West End of London.

The war was very close to home, and that closeness made the tremendous losses of the country's young manhood most keenly felt. Not that Canadian, Empire and, later, American troops, equally fine men, weren't just as tragically expended, but in their case the greater distance from home and the longer time it took news to travel somehow blunted the horror a little bit.

Charlot's company was a band of hard-working, happy clowns who'd do virtually anything to put laughter in the hearts of the audiences, which were made up mostly of men in khaki, navy blue or the paler blue of the newly formed Royal Flying Corps.

Even the Zeppelins that Kaiser Bill was sending over now to bomb London weren't taken too seriously, until I went into a nursing home in a short gap between shows to have my tonsils out. I looked out the window one night to see a Zep, pale and gleaming as the searchlights caught it. Suddenly it crumbled in flames, and you could see crewmen falling from the blazing wreckage. This was the raider, on a course to bomb the Bank of England and the Admiralty, that a young lieutenant, W. Leefe-Robinson, shot down from his little fighter plane, to become an overnight hero.

The raids continued. At first, we looked on them as a novelty. Sometimes in the middle of a show we'd run down off the stage and flock out into the Strand along with the audience to watch the Zeppelins float over, like silver fish in the night sky.

I pressed on with my new ambition to be a comedienne, aided and abetted by Lee White, who used to stand in the wings to try to make me laugh in the middle of whatever I was doing when what I was doing wasn't supposed to be funny. I was still cast as the singer of "take me back" songs. Humor was now my own idea and an all-consuming passion.

One night the idea was to wander in and out of other people's sketches, saying, "Pardon me, but you're wanted on the gramophone." Another court-martial. Another fine. It seems as if Uncle André fired me every Saturday night for six years, but he invariably relented and took me on again in time for Monday night's performance.

And still the war went on and on. Everybody was talking about America's part in it. Would President Wilson bring the United States in? Would the Yanks ever get involved? Betting that they would, Clay Smith was busy writing a song for the occasion for his wife, Lee, to sing. Being Americans, they couldn't wait to have a number ready for when the great day arrived.

A week or so earlier I'd taken on Mabel Russell's part in *Samples*, in which Lee and Clay starred. I was rehearsing at the Vaudeville one morning when Charlot walked in with a girl I hadn't seen before. A quick glance at her showed enormous blue eyes in a vivid, elfish face. The quick thought flashed through my mind: "She's clever."

"Beattie," Charlot said, "I'd like you to meet Gertrude Lawrence. She's going to understudy you."

I was young and callow enough to be elated over the acquisition of my first understudy; I proceeded to

patronize her abominably. Since then, it's become a
kind of tradition that an understudy of mine finds her
light rather well concealed under a bushel or a peck.
It's a point of honor with me to go on, no matter what.
I believe that I owe it to my audience—it's as simple
as that. Once or twice in later years I worked without
any stand-by arrangements being made. In one show,
At Home Abroad, poor Paula Trueman worked for
nine months understudying me and by the end of
the run, she'd been on stage for exactly five minutes.
(I think I must have been caught in a fit of sneezing.)

Noëly, who came very briefly on to the Charlot
scene soon after the morning when Gertie and Beattie
met, once said in a moment of generosity, "When
you read the name Beatrice Lillie over a theatre
marquee, you can be fairly certain, even if you have
had to book your seats months ahead, that she will
be there." And very nice, too. True, as well.

Gertie had long been an understudy and member
of the chorus of *Some* by the time America entered
the war. That April evening, a number of mine was
cut for Clay Smith's timely addition to the show,
which he had seemingly written overnight. He stepped
out from behind the curtains to announce his brand-
new rouser, "America Answers the Call." The front
tabs were drawn, and there stood Lee, tall and majestic
giving out in her strong contralto:

> America answers the call, America answers the
>   call—
> Tramp, tramp, tramp, tramp, tramp,
> The boys are marching . . .

There was no resisting the impulse. Standing behind
the drop curtains to hear what Clay had wrought, my

feet began to feel a twitch. In a moment, I was marking time, then I started marching myself to the beat of the drummer, to and fro behind Lee. Other members of the company stifled their giggling, but the more they stifled, the more I marched until the curtains swayed as if in a high breeze. Feeling the same impulse, Gertie fell into step behind me.

Enter Clay Smith, at a gallop. "My God, Bea, where do you think you are?"

I flicked a wrist at him (Harry Rich gesture of disdain). "The Ritz," I answered for no particular reason.

Enter Uncle André, fuming. "You," he spluttered. "Out. Ten days."

Gertie would have been permanently thrown out on the spot, except the show must go on, and she was my understudy. So he paroled me and fired her at the next morning's rehearsal. I should explain that in the middle of any current Charlot show, we were usually rehearsing for the next. I took her to lunch to console her.

In the first few weeks of our knowing each other, she had stood up so well to my supercilious airs that we were happily laying the foundation of a friendship that endured years of playing together in the same shows, sharing rooms together and then a house we took in New York. In the not too distant future, we'd be pictured with arms entwined round each other's necks or clasping hands, for all the world like the Dolly Sisters or Miss Tweedledum and Miss Tweedledee.

Charlot was great for both of us. Without him we'd have been nothing. We were almost exactly the same age. To give her the name she was born with, Gertrude Alexandra Dagmar Lawrence Klasen had started, like me, as a child entertainer at her mother's "musical evenings," singing and skipping around to:

> Oh, it ain't all honey, and it ain't all jam,
> Walking round the 'ouses with a three-wheel
>   pram,
> All on me lonesome, not a bite to eat,
> Walking about on me poor old feet.*

As we got to know each other better, we were amazed and delighted to find out how much we had in common. We had both sung from the stages of movie theatres in between performances—and, to tell the truth, so had Mumsie in her day.

Gertie hadn't been in a church choir, but she *had* appeared as a chorister in Max Reinhardt's *The Miracle*. By the time she was eighteen, she had toured through most of Britain's provinces, which sounded not too much unlike the adventures of the Lillie Trio up and down the Province of Ontario.

She hadn't been caught in a fire as we had in Cobalt, but she had known what it was like to be stranded, when a manager decamped with everything in the till in Shrewsbury, Shropshire. There had been no Harry Rich in her life to wire her the bus fare home. Instead, she'd kept body and soul together by working as a barmaid in a local hotel and was saved from the suds when another touring company arrived in town, needing a girl to sing the theme song in their show, *The Rosary*.

For years and years, Gertie and I were seldom apart. That made me somewhat intrigued to see how, in a

---

* "Oh It Ain't All Honey and It Ain't All Jam" written by George Everard & Fred Murray, 1901.

Twentieth Century-Fox production called *Star!* I was altogether erased from history. Gertie, as played by Julie Andrews (whom I came to regard as a darling when we made *Thoroughly Modern Millie* together), never had a friend named Beattie. I'll tell you what happened. The creators of *Star!* For the sake of accuracy were offered the use of my name. But in typical Hollywood style, they wanted *all* or nothing. That is to say, the right to impersonate me throughout and also do one of my numbers, "March with Me." When the answer was, "No, thank you very much," they omitted all mention of Beatrice Lillie. I was deleted from the script as though I'd never existed. Pity. I'll bet Gertie has had a good laugh at the deplorable box-office fate of an inaccurate movie.

The moral, dear, is: Refuse all substitutes and always read the label. *C'est Lady Peel qui parle. C'est Lady Quarle qui peel. C'est Lady Parle qui . . .*

Flashing back to Gertie, the luncheon table and the consolation scene; I fancy that I bought the meal, possibly with a drink to go with it, because by this time I was making reasonably good money. Gertie had been taken on by Dada at a salary of three pounds a week, and by now she had a pile of debts to pay off.

Gertie thought that, as a new girl in the chorus, she'd be out permanently for having overstepped the mark in marching with me while Lee sang Clay's tribute to America. Happily, she was wrong. She was court-martialed, but not drummed out of the service. At the special request of Lee, who didn't hold grudges, Gertie was given another chance.

Patriotic songs with a red-white-and-blue flavor, imported across the Atlantic, became all the rage. I remember tackling a ditty entitled "Shoot the Rabbit," which made war in all its horror sound like a turkey shoot and openly implored America to join in and "have some fun":

> Shoot the rabbit, shoot the rabbit,
> The old folks, young folks, all got the habit.
> When the band plays night and day,
> You act like a chicken with its head cut off.
> Johnny get your gun,
> Let's have some fun.
> Come on and shoot the rabbit with me.*

Gertie and I used to horse around backstage like a couple of colts in a meadow. Lee, whose husband had money in the show, had a liberal allowance of songs, including "Have You Seen the Ducks Go By?" in the course of which, as one contented reviewer wrote, "you may be sure there are plenty of nice young 'beauty chorus' ducks going by in the background."

Part of their dance called for them to disappear behind a wall, with only their headdresses, suitably ducky, showing over the top. Gertie liked to make her hat wiggle and waggle, and from time to time she'd pop her face up over the wall to wink at the audience. Then, out of sheer high spirits, while between my own numbers, I'd intrude on line with the regular ducklings and pop *my* head up, with a straw hat perched on my ears and my favorite false mustache clipped under my nose. You'd have *died!*

Charlot bore up bravely until our final performance, when I again joined the chorus line of baby ducks in a cowboy outfit.

---

* "Shoot the Rabbit." Copyright B. Marks Music Corporation. Used by permission.

My understudy may have been a latent star, but she needed assistance to help her shine. She had to have a chance to prove herself to Dada and the rest of the cast by playing *me*. After a certain amount of soul searching—was it the right thing to do to put friendship ahead of my public etc.?—I telephoned the theatre one morning.

"I'm in bed," I lied, in a croaky whisper, "with a temperature of a hundred and three. If it goes any higher, I'm going to sell."

So that night, with the same delicious feeling you get playing hooky from school, I took a busman's holiday and went to see Matheson Lang in *Chu Chin Chow*. I'd been itching to see it for months, but hadn't the chance to do so. I telephoned ahead for a ticket in the stalls and, with slight pangs of guilt by this time, slunk into my seat in plenty of time for the curtain. The seat next to mine remained empty until the last moment, just before the overture began. Then who should come down the aisle but Uncle André?

I wished I had the presence of mind to lapse into my prize-winning performance of childhood, pretending that my days were numbered, but I could do no more than blush, like a schoolgirl caught at the jam. I figured that someone had tipped him off when I bought my ticket. But he must have given his tacit blessing to my little plot. Apart from saying, "Good evening, Beattie; sorry I'm late," he was surprisingly docile. Maybe he thought I'd earned a night off.

In any case, Gertie appeared for me, and by all accounts, she was great.

That one chance provided for Gertie would have been enough so far as I was concerned, but fate soon entered, bearing bandages. Not to brag more than is absolutely necessary, I was in process of becoming something of an addition to the London social scene. One summer, f'rinstance, I took a house at Maidenhead, on the Thames, with Fay Compton, who played a rather large role in planning my immediate future, as we shall see. "Bridgewater Lodge" was the setting for many a frolicsome weekend party, both on and in the river.

Mother kept busy updating the scrapbooks that Pa had started. She joyfully pasted into a new, red-leather-covered tome—it looked like a cross between a hotel guest register and an oversized *Hymns Ancient and Modern* —such items as:

> IN THE PARK. Despite the cold yesterday, there was quite a decent turnout for church parade. I saw Prince Napoleon and Princess Clementine apparently consulting Achilles *(a statue)* as to which way they should go next, and he decided to go on to the Row side *(Rotten, that is)*. Many ladies riding—astride. I also ran across a merry group which included Beatrice Lillie and Eileen Molyneux. *(Eileen was the sister of Captain Edward Molyneux, the couturier.)*

One day on the Row, near the Hyde Park Hotel, one of the merry group of ladies riding astride found some lines of a lyric remembered from the good old Toronto days floating through her head as she sailed through the air off a skittish mount and landed with a considerable thump: *The next horse I ride on, I'm going to be tied on.*

Result: A medium concussion, plus a sadly bent collarbone. I was in plaster for three weeks. Fate, the true impresario, had intervened.

Gertie's star had flickered a little. She'd been given

a contract and parts in other Charlot revues. But as a
penalty for being absent at curtain time too often,
Dada had cancelled the contract and put Jessie Mat-
thews on in her place. Then he'd relented, and at
the time that a horse and I failed to agree, Gertie was
again my understudy, required to report at the theatre
every night and at matinees, too, in case of need. She
was also neatly pregnant.

You should have seen the write-ups she received
from the newspaper critics. Laced up tight by my
dresser, she went on for me, just the way it later
happened in Hollywood musicals and still happens
in the dreams of every understudy. In her autobiography, she wrote about that night:

> For the first time in my life, I knew anxiety. Bea
> was a tremendous favorite. Most of the audience
> had come on purpose to see her. Could I satisfy
> them? If I could hold that audience, if I could
> make them laugh and applaud and like Gertrude
> Lawrence, then the rest of my career was assured.
> If I failed, well—my cue came and I went on.
> Standing in the wings, watching with a worried
> look on his face, was André Charlot. I flashed
> him a smile. At eleven-thirty, after the final cur-
> tain, André Charlot kissed me on both cheeks and
> said, "Well done, Gertie."

After that, I thought maybe I'd better get back.
Uncle André seemed to be something less than
amused when I told him, "I don't know about the
horse, but I'm fit for work again." Need it be said that
he banned me from any future horseback riding in
Rotten Row or anywhere else?

Gertie and I understood each other, and so did

Charlot and I. There was *no* cattiness between Gertie and me, and Dada and I never played games. He was, besides all other qualities, a businessman, and I liked that.

As soon as I could walk, I limped back through the stage door. Gertie went off to a nursing home to have her baby, to be named Pamela, who was born prematurely on the same Monday night that I reappeared on the stage where Gertie had last played my role forty-eight hours earlier. You might call it a close call. Gertie appointed me godmother, a role I was happy to accept.

She had more courage than anyone I've known, except possibly Noël Coward. She was curiously like him in many ways. Their lives ran side by side like railroad tracks from the day they met, each eleven years old, at the classes in dance and drama that Italia Conti held in a basement lined with mirrors a few steps round the corner from Great Portland Street, London.

Gertie used to tell how Noël had a phonograph which she secretly coveted, while she owned a bicycle that he envied, though it was, in his opinion, "quite unsuitable for a girl."

Ultimately it was Noël who really brought to light Gertie's talents and provided her with the greatest chances. But he struck out when I introduced him to Charlot.

Noël was then a rather condescending young man, paper thin, with a faint lisp. He was already writing songs, and songs with a difference. Instead of the usual moonlight and roses, there was a dash of vinegar. Come to think of it, he was quite remarkably as he is today—very clever but uncomfortable to be with at times. I had met him somehow as another one of *us;* young people trying to make their mark in the theatre. Thanks to Charlot, I'd made my first dent already.

"Beattie," Noël asked, quite understandably, "do you think you could get me an introduction to Charlot?" He didn't want to try it on his own, a feeling I knew only too well.

Uncle André was rehearsing a new revue, and he'd hired a big room on Bond Street for the purpose. I'd had a call to rehearse one day, and I knew Charlot would be there, with the whole cast. I had a few qualms about asking him outright whether he would like to hear Noël, so I told my ambitious young friend, "Just come up. I'm not going to try to arrange anything special. You come up and be ready to audition."

We were in the middle of a production number involving chorus and singers when Noël walked in, pale and a little bit twitchy. The piano stopped for a short break. Charlot gave me a filthy look when I introduced this very nervous young man and said, "I just want him to play you this song he's written. It's called 'Forbidden Fruit.' You'll *love* it."

The expression on Uncle André's quizzical face said, "Want to bet?"

Noël sat himself at the piano and played, *Every peach, out of reach, is attractive . . .*

Though listening politely, Charlot could scarcely wait for him to finish. He grabbed his hand, shook it vigorously and walked him toward the door, murmuring, "Very kind of you. Thank you very much." Out went Noël, nudged by a very subtle cold shoulder. Charlot just stopped short of slamming the door behind him.

"How dare you," said Dada, turning on me, "bring people here with no talent *whatsoever?*"

Fade-out. Fade-in. Years have passed. Noëly, not yet knighted at this time but a prince among men for all that, came into my dressing room with Marina, Duchess of Kent; he resplendent in a dinner jacket as only he can be, she beautifully groomed and smiling her congratulations. This was London, near the completion of the long run of *An Evening With Beatrice Lillie.*

"You were very good, Beattie," said Noël (who *can* be patronizing), after we'd made the salutations.

"Enchanting. I shall be coming to see your show again," said the Duchess.

"You'll have to be quick," I said. "We close next week."

There was a series of bangs and clatters outside my dressing-room door. Leslie Bricusse, my young leading man, was making his first professional appearance after producing, directing and appearing in that year's *Footlight Revue* at Cambridge University, where he had taken an honors degree in languages. He had just received a second, urgent call to come and meet the Duchess. He was in his dressing room, anxious to remove his make-up before entering the royal presence. At the second hurry-up call, he raced out the door and fell headfirst down a flight of stairs. By the time he reached the bottom, he deserved another degree in languages, plus a royal warrant. Fade-out.

While Charlot was providing the opportunities for me to make something of myself, Muriel was busy exercising her talents, too. Mumsie had reason to be

proud of her girls, and so had Pa, who had arrived at
last from Toronto to try to enlist and do his bit to win
the war. He thought the recruiting officer made a
sad mistake in turning him down on the grounds
that he was a touch too old, but it was a happy day
when sometime later he came to live with us in a
house I'd taken in St. John's Wood.

My sister could fairly be described as a concert
pianist now that she had made her debut at Wigmore
Hall. She was also proving her talents at song writing,
with the result that at last I had something which had
been previously lacking—a "take me back" number
that took me back to Canada.

I introduced it at the dress rehearsal of *Cheep*,
which followed on the heels of *Some*, toward the end
of April 1917. Clay Smith and Lee White were backers
of the show, and I had a notion that Clay was none
too happy about my new number, because he suspected it would be a hit.

As Noël remembers it, this was the show that
marked the real turning point for me, "the first
time," as he wrote, "the sleek and urbane Beatrice
Lillie appeared in her true colors as a comic genius of
the first order." (Get *him!*) There are so many con-
flicting accounts of when, where and how that magic
moment came about that I'm prepared to take *his*
word for it if you are, though sometimes I have me
doubts.

At any rate, when *Cheep* opened, I was still in a
sort of chrysalis, halfway between caterpillar and but-
terfly, not yet completely out of trousers, not yet fully at home in skirts. For Muriel's song, I had to wear
the old top hat and tails, because she had me singing my "little girlie" in Hawaii, another date in Michi-

gan and a third who dwelt "amongst the golden grain
—Gee! I gotta go back again."

I recollect that the idea of a young dandy aching to
return to the Golden West was an accepted tradition
of the time which nobody considered out of place.
So, with a tweak of the tie and a twirl of the tails, I
sang about the glories of Canada:

> Oh, take me back to the Land of Promise,
> Back to the land of the ice and the snow.
> There you and I once more together will
>   wander,
> Down lovers' lane, where the maple trees
>   grow.
> Skating, baseball and canoeing,
> That's the place to do your billing and cooing.
> Oh, take me back to the land I love best,
> Back to my little gray home in the West.

Believe me, this was good, serious stuff, and the audience accepted it as such.

For the second act, I could literally let down my
hair, which reached almost to my shoulders, and put
on a long, green satin evening gown to join in a
burlesque musical act called "The Dedleigh Dull
Quartet." (Oh, we were *funny* in those days!) From
the décolletage of my dress, there protruded one large
chrysanthemum.

According to Noël, he climbed over the wall of a
military hospital in London, where he was confined
with a chill suffered as a raw recruit in His Majesty's
Armed Forces, hurried home to change into civvy
clothes and came to a matinee of *Cheep*. He apparently enjoyed what he saw in the quartet.

"She sang, in a piercing soprano, a straight popular ballad called 'Bird of Love Divine.' She sang this also with apparently the utmost sincerity, but it did *just* occur to her during the second verse to prop her music up against the chrysanthemum. I believe I was still laughing when, a couple of hours later, I clambered back over the hospital wall to be discovered demurely in bed for evening roll call."

Well, we all have to begin somewhere. I've found that men as a rule resist laughing at women. The explanation can probably be found buried down deep in the general subject of s-e-x. I must confess that a woman clown in baggy pants and a putty nose has no particular appeal for me, either.

Funny clothes aren't necessary if anyone has the right instinct for comedy. And if you haven't got that, then what's the point in trying to be a comedienne? That's what I always say. (Now do I *really*?)

I think it's important to be able to laugh at yourself before you can laugh at anybody else, and to detect and deflate pomposity or bad manners, anywhere up or down the social scale. I believe that one is either born funny or non-funny. This ability can be developed—that's within the scope of talent—to produce laughter is God-given. Spontaneity is important, too.

At one end of the social scale, there was a dowager at a party trying to be a little bit more ritzy than she could successfully handle as she boasted to me about her jewelry. "You know," she gushed, "I clean my diamonds with ammonia, my rubies with Bordeaux, my emeralds with Danzig brandy and my sapphires with fresh milk. And you, Miss Lillie?"

"Oh, I don't bother cleaning mine. When they gets

dirty, I simply throws them away."

And at the other end of the scale, we have the disgruntled cabdriver who picked me up outside the East End apartment house where I make my home in New York. I wanted to go across town to the West Side, which meant crossing Fifth Avenue. But this was St. Patrick's Day, and Fifth Avenue was closed for much of its length, so that the Irish could march up the street, as they always do, by the tens of thousands, while traffic piled up, waiting to cross.

"Goddam Irish," grunted the cabbie as we crept along. "Bunch of stupid Micks," he went on, as we slowed to a halt at every other yard. "Know what I'd like? I'd like to see 'em all drop dead," and so on until at last we reached my destination.

My *Irish* not *quite* fully up; to the fare that had clicked up on the meter, I added a dollar tip. "Something for you, driver. Buy yourself a sense of humor."

In First World War time London, all kinds of things were missing, but there wasn't a shortage of good humor. Food was scarce, and new clothes were hard to come by. Almost everything in the shops was rationed, but you could find a party in full blast somewhere every night of the week.

Some of the best parties were given by Ivor Novello, whose plays and music rival anything Noël has written, in my opinion; in fact, it's possible that his music, which is generally more serious than Noël's, will live longer, particularly among British audiences, than the more brilliant, witty works of Noël Coward.

Ivor was scarcely out of his teens. He still had something of the look of the musical prodigy he'd been as a boy—dreamy brown eyes, pale face, jet-black hair. He'd been trained by his mother, the queenly Madame

Clara Novello Davies, as a boy soprano who never sang again after his voice broke. He had become almost a national hero by writing the music of "Keep the Home Fires Burning," the marching song of British Tommies that matched "Tipperary" in its pull at everybody's heart. The lyric, by the way, was written by *an American*, Lena Guilbert Ford, who was killed in a Zeppelin raid.

Ivor lived in one of the coziest flats in London, under the dome of the Aldwych Theatre, with views of rooftops down Fleet Street and up the Strand. You got there by entering a narrow doorway, No. 11 Aldwych, then riding a creaky little lift that held no more than one at a time, and that was a squeeze.

This was the lift from which a celebrated American comedian once emerged, clutching a delicate portion of his anatomy, complaining shrilly, "I've been ruined."

In the flat, with its well sat-in furniture and lingering smell of kippers drifting in from the kitchen, Ivor gave party after party to spend the embarrassing flood of money that his song was earning for him and others who became involved with singing it. It was said he made close to £90,000 in royalties, and a single recording earned £50,000 for John McCormack, the famed Irish tenor.

Uncle André was my escort when I visited No. 11 for the first time. Ivor, a member of the Royal Flying Corps, worked at the Air Ministry in Whitehall, and he'd hurry home most evenings to be host. You could find everybody who was or wanted to be somebody in the theatre enjoying themselves in the living room, which seemed always full of flowers, good humor and Ivor's special brand of shy sincerity.

A theatre manager would have given his back

teeth to sign a tenth of them. George Robey, Violet Loraine, Gladys Cooper, Heather Thatcher, Delysia, George Grossmith, Max Darewski, Beerbohm Tree, Gerald Du Maurier, Charles Cochran, Phyllis Monkman, Lily Elsie. Gertie was often there, and, eventually, Noël was often her escort and mine. Oh, yes; we also sometimes saw the Prince of Wales.

I hadn't met Ivor until Charlot introduced me though he was already well known by reputation. I thought instantaneously, "No one who looks so absolutely like God's gift to matinee fans can possibly be human." But I was quite wrong. Ivor turned out to be the most understanding, kindest friend I had in London. The friendship continued until he died much too soon in March 1951, soon after a happy holiday we'd shared with some close friends at his home in Jamaica, "Wyndways."

According to the custom of the establishment at No. 11, Ivor's guests were expected to perform, and this was a place where we all *wanted* to do our stuff. From the moment each of us arrived, a non-stop, impromptu revue was staged to the sound of the grand piano, played by anyone with the urge to try, sometimes thumped by amateurs, sometimes resounding under the fingers of one of the master musicians whom Ivor knew, even in those early days.

Outside the blacked-out windows, under the onion-shaped theatre dome, you could hear the night sounds of wartime London—sirens warning that Zeps were on the way; anti-aircraft batteries opening up; the rattle of shrapnel from their shells falling on the roof and in the street outside.

That was the backdrop for our performances, each of us taking his turn to provide some improvised bit of song or laughter, while the rest sat around in the slightly shabby armchairs or sprawled on cushions on the floor, applauding or catcalling until it was somebody else's turn. It was at these many gatherings that my long personal and professional association with Ivor Novello began. Ivor was the composer of many of the musical numbers which I sang in those early Charlot revues, often dressed in the uniform of a Canadian "Tommy" and singing of home and mother, as in the highly popular "When I Am With Her Again" sung from a battlefield "trench" setting.

The Zeppelin raids didn't bother anybody very much. They were a kind of psychological threat which didn't work, just as the infinitely more dangerous air raids the Germans made on London in the *Second* World War didn't work either. I've always thought that the pattern of London life in wartime, of pressing on with your daily job no matter what, was established in those early years. We learned more or less to ignore the intrusion of war. I'm sure that explains to a great degree the spirit of Londoners, and the British, during the blitz of the Second World War, followed by the terror of the buzz bomb and rocket attacks.

If, as the good Dr. Samuel Johnson declared, "Nothing can make the town so fond of a man as a successful play," I should like to add that, in my experience, nothing could make the men so fond of a girl as a part in a Charlot revue, and the experience I'm speaking of came as the war drew on, oh, so slowly, toward Armistice Day.

Both officers and gentlemen became known to me, stagedoor Johnnies as well as genuine heroes. Some were bold, some were blushing. Some brought chocolates, some brought propositions. I used to wish then, as I do now, that I had a better memory for details and names, because sometimes life grows positively confusing.

We have hurried on now to the days of *Bran-Pie*, which, as the advertising claimed, had something for everybody. It had a new beau for me.

Fay Compton, who wasn't in our show but in something of her own, invited me to luncheon one day. Now it happened that the evening before I had received, in my dressing room, a basket of orchids and a card signed "Wilfred Steele." At the luncheon table in the Criterion Restaurant in Piccadilly Circus, a friend of Fay's and mine sauntered over with a very tall, fair and handsome young stranger in tow and said, "I've someone here who'd like to meet you. May I present Wilfred Steele?" At least, that's what I *thought* he said.

I gushed, "It was so kind of you to send those lovely flowers. I do appreciate it very much. Absolutely lovely flowers."

"Flowers?" murmured the fair one. "I'm afraid there's some mistake. I didn't send any. As a matter of fact, I haven't seen you in the show yet. Only just out of uniform, you see."

I plunged into the embarrassed silence. "But you must have sent them. I've got your card in my bag. Here, it says, 'Can't wait to meet you. Worshipfully, Wilfred Steele.'"

Embarrassed laughter. "But that's not my name. I'm *Bobby Peel*."

My turn to smile. "Pity! Well, do come to see us anyway, any time."

To cut a short story even shorter, he did arrive at the theatre later that week. A friendship budded, blossomed and flowered, carefully cultivated by a number of friends, first and foremost being Fay Compton.

If you can scarcely wait for the next thrilling installment, all you have to do is turn the page.

Better take a tea, coffee, or what-have-you break, first though. . . .

CHAPTER SIX

A LADY IN MY OWN WRONG

I'm afraid there's no avoiding it, as the bishop said to
the actress. We have to make a brief detour to visit
the social scene and take a quick look at the Peel family tree. After the lunchtime introduction, Fay saw to
it that Big Bobby Peel and I got to know and like
each other. I had to do a little dipping into history to
discover exactly who he was, kicking myself for not
paying more attention when I sat impatiently waiting
to grow up at a desk in the Gladstone Avenue School.

There were enough Peels, I found, to ring in the
New Year. Debrett's peerage is studded, which I doubt
is the *mot juste,* with related earls, viscounts, baronets
and knights, though it was only the baronets who
concerned me. They were all christened Robert, to
add to the confusion, and I added a touch of mine by
calling my husband "Bobby" and my son mostly
"Bobbie." (It *does* sound different, so there!)

The first Sir Robert, baronet, founded the family
fortunes as a cotton manufacturer in the early days of
the Industrial Revolution, which put factories where

farms used to be and put little children, dear God, to labor in those factories. "Parsley" Peel, as he was nicknamed from the leaf pattern on the printed calico turned out in his Lancashire works, came from a line of Yorkshire yeomen who had migrated into the next-door county, Lancashire, a scant three hundred years before today's lesson began. Yes, he *was* related to that world-famous John Peel of "D'ye Ken" fame, by two hundred years or so!

"Parsley" had a small estate near Blackburn named "Peel Fold," of which more later, but as his profits piled up, he bought other estates in Staffordshire, Warwickshire and Lancashire. In Tamworth, Staffordshire, he built a cotton factory and in 1790 purchased an ancient manor house and estates. Drayton Manor was its name and, as later reconstructed by the second baronet, it became a jewel in the glittering collection of the stately homes of England. (What a spiffing song title for someone!) Drayton Manor had one hundred and twenty rooms and fifty different varieties of trees planted all over its far too many acres.

The gardens were exceptional. A special feature was an array of terraces, each blooming with a different collection of rare plantings and borders, herbaceous, annuals, perennials and even quarterlies. These terraces were arranged in banks like a theatre auditorium. The stage in this case was a large swan lake (no, it wasn't a duckpond), upon which sailed the usual white ones and some rare black. The official title of this "Swan Lake" was "The American Pool!" How progressive and realistic! All that now remains of the classic pile is the original clock tower which appeared in all the original prints and paintings. It still stands where it was, a sturdy reminder of the golden days. Close by the manor, at the tiny hamlet of Drayton Bassett, old "Parsley" put up a little chapel (now St. Peter's Parish Church), and in the city of Manchester, where the cotton trade was booming, a lunatic asylum. You'll have to decide for yourself the significance of *that*.

As one of the mustier history books on my library shelves breathlessly exclaims, "How great are the prizes to be gained by energy, enterprise and intelligence in a free and commercial country!"

"Parsley" had already "secured a princely fortune," in the words of my old history book, when he entered politics. As a politician, his conscience started to prick him, and he strongly recommended that no child less than nine years should be employed in any factory and then not be compelled to work more than eleven hours a day; laughable now, but a tremendous gain in those days. On November 29, in the year of our Lord, 1800, "Parsley" was created a baronet, which placed him in the ranks of British aristocracy at an elevation between a common knight and the more lordly viscount.

He had six sons, five daughters and thirty-nine grandchildren, but the apple of his eye was his heir, who, of course, had been christened Robert. When he wrote his will on July 27, 1820, it was Robert who was left the biggest single share of his estate. The personal property alone of the first baronet amounted to close to one million pounds, the biggest fortune of its kind in England; in those days when a pound was indeed a pound.

The old gentleman was anxious to see that his fortune was kept intact, so he arranged a Private Act of

Parliament at the same time as he wrote his will, to make sure the inheritance went only to heirs he approved of, with no chance of slip-up.

My London solicitor once explained for me what that meant. "The funds were not only entailed in the direct line from elder son to elder son through the generations, but more than that, the settlement was not subject to normal limitation on duration, which used to be for a maximum of three generations and is now, in practical effect, for only two generations." "Parsley" had his eye on eternity, and, as things turned out, I owed him a debt of eternal gratitude for making sure that, come what may, thousands of acres of England belonged to the Peels.

The most famous of them was the second baronet, who all his life retained a Lancashire accent and dropped his *h*'s. He was very tall, six feet sixish inches—all Sir Roberts topped six feet three inches—and resolute-looking, just like the man I married, with a certain style and appearance that ran in the family. The great statesman even towered over that colossus, Wellington, by several inches. This might explain the slight amount of occasional friction which erupted between these two great Englishmen. He covered himself with scholastic glory at Christ Church, Oxford, and became the youngest Member of Parliament in history at the age of twenty-three.

Another history book describes him as "a man shy, reserved, cold, and yet hot-tempered and imperious, and most of all an unselfish character incapable of mean actions or the slightest deception—a political cavalier *sans reproche.*" To which there was added, in the nature of my husband, a touch of *laissez faire* and a dash of *je ne sais quoi.*

Everyone knows—or do they?—that the British policeman, "bobby" or "peeler," owes his nicknames to the founder of the Metropolitan Police Force, none other than the second Sir Robert. He also repealed the Corn Laws, founded the British Conservative Party and earned a reputation as the best Prime Minister the country ever had. I am sorry to list here another of his accomplishments; he established the first Income Tax, at sevenpence on the pound! But Queen Victoria was not really amused. He was awkward in society of the capital "S" kind, and she once noted waspishly that she "would like him better if he would keep his legs still."

Nevertheless, when he was killed in 1850, thrown from his horse on Constitution Hill in Green Park, she sent a wreath of gold which was buried beside him in the family vault in the little chapel his father had built at Drayton Bassett. The fortune was intact, but his heir, the third baronet, apparently set out rather promptly to demonstrate another trait in the Peel blood—that "few sons are like their father." (Did you know Homer said that? I didn't.) At any rate, it is apparently chic and right so to do. . . .

Number three it appears made his mark as one of the most reckless spendthrifts of the mid-nineteenth century, when there was a lot of competition for a reputation like that. This champion among squanderers went through his inheritance at a gallop. To pay his gambling debts, he sold off the family's princely collection of paintings. According to legend, he cut "The Blue Boy" from its frame and wrapped it around his torso under his greatcoat and sneaked it out of the house. He would have sold Drayton Manor, too, if old "Parsley" hadn't been so farsighted.

But the Peels still owned their ancestral home when Big Bobby, *Mr.* Robert Peel, who was the fourth heir to the baronetcy, began a-courting me. What the press agents wrote about him as they plastered the newspapers and glossy weeklies with photographs of us, wasn't *quite* true. He was no "heir to a great fortune," but a towering, charming young man, wondering what he should turn his hand to if he had to make his own way in the world.

Ivor Novello, always perceptive, thought Bobby was "charming, gullible and devilishly attractive" when I introduced him.

He and the rest of his family were living on limited allowances doled out by the Public Trustee. Bobby's father had scrupulously kept up the spendthrift tradition. After the Armistice, he'd gone into bankruptcy for the seventh time after relatives had scraped up £45,000 to pay some of his debts. The Peel armorial bearings included a busy bee and the family motto, INDUSTRIA, which seemed to have applied only to the first and second of the baronets.

Bobby's father, the fourth, had hoped that his son would restore the family to riches by marrying an heiress before he chose me. Bobby had been honorably discharged from the Guards with suspected tuberculosis, which proved to be only suspected. He was just back from a convalescent trip to sunny Australia, and he was twenty-one years old. Nearly four of those years had been spent in the Army. At seventeen, he'd run away from Harrow to enlist, in sunny Brighton by the sea as a private in the Royal Fusiliers Public Schools Battalion, but his height—I didn't quite reach his shoulder—had made him a natural candidate for the Coldstream Guards.

121

Backstage at the Prince of Wales's Theatre, the stage doorkeeper used to say, with a perfectly straight face, "Your young man's waiting for you, Miss Lillie; the lieutenant from the Cold Cream Guards."

By now, I was really starting to twinkle, twinkle, little star. I'd played in my first *book musical,* as distinct from revue. *Oh, Joy!* was billed as "a musical peace piece," and as a sign of the times, it boasted a genuine male chorus of half a dozen lads back from the war. As a further sign of the times, it charged the unheard price of fifteen shillings—three whole dollars in the currency of the day—for a seat in the first five rows of the stalls.

The critics thought I was very sexy in fur-lined pajamas and a white evening gown that reached down to here in the rear. I enjoyed ever minute of it, though we were all panicked by the fact that the original Broadway title, *Oh, Boy!* was considered too risqué for staid olde London. How sedate could you get? *Strewth!*

My Cold Cream Guard was a firm favorite with Mumsie, who kept busy pasting in yet another scrapbook whole pages from the society magazines with such scrumptious headlines as "A Wedding Belle and its 'Peel.'"

The four Lillies had celebrated Armistice Day, while everybody else in London went wild with joy and relief, by moving into roomier quarters, a house I had taken at 10 Loudon Road, a smart residential section of St. John's Wood in northwest London, around the corner from Abbey Road, which John, Paul, George and Ringo made famous nearly half a century later as *Beatleland.*

I don't know whether anyone but me in our family

had heard the rumor that my Big Bobby was the son of a different lily, the enchantress from Jersey, Lily Langtry. Those who knew his father weren't surprised in the least. It might have been so, who knows? I don't. Sir Robert's lawfully wedded wife, Lady Peel, was the daughter of Baron von Graffenried, of distinguished Swiss lineage. She and Sir Robert were fast approaching their silver wedding anniversary.

Rumor never bothers me; gossip strikes me as a shameful waste of valuable time. As I've always said, "Is that so? Were you under the bed?"

In the palmy days after the war, that line became something of a standard quip in London until, at one party, we sat engrossed while Constance Collier regaled us with her account of a particularly heated love affair.

She left out nothing. Everything was told in glowing detail—how often the lovers met, how many times they kissed, and how and how! When she reached the end of her story, there was a breathless pause. Thinking, "Clever me—I'll fix her," I broke the silence by asking archly, "Tell me, darling, were you under the bed?"

My friend swelled out her bosom and smiled like the Mona Lisa. I was put neatly in my place when she answered, "My dear, I was *in* it." I had learned two basic rules of comedy: don't try too hard to be funny; and don't stay with a clever line too long. Constance had topped me.

Again, there were parties, all kinds of parties, virtually every night of the week, lasting into early morning. London was racing to catch up on the good times that had been missing since 1914. The leader of the young set was the Prince of Wales, who ran second to nobody in his pursuit of a good time now that he was out of uniform—and sometimes out of favor with his father, King George V.

The young prince, boyish and debonair, was following in his grandfather's footsteps. Like Edward VII, he admired the theatre and its stars. He'd wander in backstage after dinner, tapping on the dressing-room doors to be introduced. The first time he sat in our audience, I was invited to meet him and asked to join a supper party he was giving later.

You could say that I was suddenly in the swim but, since I'd never worked at it, not in so deep as some others, like the beautiful dancer, June Tripp, who understandably was persuaded to drop her surname for professional purposes; as June, Lady Inverclyde, still a lovely theatrical ladyship, she's alive and well in California now.

Nor was I quite so much in the Prince of Wales's circle as Gertie, who was more often a guest at the parties in his flat in St. James's Palace, which were a kind of royal version of Ivor's midnight celebrations, where everyone with the taste for it had a turn at singing and dancing.

Gertie and I were forever popping in at the supper parties the Prince gave upstairs at Rule's, the little plush-and-gilt restaurant in Maiden Lane, a tomato's throw from Covent Garden, which were held in the same private room where Edward VII had frolicked with Lily Langtry. Rule's was so convenient; you could just cross narrow Maiden Lane to reach it from the stage entrance of the Vaudeville Theatre.

It all had the effect of making Gertie awfully and increasingly grand. During the early years of her career, money and Gertie were often strangers. When she had any, she flipped it away. I went to call on her once with Jack Buchanan, who was always around with us from the time of the Charlot revues. We found her installed in an enormous suite in an expensive hotel.

After she had given us a conducted tour of its splendors, Jack asked, "Why do you need a place as big as this?"

"Oh, but wait," she said. "You see, I have a chauffeur and three mehds."

"Three whats?" I said.

"Mehds."

I still didn't get it. "How do you spell it?"

"Mehd. M-A-I-D. And then I have a butler—"

I don't remember whether it was Jack or I who threw the first cushion at her. I know we knocked her down, literally. It did her good now and then. She was a darling, but she sometimes behaved like an Empress of China.

If we knew of a good party, we'd *go* whether or not we were asked. My companion in gate-crashing was often Fay Compton, who, before Bobby Peel, liked to keep an eye on me to see how the big romance was proceeding. The two of us showed up one evening at a highly elegant affair in Park Lane, where a receiving line was slowly winding its way from the marble-floored entrance hall to the top of the magnificent staircase a full floor above. There at the top stood Milord and Milady, to greet every guest while the butler announced each name loud and clear in a terrifying baritone.

"The Right Honorable the Earl and Countess of Whatsis," boomed the flunky in a bass voice loud enough to rattle the windowpanes. Smiles and limp handshakes among four. "Her Grace, the Duchess of Whodat." The same again, please, for three this time. "The Right Reverend John Clench, Bishop of Pishill-over-Lyme." Somber salutations.

I started to get the feeling that Fay and I were going too far as we ascended the social staircase, step by step, caught between an Order of the Bath and a diamond tiara beneath us and a solitary gentleman in immaculate evening dress just ahead of us on the stairs.

"His Excellency, Count However and Her Highness the Princess . . ." Only four announcements to go and we'd be at the head of the line, confronting the human loudspeaker. Courage failed me. I flipped up the black coattails of the man ahead of us and peeped inside.

"Quarter past ten," spake I, in a terribly Park Lane accent. "Time to go." Clasping hands and clutching evening bags, Fay and I turned tail down the staircase and escaped, still incognito and incorrigible.

This was an era, you may have read, when many a noble crest got decorated with a dab of greasepaint. Half the eligible peerage of the realm hung around stage doors, eying the eligible talent. Buttercups and daisies were grafted on to all kinds of family trees. "To knight, at 11:30" was a way of life. Every dancer in the chorus could tell you what happened to Gertie Millar, who became the Countess of Dudley when she married the Earl of same in 1924. Only P. G. Wodehouse could have invented the goings-on when a girl who knew how to say "Yes" and when to say "No" might make it with very little trouble from theatrical digs to the ducal suite. And Wodehouse didn't have to—it was all there to see ready-made. Being blessed with the conviction of true love I was luckily an exception. Marrying Mister Robert Peel was too good to be true. . . .

One of the headlines read, "Baronet's Heir Weds Actress," and scarcely any reporter could refrain from "theatrical romance." Big Bobby and I were married in the old-fashioned church that the first baronet had built, St. Paul's, in Fazeley, near Tamworth and Drayton Manor. My father, as to the manor born, very distinguished in a top hat and morning coat, gave me away. Muriel and our friend, Ida Morrison, in canary-yellow chiffon velvet, served as bridesmaids, carrying bouquets of daffodils. I had a Page to carry my train—brocaded satin with ostrich feathers, no less, in one corner. He, bless his heart, was Anthony Pelissier, Fay's son by her first husband, bearing up bravely in a pink satin Charles I suit.

Fay was there, of course, and a special train from London brought a lot of my friends from *Bran-Pie*. We had music enough to please even Mother, from "The Voice That Breathed O'er Eden," played while we followed the choir and clergy to the chancel step (kneelers embroidered in the Peel family colors), to Mendelsohn's "Wedding March" when we left as man and wife.

It was quite a day, a truly English rural fête, complete with evening fireworks, cheering villagers and two triumphal arches, one wishing us "Long Life and Happiness," the other "Health and Happy Days."

As we drove, oh, so sedately, through the Swiss Lodge entrance into Drayton Park, there were flags spanning the driveway, and more flags in the Statesman's Gallery of the house, where my mother and father gave a reception. I had a very clear impression that it was all like a fairy tale, but if I was impressed, it was nothing compared with the sensations experienced by a writer for that famous shiny weekly, *The Tatler*. The style reflects those gentler days.

"After the ceremony, I drove to Drayton Manor, where a sumptuous repast awaited the guests, perfectly purveyed by the Pattison-Hughes Catering Company, Ltd., Albany House, Dalton Street, Birmingham; and exceptionally well done it was, too, down to the smallest detail. The beautifully modelled wedding cake was provided by Alfred Hughes and Sons, Ltd., Birmingham, and many were the comments on its excellence. As one guest truly remarked to me: 'It was obvious it had been made from the finest materials, because, unlike ordinary wedding cake, one positively enjoyed eating it!' With this sentiment, I cordially agree.

"This firm's famous biscuits were very much in evidence at Christmas time in the various London stores. No doubt you noticed the richly handsome leatherette boxes containing Hughes' Floral Chocolate Biscuits; choice example of the biscuit-maker's art, embellished on top with crystallized flowers. Sugar wafers and rich dessert biscuits are two other of their very popular afternoon and after-dinner dainties. If you have not yet tasted these, you have indeed a treat in store. Hughes' Gold Medal Cakes need no advertising comment other than to say that they are as delicious as Hughes' biscuits.

"The photographers and the 'movie men' were strongly in evidence and Miss Lillie (Mrs. Robert Peel) and her husband were much photographed. Everything was carried out in the best style, and the Pattison-Hughes Company must be congratulated upon that—I heard countless compliments paid to the excellence of the catering arrangements.

"Drayton Manor, with its parquet floors, fountained conservatory, and wonderful gardens and vinery, reminds one of a scene out of a film. When I left, I came away with the impression that the catering is the corner-stone of a successful wedding, and if that is so, then Miss Lillie's reception was indeed a huge success—thanks to the caterers, the Pattison-Hughes Catering Company, Ltd., Albany House, Dalton Street, Birmingham." Get *him!*

Well, we knew after that, at least, that there would be no crisis in our lives together that a nice Floral Chocolate Biscuit couldn't cure. At the time, Bobby was trying his hand at selling used cars. Poor Bobby was always trying something. Even then, he felt the inadequacy of simply being the great-grandson of the great second baronet. He desperately wanted to be a useful and needed member of the citizenry and a good husband. I was supposed to be giving up acting temporarily, but as I'd told another reporter, one less overwhelmed by the catering, "Leave the stage? I'd be like a duck without a pond."

When evening came, they shot off the fireworks against the chilly January sky. In a shower of confetti, Bobby and I drove away with fresh cheers dinning in our ears. We were off, we said, to the South of France for our honeymoon. It was a white lie. After idling around in the car for hours, waiting for the last guests to leave, we went back to Drayton Manor, to spend the first night of our marriage in the quarters we always occupied during the comparatively little time we spent there; in the Bachelor's Wing!

Neither of Bobby's parents had come to the wedding. His mother, Lady Mercedes, stayed in Switzerland. His father pleaded illness, but he sent a diamond bracelet as a gift to me, an heirloom that somehow escaped being caught in the net of bankruptcy. The same held true of the beautiful yards-long strands of the Peel pearls that Bobby gave me.

Before too long, he gave me something else, too, that turned out to be important in preserving for a while longer the inheritance left behind by "Parsley" Peel.

Bobby didn't pretend to have any ability to handle money. When any came into his hands, it stayed only briefly. And he had champagne tastes. He was known, for example, to buy a new dress shirt every morning for that evening's wearing and throw yesterday's away rather than bother sending it to the laundry; a fascinating concept really.

Muriel thought that for my own good a marriage settlement would be in order. Our friend Ida Morrison, who'd been one of my bridesmaids, was the sister-in-law of a distinguished solicitor well-known among theatrical people. She arranged the introduction. In his offices in a magnificent Georgian house in The Temple, between the Strand and the Thames, Theodore Goddard drew up the document on my behalf. Bobby signed it, to resettle his life interest in the Peel Settled Estates so that the property would be kept intact for the next generation. We both wanted a next generation.

On the morning after our wedding, we peacefully set out on our honeymoon for the second time. We made it to Monte Carlo with no further delays. Perhaps it was the wrong place to have chosen. Anyway, in the first few days, I had an inkling of Theodore Goddard's wisdom.

Big Bobby loved to gamble. Nothing pleased him better than to while away the hours at the roulette wheel, which bored me stiff. As the evening wore on, I decided that I'd leave him to his favorite pastime and go to bed reasonably early. He had started playing number seventeen and was sticking to it when I went back to our hotel.

I fell asleep, not exactly overjoyed, and I felt even less joyful when I woke at 6 A.M. to find I was still alone. I thought, "I have to give him a lesson and, I hope, a scare." So I hurried into some clothes and went off to a different hotel, the Hotel de Paris, where a friend of mine, Julia Thomson, was staying.

My telephone call from the lobby woke her. "Can I come up and stay with you for a while?" I said.

"Of course," she said. 'But what's all this about? This is your honeymoon."

"It is? I'll explain upstairs."

I waited with Julia for an hour or two, very pleased with myself and my little scheme for teaching my new husband better manners. Then I made my way back to our hotel. "He's going to be worried stiff," I thought.

Not at all. He wasn't in our rooms. He was still at the tables in the casino! It was hours later before he turned up, heavy-eyed but exuberant, airily proclaiming, "Sorry about all this, my love. Had a bit of good luck. Stayed with seventeen and broke the bank."

A moment for that to sink in. "That's wonderful, darling Bobby. But you look so tired. Did you win a lot of money?"

He grinned. I almost forgave him! "Only ten thousand pounds."

The Lord, we are told, giveth and taketh away. The next forty-eight hours tooketh. I tried to insist that we take the lovely loot and hurry on somewhere else, or even go home. But a sudden strike canceled all the trains. We had to cool our heels until the railroad was running again. I was certain that the strike had been called for the sole purpose of keeping the winner in Monte Carlo. Though I begged him not to, back to the casino the next night went Bobby, with his ten thousand pounds. When he returned to the hotel the *following morning*, his face told what had happened.

Just for the record, I asked, "Did you lose it all?"

He nodded. "And a lot more."

But the honeymoon was by no means over, not so far as our travels were concerned. We quarreled, you can imagine, when he had to borrow money to settle the hotel bill and hire a car to get us home. But he had a wonderful sense of humor which, in those early days, made quarrels seem foolish. And I had an Irish temper which made quarrels inevitable, though, let's face it, there was provocation. Sometimes.

Back in London, I once flared up at him while we were out walking on Bond Street where excavating was going on for a new building. We paused for a moment, our voices rising, beside a wooden barricade guarding a deep pit half-filled with rubble.

I tugged off my wedding ring and hurled it into the hole. "That's what I think of you," I shouted.

He turned on his heel and strode away. I went off in the opposite direction. After a moment, I looked back over my shoulder. But Bobby didn't.

An hour later, I returned to the scene of my crime. I lowered myself very gingerly into the pit, gathering dust and grime all over my clothes. I took off my gloves and sifted through the rubble. It was useless. I kept sorting through broken bricks and bits of concrete until my fingers were sore.

Then I began to smile. "How silly of me!" I thought, guessing what must have happened.

I telephoned around town for my bridegroom and finally found him at one of his clubs. I told him how sorry I was for my anger. "I'm so happy," I said, "that you didn't lose your temper and went back and found the ring for me—"

"Not I, my dear girl," Bobby said. "I never go back."

A taxi took me from the telephone call box to Scotland Yard, headquarters of the London police. The duty officer heard out my story. He was very polite and quite friendly. Ever so gently he made his recommendation. "Perhaps, if I may say so, madam, you would be better advised to see a doctor than a detective." Get *him!* Happily, Bobby soon had the site searched thoroughly and the ring was found!

From London we continued our honeymoon in New York. Aboard ship, at the Manhattan pier, Bobby attracted a certain amount of newspaper attention by climbing the mainmast of the liner in which we'd crossed the Atlantic.

He fancied he may have discovered another way to make a living; he'd taken up writing for the movies, with the intention of our going to California. I'd "do cinema work," as they quaintly described it in the gossip columns, while he'd shine as a scenario writer. He completed one script for something he called *Within an Ace of Death.* He entered it in a competition and won a hundred pounds. Thus began, and ended, his Hollywood career.

There were various moves to get me to work in

New York on that first visit. Flo Ziegfeld wanted me for the latest edition of his *Follies,* which had grown more dazzling with every year that passed since he staged the original show in 1907. Ziegfeld used to proclaim that "He who glorifies beauty glorifies truth." I wasn't quite sure what that meant, but I was ready to be glorified by anyone who wanted to try. There was no doubt at all in my mind that I'd be going back to the theatre sooner rather than later. However, there was a small but growing obstacle in the way of my taking up Ziegfeld's offer and signing a contract with him. I just happened to be pregnant.

Half a lifetime went by before I finally appeared in a *Follies* show (which would probably have been better if known as *An Evening Without Flo Ziegfeld* or perhaps *Another Evening With Beatrice Lillie.*)

As a place in which to have a baby, Drayton Manor was about as cozy as Castle Dracula. So far as anybody could calculate, it would have cost somewhere between ten thousand and twenty thousand pounds a year (when there were near enough five dollars to the pound) to keep up the ancestral home in reasonable style. You mustn't imagine that there was anything like that kind of money to be spared at the time.

The house was so enormous that it was uninhabitable unless you shut off some of the wings, which meant dragging out furniture and putting it in storage. Tamworth was a long, long way from London, too, and I wanted my baby born there. So it was time to start looking for a nice little house, not too far from the rest of my family, where the stork could make his call. St. John's Wood was again the answer. We found just the place on Marlborough Road, London N.W. 8.

Meanwhile, the English countryside and I struck

up a warm acquaintanceship, though we didn't really become close friends. The Peel estates were beautiful to visit, but the joys of the squirearchy weren't really for me. Drayton Manor's coverts were renowned for foxes, and the South Staffordshire Hounds made a great fuss whenever they arrived. But I wasn't much interested in foxes until they reached the furrier's shop-window.

Bobby had been brought up on guns, and there'd been his army years on top of that to make him an expert shot. Shootin' had no more appeal for me than huntin' or fishin' until one evening, years later, some friends took me to a rifle range in a club in Chicago. Now *that* was different. I found, to my delight, that I could annihilate clay pigeons, ping-pong balls and wooden ducks by the dozen. For the longest time after that, if anyone was looking for yours in the cause, I could be run to ground in the shooting gallery of the nearest fun fair, armed to the teeth, blazing merrily away.

Cricket was another of Bobby's passions. He had played for Harrow, and to prove that he could turn his hand to almost anything, he once got so far as writing a book about the game. *How Not To Play Cricket* was its title, and it sold quite well.

Bat-and-ball games, however, were not for me. I couldn't keep a straight face, much less a straight bat. Bobby was captain of the local team, which played on the grounds in Drayton Manor Park—we had something for everyone, foxes, deer, trees, flowers and people.

The first time cricket was played that summer, I thought I would play the charming gentlewoman and while away the afternoon in a comfortable deck chair, entertaining our guests under a shady tree. We would clap politely at the best bits in the game and summon up a resounding cheer for the winners. I could see it all in my mind, the spirit of rural England at its best, though I hadn't the least idea what cricket was about or what the difference was between the umpire and that silly mid-on. (For the benefit of the uninitiated, *silly mid-on* is one of the fielders, and not an item of ladies apparel.)

I dressed for the part in eau de cologne and cool chiffon and wafted down to my deck chair, chattering like a canary to our guests. It seemed to me that the game had scarcely begun when my ears caught the cry, "Over!" Once again, for the non-cricketers in our audience, I must explain, in the light of latter-day knowledge, that the cry of "Over!" is a signal for the two batsmen to change ends, proceeding ceremoniously from one wicket to another; roughly like an inning in baseball.

But I then thought "Over!" meant the whole game had finished. I sprang lightly up from my deck chair, smiled brightly to the company and said, "Well, that's that. Shall we go in and have some tea?" I couldn't wait to get away. Cricket was too slow for a Canuck weaned on baseball.

My son was born in an upstairs bedroom in the house I'd rented in St. John's Wood, no more than two minutes' walk round the corner from the other house in Loudon Road, where Mumsie, Pa and Muriel continued to live. Through the big panes of the bedroom windows, you could look down the curved driveway or up at the gray December sky.

It was the style then to have your baby at home, with the doctor coming in for the main event and a nurse staying on afterward. It was also the style then not to make things any too easy in childbirth. I had planned for everything, really, but the pain. I had a lovely little cradle made and placed next to my bed, ready for *him;* I was determined to present Bobby with a son and heir.

The first thing I remember after Little Bobbie was born was the nurse carrying him into the room. I can just see it now. She bathed him in the little tub that was waiting, then popped him into the cradle beside me. She saw that I was conscious and said, "It's a boy, Mrs. Peel."

I couldn't take my eyes off him. Everything was suddenly calm and quiet, and I kept thinking, "This can't be true. He must be somebody else's baby."

My husband had come up from Drayton Manor in time for the birth, to stay in another room. He came upstairs as soon as he'd had the news from the doctor. "It's a boy," Bobby said over and over. "Robert Peel, and he'll be *Sir* Robert Peel, the sixth baronet, one day."

My husband, like me, kept staring and smiling at our son; he didn't even look at me. Not a word. Nothing. Then he went off downstairs to telephone everyone in London: "It's a boy, Robert Peel. *Sir* Robert Peel one day."

That night, the nurse stayed in my room. I couldn't sleep. I heard a little cry and didn't know what to do for worrying. "Can't you possibly bring him in?"

"It's too early," she answered, her voice as crisp as her apron.

"But he's crying."

"Well," she said. "We usually wait."

"What if he's hungry? Shouldn't you bring him to me?"

"We usually wait just a little bit longer," she said.

I took her word for it finally and contented myself with just thinking about him. Oh, he was very handsome, just like his father! One day to be Sir Robert, the sixth baronet. . . .

CHAPTER SEVEN

BEATRICE LILLIE STRIKES BACK

I hold firmly to the view that a baby's best friend is his mother. I feel so strongly on the subject that I once made a recording to elaborate on the theme; you might like to hear it sometime. I suppose it is possible to argue that the obstetrician plays an important role in the infant's young life, but they see so little of each other later on that they're more likely to end up mere passing acquaintances rather than real friends.

The nurse who first pops him into a bathtub and dandles him on her knee must be an important figure in a young man's life, but she, too, is usually only a fleeting fascination. Strangers on the street who kitchy-koo him, the policeman who returns his smile, the relatives on both sides of the family who detect resemblances between the young sprig and Uncle John or Grandpa Robert—none of them, I insist, means so much to him as his mother.

I was not sure, however, that Little Bobbie looked on me as his best friend as he started to grow up. In the first Spring of his life, I found myself increasingly dissatisfied with my life, which was so far removed from everything I'd been brought up on. The little duck had a yearning to go back to her pond, to forget for a while the manor, the swans, the total of seventeen thousand acres and everything that went with them.

For a while, I had if not the best of two worlds, then a good helping of pleasure from both. I could watch Little Bobbie grow, and I had the joy of working again in the theatre. There was a little front yard with a young fruit tree in its middle at the house on Marlborough Road. That's where the perambulator used to be put. Under that tree he used to play when perambulator days were over. The tree's still there, and so is the house, but the street number has been changed.

One of his first toys was a rubber plunger of the kind known as the "plumber's friend." He must have helped himself to it in one of the bathrooms and made it his own. He used to wander into my bedroom in the mornings before I was awake. I'd be roused by the special sound of the plunger being thrust against, then pulled off, the walls. Such beautiful wallpaper, too! *Thunk* . . . plop . . . *thunk* . . . plop.

My little Bobbie was only four months old when I first went back to work. There is some confusion about what I went back to work in. Friends and archives insist that I opened at the Playhouse Theatre in the ageless old farce which was one of the things Ivor Novello had seen on his first visit to New York after the war ended. But *Up in Mabel's Room* would be nothing I should choose to be remembered for, so I refuse to remember it except possibly as a conditioner for the real thing. But its run, if any, was blessedly brief, so I had the chance—and I'm more or less sure I took it—to open in two more shows before the year was over. *Now and Then* and *Pot Luck,* both at the Vaudeville Theatre, were revues, the kind of thing I should have been able to do without a tremor. I always was and always will be rather partial to a tremor, or even two.

Keeping busy was the main thing. It was and still is a better antidote for depression than buying a new hat, and I'm a great believer in the *chapeau* treatment as a cure for gloom, preferably one with a red bird or something equally sensational on it, to make people on the street turn and gape with amazement.

Mumsie was happy to serve as the supervisor of Little Bobbie's upbringing more and more as time went on. It was her grandson, in fact, who was responsible for dubbing her "Mumsie"; she refused to be "Grandma." One day when he was still very young, scarcely a wink older than three, she brought him to the theatre to watch me. He was with her in a box all through the performance. When it was over, he had only one comment, said with something that combined outrage and sorrow: "People *laughed* at you."

Just for a moment, I wished that they hadn't. For future attendances at the show in which I appeared, he'd sit on the floor, out of sight of the stage, as soon as Mumsie brought him into the box. And he'd stay down there until the last curtain was down. It took him a bit of time to grow out of this habit and face his mum from an audience.

But I'm skipping ahead of myself, which is a dangerous thing to do because you never know who will catch up with you on the bias. I continued to lead the life of a busy little Bea, opening in a new show almost as soon as the current one closed.

Once again, Uncle André was planning a new revue. He hit on something that sounded as all-inclusive as the London telephone directory, *A to Z*, but early on I was smitten by some variety of hostile bacteria and couldn't accept his kind request to star in this production for more than a minute.

So at the suggestion of Dada's wife, Flip Charlot, Gertie stepped in again for me, sang "Limehouse Blues," and climbed another rung or two up the ladder to stardom.

I ascended a few steps myself in a show that followed on the heels of *A to Z*. Two of the Lillie Trio had a share in *The Nine O'Clock Revue*, which, hard to believe, was *not* a Charlot production. I was number one of the nine performers; my sister had written the music, in collaboration with an elegant young man named Ord Hamilton, who subsequently went onward and upward with the arts to write a smashhit number entitled "Blasé." (You're bored, When you're adored; You're blasé.) 'Twas a camp.

But Muriel was more interested in the man who wrote the lyrics, Arthur Weigall, that Inspector General of Antiquities for the Egyptian government I told you about. It was Arthur, you may recall, who had designed "The Spirit of Egypt" number for *Now's the Time*, which became Phyllis Monkman's coming-out party. If you fancy you again detect the scent of orange blossom coming your way, you won't be far wrong.

Muriel was fond of saying, "When my sister sings my songs, I never know how they'll come out." She created them as gems of classical music ("Maud," for instance), and I would promptly convert them into classics of a different nature, comedy; something for

which Muriel, ever the purist, has never really forgiven me. She and Arthur together wrote one song
that's still a favorite of mine; hope I get it right this
time, Muriel.

> When I'm feeling lone and sad,
> And when I've got the blues,
> I love to hear the squeaking
> Of Susannah's Sunday shoes ...
> I love the twanging of the old banjoes,
> I love the haunting music of the piccolos,
> I love the crying of the cockatoos,
> But best I love the squeaking
> Of Susannah's Sunday shoes.*

There was another gentleman connected with *The
Nine O'Clock Revue* whom I once trusted with my
bank account. I trusted him because he was something of a charmer and well-known in the London
theatre for several talents, including acting, producing and writing. I discovered that he also had a talent
for taking my money at a time when I most needed
it. But he wrote one of the sketches that I still do now
and again, and frankly I find it's too much hard work
to hate anyone. As I'm lazy at that kind of thing, let's
just call him Mr. Nameless.

It was *The Nine O'Clock Revue*, produced by Mr.
Dion Titheradge, that proved to be the ticket that
first took me to the United States under the wing of
Uncle André. His tremendous success with revues had
made him the apple of many an American producer's

---

* "Susannah's Squeaking Shoes (Weigall-Lillie) Copyright ©
1923 by Cecil Lennox & Company. Copyright renewed. Used
by permission of Warner Bros. Music. All Rights Reserved.

eye, but Charlot had turned down all offers to open on Broadway.

Then over the seas came one Archie Selwyn, who had a *theayter* of his own named for himself on West Forty-second Street. He wanted the best numbers and the best talent *from all the Charlot revues* put together for New York. Uncle André liked the idea and proceeded to sign on Jack Buchanan, Herbert Mundin, a Lancashire comedian who had appeared three of four times in Charlot shows, and Gertie, who was now playing together with Noël in a revue he'd written with Ronald Jeans, *London Calling*. As you may have assumed, Uncle André gave me the nod as well, *and first billing, I'm happy to say.*

We'd heard a lot about New York from Ivor Novello, who had recently returned from a very star-spangled visit there. Two of his movies, *Call of the Blood* and *The Bohemian Girl,* had already made quite a splash when he was invited by D. W. Griffith to co-star with Mae Marsh in *The White Rose,* to be filmed in Florida. American newspapers couldn't decide whether to call Ivor "the handsomest man in England," a "Greek god" or "the most gorgeous profile to be seen on the screen since Francis X. Bushman."

Ivor was as embarrassed as Gladys Cooper for the "romance" that the Griffith press agents invented between them—he'd played a Polish patriot and she a gypsy in *The Bohemian Girl.* It didn't help to damp down the rumors when Ivor and Gladys went around New York together, pursued by photographers whose pictures appeared under headlines like, "Will Love Find A Way?" There was an obstacle, however, in the person of H. J. Buckmaster, to whom Gladys was still married at this time.

Besides all the excitement and razzle-dazzle Ivor

had led us to expect in New York, I had a strong suspicion that I'd run into something called homesickness there. But the show must go on, and I left Little Bobbie in Mumsie's care. I'd had three consecutive Christmases with him, but the fourth had to be missed. Gertie, Jack Buchanan and I sailed with Dada in the *Aquitania,* the last ship to leave Southampton before December 25.

I had more fun than I'd expected. Gertie and I made a shipboard friend of one of the season's glamor boys, Alastair McIntosh, who later married Constance Talmadge. When Gertie, Jack and I mentioned to him that we'd no idea where to stay in New York, he ordered another little drink all round to dissolve our fears.

"I'll fix it for you," said Allie. "My friend William Rhinelander Stewart just about owns the Hotel Ambassador on Park Avenue. That's the place for you. I'll send him a radiogram."

We docked on Christmas Eve 1923. I was up like a lark—or maybe a sea gull—to see the famed Manhattan skyline. The minute I saw the skyscrapers, I had an idea that somebody had shot a hole in my middle. I was homesick from the moment we walked down the gangway.

"This," I told myself, "is a Great Hazard." Glancing at Gertie, I could see that she thought so, too.

The pier was chaotic with passengers, porters, reporters and customs men sniffing like bloodhounds in their search for bottles of liquor which the thirsty were trying to sneak in to help break the great American drought. But good old Allie McIntosh had been as good as his word. William Rhinelander Stewart, who looked vaguely like Howard Hughes, was waiting to welcome us.

145

He was *very* society, but a wonderful guide to the social life. We whizzed away in his limousine to the Ambassador. He had reserved two suites, one for Jack, one for Gertie and me. Our eyes took in the chandeliers and candelabra, the velvet curtains; our cheeks glowed with the warmth of central heating; our feet sank in the deep carpets.

"This is the life," said Gertie, grandly draping herself across an armchair.

"Amen," said I, swinging from a chandelier.

The rude awakening came approximately forty-five minutes after we'd opened our eyes the next morning, skipped to the windows to goggle at the view up and down Park Avenue, then reveled in our respective marble bathtubs. Gertie picked up the white telephone to order breakfast.

"What do you care for, madam?" said Room Service.

"Oh, anything at all. I'll leave it to you," said Gertie, grandly.

In a matter of minutes, a parade of waiters arrived, each pushing a little serving wagon. As they whisked off the silver dish covers, we contemplated sausages, eggs, slices of ham and bacon by the dozen; a bakeshop's fill of toast and muffins, firkins of coffee; and glistening sections of a fruit neither of us had set breakfast eyes on before, called grapefruit.

"Pretend not to notice," I whispered to Gertie.

"Merry Christmas, darling," she replied.

"Merry Christmas," said the captain of the waiting band, flipping over the check on its own little silver platter and flourishing a pencil.

"Would madam care to sign?"

Why not? I applied my neatest autograph.

My appetite was already fitful; I was still feeling

146

queasy about the Great Hazard that lay ahead. Reading that check chased away every trace of hunger. As soon as the waiters had bowed themselves out, I cantered to the telephone without so much as a nibble on a piece of toast.

"Jack," I said, "have you had breakfast?"

"Merry Christmas, Bea. Yes. It was rather nourishing, as a matter of fact."

"Merry Christmas. Did you see how much it cost?"

"I didn't really notice."

"We got a bill for twenty-five dollars. Excluding tip. For two. For breakfast!"

Jack was in the same predicament as we were. We didn't know yet whether *André Charlot's Revue of 1924*, as it was going to be billed, would succeed or flop with American audiences. We had two weeks of rehearsals, an engagement in Atlantic City—in midwinter yet!—and we had to live until then on limited spending money.

"I'll be right over," said Jack, quick of mind as well as of foot. "Let's start packing," said this canny Scotsman after we'd counted out all our money on one of the beds.

"We must be dignified about it," said Gertie. "Think of Will and dear Allie. They made the reservations for us."

Jack put a call through to Archie Selwyn. He suggested we try the Algonquin, owned and run by Frank Case, whom Archie and half of the rest of New York seemed to know.

Not knowing when we'd eat next, and wishing to obtain full value, Gertie and I each forced down a hearty breakfast, helped by Jack, whom we pressed into service to take his second start to the day. Then we pooled our resources and let Jack pay the bill for our beds and breakfasts when we checked out.

"We'll need a cab, of course," said Gertie.

"Can we afford it?" I asked Jack.

"Not really, but you know Gertie."

We had all our luggage loaded into and onto a yellow taxicab, tipped the bellboy and the doorman for Gertie's sake, entered the cab, and then got out again as soon as we were out of sight. We then made our way to the Algonquin, carrying our own suitcases.

This looked much more like our present financial style, with well sat-in settees and a stately grandfather clock tick-tocking in the lobby, and a room for Gertie and me that could have come straight out of the old King Edward Hotel in Toronto. It was a good place to stay for our introduction to life in New York during the great drought.

There was more drinking than we'd ever seen before. There were more drunks, too. With Will Stewart and Allie to guide us, we were at a party every night. Prohibition, we concluded, was an awful joke. You could get liquor any time, anywhere, in bottles, speakeasy bars or bathtubs. Because everybody thought I was English, I'd sometimes be asked around to tea, but that wasn't what was served in the cups, chum.

In the oak-paneled dining room of the Algonquin, there was a table at which Frank Case sat for lunch. It was a piece of furniture that became as famous as King Arthur's at Camelot. Gertie and I stumbled onto one of the early meetings of Frank Case and his knights. Gertie rather timidly asked if any of them knew a columnist she'd heard about from Will Stewart—O. O. McIntyre. There was a breathless hush. Who were *we* to realize that the Round Table regulars, perhaps unjustly, regarded the man from Ohio who wrote "Bits of New York Life" as a mangler of prose and a thief of other men's material?

But the *gaffe* was forgiven, and we were invited to have a chair pulled up for us at the Round Table the first time we saw it. From then on, we were included among the regulars, helped by the good offices of Marc Connelly, the playwright, whom I'd met in *The Nine O'Clock Revue* days. Before luncheon was over, we excused ourselves, counted our pennies and did a bit of hasty shopping. We hurried back to the table, to make amends for McIntyre with a big basket of fruit, which had five bottles of pop hidden under the pineapples and oranges.

The following morning, the telephone in our room rang just as I'd gotten into the bath. I answered it, dripping water on the carpet, clutching a towel.

"Is this Miss Lillie from England?"

I allowed that it was, though the voice sounded like a stranger's.

"This is the New York *Sun*. We'd like to know your feelings, Miss Lillie, about the death of President Harding."

"Who?"

"Our President, Miss Lillie. Warren Gamaliel Harding. He's dead. How do you feel about it?"

"Well," I flustered. "I mean, it's a great loss, isn't it? A man like that. What a terrible thing! How will you find another President?" I hadn't the least idea.

The voice at the other end changed. "Can we expect bigger and better things from you in the future?" said my caller. "As a matter of fact, Harding died last August." He hung up before I could wish him the compliments of the season or whatever else was on my mind. But he called back later to identify himself and invite us to lunch again. It was Marc Connelly, that priceless man.

Gertie liked to pretend later that she loved New York at first sight. As a matter of fact, she thought Broadway by daylight was dirty and depressing, and so did I. We had little confidence in the show we would be starring in. We felt even more pessimistic after a week's tryout in Atlantic City. Americans simply didn't seem to get the point of what I was supposed to be doing. At least, not Archie Selwyn.

As soon as Ivor had arrived back in London, he had gone to work for Charlot, writing the score for still another revue called *Puppets,* with Dion Titheradge supplying book and lyrics. Uncle André had taken one of the songs, "March with Me," and given it to me for the New York show. It's sung by a very dignified and slightly matronly Britannia, who runs into trouble with her spear, her shield, her helmet and her feet.

I was my usual miserable self at rehearsal, keeping the performance sharp and clear in my head but waiting for the response of an audience to tell me how to develop it. *Then* you feel almost as if the Good Witch of the East has inspired you with a tap of her wand on your shoulder. That's how I used to describe the feeling in a kind of personal shorthand: "The *wand* is on."

Archie Selwyn knew nothing about this and wouldn't have cared if he did. "When's she going to *do* something?" he kept nagging Charlot. "That number will die on Broadway. You ought to cut it."

The end not only of the song but of the show, too, nearly came in Atlantic City. Someone had booked us to do bits from the revue at a charity benefit. The local élite had forked over something like one hundred dollars a seat. They reacted, we thought, as if a dollar would have been plenty, with ice cream thrown in free.

"We can't open in New York," said Archie Selwyn, wrapped in gloom and a heavy overcoat. "Americans will never fall for this English stuff."

He changed his mind so reluctantly and reprieved what I thought would be my best number so grudgingly that when we returned to the Algonquin for the opening at the Times Square Theatre, I didn't even bother to unpack. I could see it all as clear as day: I'd be sailing in shame for home on the morning's tide.

But have I got newsboys for you! You've never seen such reviews as *André Charlot's Revue of 1924* was given by the whole gang of critics—Alec Woollcott, Ring Lardner, George Jean Nathan and the rest of them. Casting modesty aside for a moment (get over there, poor thing!) and blushing not a whit, I shall permit myself to quote but one set of headlines which were plastered all over the readers:

LONDON STARS TRIUMPHANT
NEW YORK SURRENDERS TO
CHARLOT REVUE GIRLS
FIRST NIGHT SCENES
*Beatrice Lillie Takes First
Act "Call" in Kimono*

And, my dear, every word was true. I was a first-act call girl, dragged protesting, but not too hard, from my dressing room, because the audience wouldn't stop applauding until I skipped out in front of the curtain. What do you think had stopped the show? Not "Tea-Shop Tattle," in which I played Gwladys, a supercilious waitress, with acknowledgments due to Lyons Corner House, Piccadilly, and Harry Hart, that agent who kept his business in his hat.

No, it was "March with Me," the number Archie Sel-wyn threatened to kill because, as he had said so fastidiously with best Broadway understatement, "It stinks."

Herewith a sample of the lyric, though please be ad-vised to picture me roaming the stage as Britannia:

> March with me to the roll of the drum,
> March to that rousing tune.
> March with me to the call of the fife.
> March, March, April, May and June.
> Canada! Australia! South Africa!
> To merely name a few.
> Thirty days hath September
> April, June and November.
> England is proud of you!*

In the audience sat Will Stewart and a number of what were called in those days "young men about town," the devils. We heard that Marion Davies was out front, too, and Adolph Zukor and Gene Buck and Doris Keane and heaven knows who else. It seems that anyone we'd ever heard of and everyone I've met since was there that night.

We got to meet some of the audience rather inti-mately for a moment or two after the performance. Led by Will Stewart, they were waiting for us when we came out of the theatre, to hoist me on their shoul-ders and carry me to the waiting car. Corny? Of course, but wonderful to glance back as we drove off and see the electric light bulbs above the marquee

---

* "March with Me" (Furber-Novello) Copyright © 1924 by Harms, Inc. Copyright renewed. Used by permission of Warner Bros. Music. All Rights Reserved.

spelling out a sign that was obviously going to be up there for many months: CHARLOT'S REVUE.

But wait! The "C" was slowly blinking off and on. What kind of show *was* this? Shrieks of laughter. Athletic congratulations. Whee!

Since those delicious, delirious early days in New York, I've often blushed over some of the things the critics have written. "She is the funniest woman in the world" and so forth and so on. That kills me. It has been said so often that I've wished they would write something along the lines of, "Bea Lillie is not worthy of this revue; it's too clever for her." It's a tradition, let's face it, for every comic to want to play Hamlet. (But I'd want to be Ophelia.) Though I have enjoyed a fair share of absolutely brilliant material (chiefly musical numbers and sketches), if there is one small regret, it is that I would rather have (and have had) better production material in the "book musical" portion of my career.

I had no such thoughts at this time. I swallowed every word when O. O. McIntyre told his readers in a memorable phrase he made up on the spur of the moment, that I was "one of the new toasts of the town," and it went down with butter on both sides. I accepted, as though it were my due, a loving cup presented at the stage door after one matinee which was thoughtfully inscribed, "To Beatrice Lillie— Champion Comedienne Forever."

We had originally been booked for a run of six weeks. As it turned out, we stayed for nine months. We could have lasted nine months longer. The show was sold out at every performance, and Archie Selwyn saw to it that we gave the full measure of eight performances a week. In the spring, Jack Buchanan, always a businessman as well as an actor, had to sail home to meet previously made contracts, and little Nelson Keys, perpetually nicknamed "Bunch," came out to take his place.

When Gertie and I saw that we were likely to be in for a long run, we decided to rent a house together, a roomy place designed by Stanford White on West Fifty-fourth Street with a tiny garden that caught the sun. It would be a much better home than a hotel for Little Bobbie to stay in when he came to stay with me.

Mr. Charlot's two young ladies, said one society column, had taken the house to "return some of the entertaining that has been so constantly done in their honor. In private, as well as in public, they have created a most favorable impression." Get *them!*

Flo Ziegfeld, in a petulant mood, threatened to sue to keep "Bunch" from joining Charlot. The maestro of the *Follies* was stung by the critics, who kept advising him, free of charge, that long-stemmed girls weren't enough to please American audiences now that they'd seen our brand of entertainment. But Ziegfeld's claim that "Bunch" had signed a contract with him wasn't true, and Nelson Keys made his New York debut with us. It was one of the few times in my life that I towered over a leading man.

Gertie and I did our best to live up to our reputation. As the newspapers reported, we were "companions in a thousand frolics and we'd brought a whole new concept of theatre and comedy to a grateful America." There were photographs of us, looking like Thérèse and Isabelle, in the rotogravure. We made our house a kind of equivalent to Ivor's London flat, a perpetual open house for composers, playwrights, newspapermen, our Round Table friends, anybody from the theatre, everybody visiting from London. All our British friends told us we were Britain's secret diplomatic weapon in America.

Fanny Brice came around to visit after she'd seen a special midnight performance we gave so that people in other shows could come to take a look at Charlot's "harlots" in action. There was some idle gossiping over whether Fanny and I, the Queen of American comedy and the new girl from London, would start a-feudin', but we disappointed those well-wishers and hit it off from the beginning, in later years becoming close friends.

Jules Glaenzer of Cartier's, a great party thrower and theatre fan, used to come to our drawing room, and we'd go to his. Jules gave so many parties that he was known to everyone as "Shush" Glaenzer as a result of his habit of circulating among his guests at the height of their merrymaking, trying to "shush" them into temporary quiet. He'd obviously once had a mammoth complaint from the neighbors.

Jules had two or three pianos in his house, and we had only one, but ours was the one at which Vincent Youmans sat down and wrote "Tea for Two." (We seldom touched the stuff except for breakfast. And oddly enough, we seldom sampled the hard stuff, either, apart from a sip of champagne now and then. I tippled on water, ginger ale and an occasional beer.)

Alec Woollcott was always in and out, solemn and cuddly, telling us that nobody had been welcomed as we were since the time of Jenny Lind.

Will Stewart still paid court and sent a gardener to plant flowers in our little back yard. A long list of young gentlemen could be relied upon to supply bouquets, assorted viands from the five-star restaurants and lashings of champagne, champagne, champagne. (Where *could* they have found it?)

Condé Nast, whose publishing business produced *Vogue* and other magazines, occasionally stopped by. It was under his palatial roof in Connecticut that I met, among hundreds of others, Josephine Baker. She'd made her reputation as an American in Paris by dancing in a skirt of banana leaves. She hastened to explain, in perfect pidgeon French, how much she admired me and what a brilliant performer, so funny, ooh-la-la and la-de-sangy-da.

"Honey," I interrupted, in a *moonlight-and-molasses accent*, "y'all so *kind*. Ah think you're just great, *too*." She got the point, came off it, and we became fast friends.

The social register at 48 West Fifty-fourth Street really started to ring, however, when the Prince of Wales passed through New York on his way to his ranch in Calgary. There were quite a few old friends of Gertie's or mine in his party, and we were always glad to see them when our doorbell rang.

The Prince was billed as a guest of honor at a benefit performance at the New Amsterdam Theatre arranged by Mrs. William Randolph Hearst for her Milk Fund. All of us from *Charlot's Revue* contributed our efforts, and so did everybody from the rival musical attraction on Broadway, the *Ziegfeld Follies*, including Will Rogers and Lupino Lane, as masters of ceremonies for the complete affair.

A box was bought on the Prince's behalf, but he pleaded a previous engagement. The British consul general, Sir Henry Gloucester Armstrong, showed up in his place. The Hearst newspapers, however, still considered the night to be "an artistic triumph" and the audience "by far the most distinguished of the season."

Gertie and I, with the rest of our people, had the chance to meet the old St. James's Palace circle, though, in Southampton, Long Island, during the summer, when two local potentates arranged with Archie Selwyn and his brother, Edgar, to close the theatre for a night and import the whole production to play in the garden of the Parrish Art Museum. The Prince was a visitor in Southampton, and the gossips struck again.

On the instructions of Uncle André, Gertie and I afterward turned away every reporter's questions by saying, "Mr. Charlot will not allow us to talk about it." It would have been simpler—but maybe less intriguing —to dampen the rumors by repeating what the Prince had said after he'd appeared so regularly at *The Nine O'Clock Revue* that he was asked about his feelings toward the leading lady.

"Certainly I'm in love with her," he said, with a very straight face. "Who doesn't love her? She reminds me of my grandmother, Queen Alexandra."

We had one very special guest in our house that summer. Mother brought him over in the *Majestic*. Little Bobbie was the best cure for chronic homesickness that anyone might imagine. We filled the house with plush-covered jungle creatures of every conceivable size and breed from ants to zebra. We strung the back yard, filled with flowers now, with balloons.

After seeing a matinee and being persuaded to watch "March with Me," Little Bobbie suddenly took a fancy to assisting me through doors just the way the chorus girls did in their desperate efforts to keep poor Britannia on her feet. (Child psychologists may be heard from.)

I suppose I should now let you in on the fact that

Big Bobby was back in Australia. He'd gone out there to try his hand at sheep farming in the hope of making his fortune. This should not be taken as any kind of reflection on the degree of concern he felt for Little Bobbie. In *some* aristocratic families there was a traditional style for dealing with sons. After inspecting the newborn infant, the father said, "Now take him away and bring him back when he's reached fourteen."

There's one story about our son that fits here, though it happened the following Easter, when we were back in England together. I took him to church, the first time he'd been old enough to attend a grown-up service.

"Bobbie, dear, tell me what Easter is about," I said as we walked down the front steps after the benediction. He explained how Jesus had been born again.

"Now tell me about Good Friday."

"Oh, well, you see, Robinson Crusoe had a friend . . ." he began.

Cut back to New York, where *Charlot's Revue* played to packed houses throughout the sizzling summer. At the end of September, we were going on a prestige tour for six months, starting in Philadelphia, then on to Boston, Toronto, Detroit and Chicago, winding up with weeks of roving in the Midwest. We had become the most imitated show on Broadway and everywhere else in the country, too.

One commentator wrote: "Every native musical production that has appeared since the advent of the *Charlot Revue of 1924* has wisely endeavored to copy the technique." None of us—not forgetting Florenz Ziegfeld—fully realized at the time that a new era in the American musical theatre had dawned, in fact.

The days of overstaffed, overstuffed, overproduced extravaganzas were coming to an end, declining in popularity, making way for the Charlot-style show, light on décor but heavy on talent.

Following tradition, we closed on a Saturday night. The front rows of the orchestra of the Selwyn Theatre —we'd been moved two theatres westward along Forty-second Street from the Times Square Theatre to make room for "a musical knockout" entitled *Mr. Battling Butler*—were jammed with theatre friends, newspaper friends, social "friends" and "repeater" fans. Most of them knew our words and music by heart, and they joined in the singing all through the show.

In one athletic number ("Why she doesn't break her neck, I'll never know") I used to escape from a mad apache by jumping off the apron of the stage and crawling between the front row's knees and the brass rail of the orchestra. On this night, I paused for a moment that became minutes, while the audience howled, on the well-padded lap of Alec Woollcott.

When the final curtain fell, we were bombarded with flowers. Then the orchestra played "Auld Lang Syne," and everybody, on stage and off, sang it through together. We all clasped hands, audience and cast, hundreds and hundreds of us, in a daisy chain which progressed slowly around the inside of the theatre. Those *were* the days, I tell *you*. And the nights.

When Gertie and I emerged from the stage door, the crowd was blocking the traffic on Forty-third Street. We were picked up bodily, hoisted onto the roof of our waiting car and followed back to Fifty-fourth Street by a parade, singing the songs we did in the show.

We will now proceed to Chicago, where my dressing

room was rifled and all my costumes stolen. It was there, too, at the Ambassador East Hotel, that I received a cablegram from London telling me that my father-in-law was dead. Big Bobby was now the fifth baronet, our son the new heir apparent, and I was Lady Peel. Apart from little diversions like that, I enjoyed Chicago immensely.

Oh, yes. Did I mention the date? It was Friday, February 13.

160

CHAPTER EIGHT

LILLIE DACHE . . .

In those long-lost, innocent days before he tried out his hand as a producer, when he was writing some of the sharpest criticism the theatre has ever seen, Kenneth Tynan concluded that my title "sits on her like a halo on an anarchist." *O, tempus. O, mores. Oh, Calcutta!*

It may not be a perfect fit, but, to tell the truth, I've grown to like it, kind of. Being every *other* inch a lady, like almost everything else in life, is a mixed blessing. You get used to it as time goes along, the way your feet grow accustomed to a pair of tight shoes. Either the shoes stretch or your feet grow corns, but ultimately shoes and feet get along together.

In America there was a problem at first with some audiences. Once, I appeared in Kansas City on a vaudeville tour and bowed at the end of my act, the customers in the first few rows of the theatre stood up in unison and bowed back! They thought that was the way to behave in the presence of a Genuine Lady. An immediate investigation brought the answer.

161

An overly zealous local entrepreneur had seen fit to "bill" me all over the city as "Lady Peel, direct from London and The Palace." If he had taken the trouble to get it right, the ads would have said, "Beatrice Lillie, direct from the Palace Theatre, New York." The whole thing served a useful purpose, however: from then on, I made sure that Lady Peel wasn't allowed within a country mile of a theatre where Beatrice Lillie was appearing.

One of the few places where I am consistently "Lady Peeled" is in Tiffany's glittering emporium, where one special dignitary usually helps me. The following dialogue ensued on an afternoon years ago:

DIGNITARY: If you will turn your head ever so slightly, Lady Peel, I will fasten this necklace. (I *loathe* this sales technique.)

MILADY: Righto, buster. Now then, may I see a coronet, please?

DIGNITARY: Oh, I'm so sorry, Lady Peel, but we don't have a coronet at this time.

MILADY: No? Well, it doesn't matter really. In any case, I don't know how to play one.

Meantime, back in Chicago I appeared as usual on stage the day the cablegram arrived with the news of the death of my father-in-law. Reporters asked the same question that had been asked when Big Bobby and I were married: would I be Giving It Up? The answer, of course, was No. I'd learned that I couldn't just be Mrs. and now Lady Peel. I knew now that the theatre was my profession, my hobby, my life. (And besides, just between us, we needed the money.)

Drayton Manor was, to put it mildly, a drain on the

pocketbook. By all accounts, the property would be worth more if the house were torn down. It stood on ground that was rich in coal. We had one or two offers to buy the mineral rights, but nothing came of them. We couldn't really decide whether we wanted the Peel estates turned into a coal mine. We should have known better.

There was no Gertie around to sit and have a good gossip with. She had picked up a cold when we were playing in Boston. She'd neglected it, and when our company reached Toronto, I was as much concerned about her health as I was about being back in the old hometown for the first time since I'd left it for England and a whole new world.

But reporters were in and out of our top-floor suite in the King Edward Hotel most of the day. The newspapers were full of the Toronto girl who had "dazzled London and New York." I was happy enough that I'd been able to talk Uncle André into including my native heath on our travels with the show. Every ticket was sold for every performance, and there were parties every night.

It was impossible to persuade Gertie to rest. On a Thursday evening, after the performance, we were off, as usual, in search of recreation, but Gertie collapsed in our host's living room. Someone took her back to the hotel. She woke me early the next morning and asked me to take her temperature. One hundred and four degrees.

"Back to bed," I said, suddenly wide-awake. "You need a doctor."

An ambulance whisked her off to Wellesley Hospital. Double pneumonia and pleurisy. She was desperately ill for three months and more, too ill to understand when the revue completed its Toronto run and the

163

company had to move on to Detroit.

I didn't want to leave. I tried to tell her what I felt, but she was delirious. I wondered if I should ever see her again. But Gertie's courage and determination didn't fail her. As soon as she could travel, she went off to the Riviera to recuperate. We cabled her when Charlot's company finally reached the end of its travels, and I sailed in the *Olympic* for home.

The ship stopped at Cherbourg first before docking at Southampton. There on the pier of the bustling French port stood Gertie, waiting to join us so that we could arrive back in England together. She had looked like a ghost, lying in the hospital bed, when I'd tried to say good-bye. Now thank God, she looked wonderful again.

Except for affairs of estate at Drayton Manor, life was becoming rather heady. Little Bobbie was growing up, a bright, handsome boy, almost ready to start in at the Arnold House School, just across Loudon Road from the house in St. John's Wood. I'd been Lady Peel for almost two months now, and I was beginning to enjoy it. And what did the New York newspaper say when we left? "Famous Beauty Sails on *Olympic* for Europe After Successful American Tour." Well, that was *m-e-e!*

I had some other memories of the more than a year I'd been away. The day's train ride from Toronto to Detroit, wondering if Gertie would live or die. The view of a boiler factory from my bedroom window in St. Louis. The dynamite blasts of the excavators working next door to the hotel in Baltimore. The bill for fifty dollars' worth of telephone calls. Ah, the lay public (love that term!) always fancies the life of glamor that we lead in the theaytah.

As a farewell note for the newspapers, I wrote,

"Many of you who remember me in the Crimea, where I led the Light Brigade, think that I am just a silly little girl. I am not, really. Beneath all the *tinsel* —and shall we say greasepaint?—beats, as best it can, a badly broken heart. Because I'm leaving, and I love you."

Charlot's plan was to cash in on our success by reopening a new version of the revue in London with we "originals," before he took us back to America with a new production, to be called *André Charlot's Revue of 1926*. He had no trouble finding an audience for our London opening at the Prince of Wales's Theatre, on March 30/31, 1925. So many people wanted seats that he decided to have two first nights on the same evening, one starting at 8 P.M., the other at midnight, with special buses laid on to take the second first-nighters home. The midnight show was the first of its kind in the modern London theatre.

My dear, you should have been there. There were thirty-one—count them, thirty-one—stars of the stage and silver screen in the boxes and stalls. Jack Buchanan, who later joined us in July, was typical, coming over from the Empire Theatre when his own show was over. Like Jack, most of them just had time to change from theatre costumes into evening clothes. During one interval, they all trooped up on stage with us for a swallow of champagne. Noël, who'd written some of our new numbers, sat with Lillian Braithwaite, John Barrymore with Lady Diana Duff Cooper (not to be confused with Gladys Cooper, the *Bohemian Girl*) and Ivor Novello. George Grossmith, my leading man in a later Hollywood movie, *Are You There?*, appeared in a box sporting a monocle, *and* so did his boxmate, Heather Thatcher. Zena Dare wore black, and Tallulah Bankhead a mammoth bunch of orchids. There sat Fay Compton and Leon Quartermaine, Phyllis Monkman all in pale pink and gold tissue, and Fanny Brice in the flesh.

I was a trifle uneasy about Fanny. We had barely met as of then, and I was doing a burlesque of her, while Gertie mimicked Sophie Tucker, the "last of the red-hot mommas." This was a new sketch we'd worked out, dressed as twins in baby carriages and playing ukeleles. According to the program (if you can stand it), we were the Apple Sisters, Cora and Seedy. I needn't have worried; Fanny loved it.

Outside the theatre, the night was filled with cheers from the hero worshipers and autograph hounds who jammed the streets between Piccadilly Circus and Leicester Square. Inside, it was *darling, darling* all the way, breathed by everyone to everyone else from lights up to lights out. On stage, behind the house curtain, it sounded like waves washing a beach—rather dreamy, really.

Toward the very end, around 3 A.M., the performance sagged just a little. Counting the hectic afternoon dress rehearsal, this was the *third* time we'd done our stuff in twenty-four hours. But good old "March with Me" roused 'em and got their eyes open again, as it always did. In a minute or less, the tears of laughter began to drip.

Before we'd finished, it was past three-thirty. Crowds were still waiting in the streets. The only way Uncle André could start the audience going home was to make a curtain speech.

"Gertie," he said, sounding *exactly* like Maurice Chevalier, "has fully recovered from a serious illness and Beattie from a serious title. Although I am not paid to do this by the people concerned, I am going to read to you a list of places now open where

166

those of you who are hungry can get some breakfast."

We opened in the spring and ran until autumn came. Then, in spite of full houses, Uncle André said it was time to pack again and go back to New York. Secretly, I shouldn't have objected very strongly if we'd closed a few weeks earlier, so that I could have had a week or so off, to rest me wee bones. But it was a summer of sunshine, and the best of being sunburnt is that you look well even if you're not. Remember, dear, it's not how you feel that counts—it's how you look. (Get *me!* That's a quote to be quoted.)

Between leaving New York and returning there, another change had come over, and perhaps overcome, your theatrical correspondent. I'd left with two long braids of hair which, one reporter wrongly guessed, "have never been bobbed and never will be." Did I show *him?*

Max Aitken, the forceful little Canadian who founded the London *Daily Express* and later became Lord Beaverbrook, gave a weekend party aboard his yacht. Not exactly a romp on the high seas, because we stayed most of the time in Southampton Water. Max had some advice to offer on how to raise Little Bobbie in the footsteps of the illustrious second baronet. "Bring your boy up," he said, "on the Bible and the life of Sir Robert Peel."

There was quite a gaggle of us aboard, ranging, in alphabetical order, from Michael Arlen, who had just written *The Green Hat*, to H. G. Wells, who had just invented science fiction. Lloyd George, the recent prime minister, was afloat with us, too, and so was Frederick Lonsdale, the playwright, with his two children.

It was the two children and Michael Arlen, I suppose, who were together responsible for the Lillie

Eton crop. The children had lovely short hair, and when they went swimming, it dried in a moment, wink or thrice.

Personally, ever since the war—the *second* one—I've always gone in the water with my hat on. I just sort of paddle and never get my head wet. But in those early days, Michael Arlen said, "You should have your hair cut. It would suit you better. And think how convenient when you go in the water."

Taking a fast peek at Lloyd George, who had a mane of white hair, I tended to agree. I think that in my continuing dreams of glory I perhaps saw myself as another Gertrude Ederle, thrashing across the English Channel. Impetuously, I snipped off my braids, took a dip, then carefully pinned back the severed hanks of hair. As soon as I got back to London, anonymous under a large hat, I walked into my friendly local *coiffeur* to survey the havoc I had wrought, carrying my hair in my handbag.

When I looked in the mirror, I felt like a green coconut. So I had him make the braids up into two wound-around plaits, like the earphones of a stereo hi-fi set. For quite a while, for all public appearances, I wore my earphones, attached to my head by rubber bands. No one knew the difference, but the feeling of freedom without them was positively sensuous.

I liberated myself at a party one night, where somebody with a very good voice was singing. I said, "I can't hear you," and lifted this thing off my ear. It came away in my hand and fell on the carpet. After that, the mask was off. No more earphones for me. I auctioned them off for charity.

I sailed, without braids but with Big Bobby, in the *Caronia* when Uncle André took us back to America for the newest version of his revue. The three originals

168

—Gertie, Jack Buchanan and I—were back together again. "It was not a performance—it was a reunion," wrote Alec Woollcott after our opening night at the Selwyn Theatre.

With fond thoughts of Channel swimming, I'd introduced an impression of Gertrude Ederle which the audience swallowed by the gallon. And I'd discarded Gwladys, the teashop waitress, in favor of Florence, a sprightly housemaid who, in the inscrutable wanderings of the sketch's plot, got to telling a startled visitor about an imaginary trip to Africa.

FLORENCE: Oh, yes we had quite a safari—*quite* a safari! We shot a lot of elephants, tigers, lions, canteloupe and rats. We shot a lot of rats—really! Pardon my rumbling—rambling.

VISITOR: Did you get a big bag?

FLORENCE: How did that go again?

VISITOR: I said, did you get a *big bag?*

FLORENCE: Natu*rally.* We had to—to put the elephants in. We wouldn't want to drag them through the jungle by their tusks, you know, so they had to go in the bag.

VISITOR: Did you get a bison?

FLORENCE: *Comment?* I beg your pardon.

VISITOR: I said, did you get a bison?

FLORENCE: A bison? Oh, good Lord, no! We had to wash in a bucket. We roughed it out there. D'you know, I didn't see a bison the whole time we were out there? Nothing but buckets.

Even with jokes like that, we were a bit surprised when the show closed rather earlier than we had expected in New York, though we had a goodly run, and we were off on the road again the following summer. During the Broadway run, I first appeared in Cabaret, at Charlot's new Rendezvous Club, and found I enjoyed leading this doubling life. Somewhere along the route of our tour, a newspaper interviewer came up with a story whose headline told the story of my life to date: "Beatrice Lillie Finds Title Makes Little Difference: Fond of Salt-Water Taffy."

But in Chicago I was handled more professionally. Some of the sting of having been robbed there—and first dubbed "Lady"—the last time around had been eased when I claimed the loss of my costumes on my American income tax return and was allowed to deduct the magnanimous equivalent of two hundred pounds. This was one of the very few victories ever won in my hassles with tax collectors on both sides of the ocean.

What I *really* liked best about Chicago was Ashton Stevens, the drama critic of the *Herald and Examiner.* I found him personally engaging, brilliant and kind, perhaps at first because he seemed to think much the same about me. His review, after we opened a several weeks' run, sounded suspiciously like a *billet-doux,* and I shamelessly quote:

"What shall I say about Beatrice Lillie that I haven't said before? That her little dark head is dearer and more Chaplinesque than ever for being bobbed? . . . My admiration for this heaven-sent lady is so great as to render me worthless as her critic. She could make me laugh reading from the telephone book—or cry. That's her spell."

Is there a woman in the house who doubts that this was music to my auditory canals?

On our closing night at the Selwyn Theatre, in Chicago, Ashton sat in the front row with Gene Markey and Charles Collins, pelting me with flowers. But they weren't bouquets of orchids or carnations or roses. These were withered blossoms and dry sweepings, all that was left at the nearby florist's, which was long since closed for the day when Ashton—ever the working journalist—arrived.

As Ashton told me later, only the porter remained in the place. He would accept no more than fifty cents for these pickings, and he thoughtfully refrained from ringing up the transaction on the cash register. But to me those secondhand blooms were as fresh as the rogues who threw them over the footlights. I'd had all manner of posies from a prince, dukes, earls, and a baronet, but never from hard-working newspapermen.

I wept as I tried to thank them, standing right there on stage. I saw that Ashton was weeping, too.

Until he died, he continued to write his public love letters. "I think that she was born the way she is," he once remarked, "that fairies at the lying-in beaned her with tiny golden hammers."

"Next time you write that," I told him, "make it *angels*." He was a great gentleman, God bless him.

Westward rolled the *wagon-lits*, until we arrived in Los Angeles. We opened in Hollywood's El Capitan Theatre the same night as El Capitan itself, a huge, slightly gaudy structure with every modern convenience. The owners had summoned up their courage and charged fifteen dollars apiece for orchestra seats, which was a fortune at the time, so we knew we had to give the audience their money's worth.

Our *debut* was like a movie première, complete with searchlights and a mob wrestling the police to catch a glimpse of the stars who flocked to the show. We were rushing around backstage, getting ready for our first entrance, when the solemn notes of "God Save

171

the King" boomed out from the orchestra. We stood rigidly to attention, muttering to ourselves, because we were all too green to recognize that, to Americans, this was "My Country 'Tis of Thee."

We kept our eyes on one of the boxes. In it sat Charles Chaplin and his wife of the time, Lita Grey. In the front row, Pola Negri, like a white orchid, whispered sweet nothings into the gallant ear of Rudolph Valentino. Charlie spent half the time standing on his chair to watch us, which was apparently unheard of, since he was notoriously restrained on the few public occasions he chose to attend.

Another great comedian who'd been sitting in the audience had a different method of demonstrating his attention. After the opening, Buster Keaton came to the hotel where we were staying and spent the night lying in the corridor, guarding my bedroom door like Old Dog Tray.

When closing night arrived in due course, Hollywood's males were out in force again, crowding the orchestra seats. Gertie, Jack and I wondered what had gone wrong when we saw them filing out one by one toward the end of the final act. We had no time to worry too much about it, however, because the pace of any Charlot revue was fast and furious.

We seemed to have mislaid bits of our costumes for the finale, which had Jack in Scottish kilts, Gertie dressed up as Flora MacDonald, and me as Bonnie Prince Charlie. In the middle of Jack's opening song, we saw where the men who'd been out front had gone. Out from the wings, they marched in procession, each with his trouser legs rolled up above his knees.

Rudolph Valentino had Jack's Scots bonnet pulled down over his swarthy sideburns. Charlie wore his dinner jacket tied around his middle as an improvised

kilt. The Marx Brothers had brought false beards.
Richard Barthelmess had borrowed his wife's tartan
tam. And John Gilbert, the great lover, quite for no
reason, had picked up a ladder somewhere to carry on
his shoulder.

It was my turn to stay behind when the Charlot
company said farewell and took the train back to New
York, to sail for home. After a brief stay at the famed
Garden of Allah Hotel, I rented a house atop Fairholm
Drive, in the Hollywood Hills, just off lower Laurel
Canyon. Gertie, feeling fine, was off for a holiday in
England before she took up a New York contract to
play in *Oh, Kay!* with music by George Gershwin,
who'd also been one of the regulars at our Fifty-
fourth Street house. George liked to sit at our piano
and play for us, long before publication, the music
that became world famous. During the summer he
did the same thing on Fire Island, in those days a
peaceful retreat for the likes of us beautiful people.

As a result of our El Capitan capers—"Hollywood
Capitulates to the British Invader"—Metro-Goldwyn-
Mayer had signed one British invader to make a
movie. I was going to star-de-dah in something called
Exit Smiling with Jack Pickford, brother of the celebrated Mary and another Torontonian. I hadn't much
time to sample the local *joie de vivre,* but I was determined to give it a try.

Jack Gilbert and Greta Garbo were making eyes at
each other, and she spent a lot of her time visiting his
house, one of the first to be built on the peaks of
Beverly Hills, reachable only by a winding mountain
road. This was long before she took off and fled for a
while to Mexico, with Jack following fast after her.

She'd not long arrived from Stockholm and she
hadn't even had time to change her friendly, fun-lov-

ing way of life. She was *seldom* alone; she loved people and parties. Her first Hollywood movies—*The Torrent* and *The Temptress*—made her an instantaneous queen, and now *Flesh and the Devil*, with Jack Gilbert as costar, was ready to raise more goosebumps in the stalls throughout the country and the Western world.

Jack really believed the studio press releases that dubbed him "The Great Lover," and he did his damnedest to live up to his reputation. Whatever his latest role on the screen, he continued to act it out off screen. His neighbor on the next Beverly Hills mountaintop, the director King Vidor, once remembered:

"If his new assignment were a dashing Cossack officer, Jack would hire Russian servants in his household, and guests would be entertained with a balalaika orchestra while they were served vodka and caviare." Nothing obvious, mind you. . . .

Jack had a talent for backing into trouble. He woke up one morning in his mountaintop home to hear terrible ripping and wrenching noises coming from downstairs. He rushed out to see what was going on and found a municipal demolition crew removing a corner of his living room which jutted out too far on his property in violation of the local building code.

He bought a boat around this time, a beautiful schooner, which he christened *The Temptress* (aha!). He spent months refitting every cabin and every bit of equipment as a labor of love before he announced that *she*—no, the boat—was ready for inspection by his friends. *The Temptress* looked highly seductive, riding at anchor off Catalina Island one Saturday morning.

Jack, trim as a trivet in his yachting cap and blue

blazer, ferried his guests aboard in a spick-and-span dinghy, then escorted them from stem to stern, showing off his two-masted treasure. One of the guests, Norma Shearer, had a question for him.

"We thought we saw Greta aboard through our binoculars. What's happened to her?"

Jack gave no answer. Nobody saw her, and the only way she could have avoided them was by hiding in the crew's quarters. *Watch it!*

Now without even knocking, the notion entered my head that I should contribute a little something to make sure that the course of this true love did not run altogether smoothly. I'd no real thought of competing with Garbo, who was the queen of all she surveyed at MGM. And there was Nothing Like That so far as Jack was concerned. But I fancied a bit of mischief at their expense. They took themselves *so seriously,* and I'm always tempted to try puncturing solemnity wherever it appears.

So I began sending Jack one anonymous red rose every day, with an unsigned note, ostensibly written in the toils of passion. I itched to know what effect, if any, it had on the lady who was rapidly becoming famous in the publicity handouts as "The Silent Swede."

The thought was in my mind, or whatever passes for it, one evening as I wandered in a new convertible around the winding then dirt roads of Beverly Hills. At one particularly sharp turn, I forgot for a moment which country I was driving in. I yanked the wheel too hard, the wheels skidded in the dust and the car rolled onto its side. It was quite spectacular, rather like a finale of "Gang Busters."

My own performance wasn't so bad, either; I'd rate it "GP," parental supervision advised. I jumped out before the convertible finished upside down in the middle of the lonesome trail and landed on my hands and knees in a flurry of dust and pebbles. Ouch! I was shaken, scraped and bruised. Really.

The nearest house was King Vidor's. So I dragged myself to his front door. When the butler answered, I gather that I fainted in his arms, muttering that I wanted to see Jack Gilbert. Cut.

Down the road drove King Vidor and his wife, Eleanor Boardman. Their car's headlights picked out my wrecked convertible. Very gingerly, he got out and looked inside. No mangled remains, but a hand-bag with a driver's license—Beatrice Lillie's. The Vidors, with the help of their headlights, scoured the hillside for the *corpus delicti*, then decided they had best go home and telephone the police. But nobody was there.

Their butler, British to the core, Maud, had most kindly conducted me to my chosen destination. I was back on my hands and two skinned knees when Jack opened the door, dazzling in a blue brocade dressing gown and open-necked silk shirt.

"It seemed to me," King Vidor said afterward, "that he had anticipated the scene he was about to play and had carefully dressed for the part."

"Good God, Bea," Jack gasped in his high, thin voice. "What's happened?"

I managed, "Heard there was a party. Came."

He had the butler carry me to a divan in the living room. By this time, Mr. and Mrs. Vidor had sped round to their neighbor's. "I'll call a doctor," I heard King say.

"No, please," I mumbled, eyes still shut.

Jack fell to his knees beside the divan and grabbed

my hand. "Speak to me," he whispered. "Speak to me, Iris March."

Iris March? Of course, I knew her. She was the invention of my tonsorial friend, Michael Arlen, the heroine of *The Green Hat*, who kills herself for love by bashing a tree with her car. And who was going to play in the movie version of his novel but dear Jack and Greta?

I opened my eyes in a hurry and stared at Jack. The cad! He was pacing the floor like a madman, weeping, "She must not die. Iris March must not die."

I started to sit up, but he got to me first. With tears streaming down his cheeks, he threw his arms around a set of shaking shoulders and pinned me with a great big kiss.

But I was wrong. Garbo wasn't at his house that day. Pity!

There was another establishment we used to visit that was even more remote and infinitely more pretentious. As soon as La Casa Grande, the main house on the 275,000 acres of San Simeon, was completed in 1925, the mistress of the castle, Marion Davies, used to invite a slew of friends there. I don't believe that all three of the guesthouses were finished then, with fifteen rooms apiece, but La Casa Grande has one hundred rooms, including thirty-eight bedrooms, so space was not exactly at a premium.

The first time I was invited, I was a touch afraid of being informally introduced to a few of the lions, leopards, wildcats and polar bears that roamed the place, according to what I'd heard. (Oh, yes, there was a herd of bison, too, and one elephant, but we didn't bag him. I still had my bucket, though.)

177

What shook me more, however, was the sight of one castle, Italian, used, complete, lying around the lawns, packed in numbered crates. And what shook me most was dinnertime at La Casa Grande. We were invited to gather in the Assembly Hall, which was four times bigger than any hotel lobby, with carved choir stalls on each wall and a sixteenth-century French fireplace big enough for the likes of me to walk into without ducking.

Punctually at seven-thirty, William Randolph Hearst descended from his quarters in the Celestial Suite, which occupied the castle's twin towers, riding in a converted confessional box that served as an elevator. San Simeon appeared to be one of the few gathering places in the whole United States that was officially dry. So after toying languidly with tomato juice, ginger ale or some such refreshment, we progressed into the refectory.

This was supposedly William Randolph's favorite rendezvous. If Big Bobby had been there, even he could have walked into the fireplace with no need to bob his head. More choir stalls lined the walls. Banners which had been shipped from an Italian monastery hung from the ceiling. Statues of the saints were in each and every niche. Paper napkins and catsup bottles were on the three enormous antique tables, which could seat a hundred and more guests. Bootleg gin was introduced into the guests' water carafes unknown to W.R.H.

This final touch of timely hospitality was supplied by our hostess, Marion Davies, a warmhearted, understanding woman. She was described by my distant relative, George Bernard Shaw, on his one and only visit to the little hideaway as "by far the most attractive of the stars who are not really eighteen." Mr.

Shaw and I developed a sort of nodding acquaintance-ship, but that came later.

For reasons none of us questioned but sometimes gossiped about, Marion could do no wrong as the brightest star of Cosmopolitan Studios in the opinions of the critics employed by Hearst newspapers and magazines. Every day, it seemed, one or another of his publications ran a story about her. I remember being at a party somewhere with Charles Chaplin and seeing, down below us, the million and one lights of Los Angeles flicker on as night fell.

"I suppose in a minute," said I without thinking, "they will all come together and spell out 'Marion Davies.'" Marion loved that when she heard it. We had some happy times together as good friends.

San Simeon allegedly had some forty miles of trails for horseback riding, which was another of the standard pleasures of the place. On one weekend there, I ventured to deposit myself in a saddle and went off riding in the company of Valentino. After twenty minutes, I was breathing harder than the horse, which I succeeded in wheeling around, to head back toward a secluded hammock under the trees, where I could dismount and rearrange myself.

Rudolph, however, turned around, too, and followed me, the Latin lover to the life in his white shirt and adhesive riding breeches. For reasons not to be questioned, he took off his wrist watch before he struck up his overture. I did my best to convince him that, saddlesore or not, I could never be *that* kind of girl. But his wrist watch was still in the hammock the following morning. Who was I to quibble?

So far as I could gather, Hollywood was educational in a special sort of way, and the climate was nice, but more than that I could not say. The job I was doing in *Exit Smiling* didn't strike me as anything to set the world on fire. Most of the time, I couldn't make out what the movie was all about. Neither could anyone else.

The director, Sam Taylor, who politely smiled when I nicknamed him "Mr. Guggenfish," apparently had very little more idea than I had about what I was supposed to do. Sweet reason had no part in making movies, and there was no audience to learn from—only the grips and gaffers and the rest of the nice people who made up the tribe of strangely named apostles of the faith.

I'd try to introduce a fitful note of humor before we started to roll 'em. "Now, boys, be careful to get all my nose in this scene."

After the first laugh, nobody paid much attention. I was used to working for months to perfect a gesture or a piece of business. Here, we were due to finish in five weeks, and it was hard to believe that these disconnected scenes could possibly be patched together to make a movie with any kind of plot.

The author of our epic was Marc Connelly, who had already made a Broadway reputation with *Beggar on Horseback*, though *Green Pastures* still lay over the hill. He traveled to California with us for this, his first movie script. I doubt whether "De Lawd" himself could have made much sense of the goings on at the *Exit Smiling* set.

I was Violet, an aspiring and perspiring young actress who served as factotum, dog's body and general understudy to a theatrical touring company which had the good sense never to play in the same town twice. The best gag, I reflected, which Marc said was not of his writing, was a subtitle: "She played 'Nothing' in *Much Ado About Nothing*."

Jack Pickford was the hero, a bank clerk wrongly suspected of theft, who even more wrongly suspected himself of being an actor, according to the ramifications of the plot. Franklin Pangborn, who turned up again later when we made *Dr. Rhythm* with Bing Crosby, played Cecil Lovelace, the touring company's leading man, swishing around in a style the censors disallowed for years after that. Harry Meyer, a stalwart of Chaplin movies, gave a neat performance as the villain. Doris Lloyd was a tower of strength as the tippling leading lady.

When Sam Taylor announced that the shooting was over, I couldn't believe that we'd completed a picture. They assured me that it was "in the can," but I wasn't sure *where* that was. For the longest time, I refused to see *Exit Smiling*. It's an awful feeling to sit watching yourself, knowing there's nothing you can do about it. Yet, headstrong chit that I was, I still fancied I'd like to do another comedy, provided we wouldn't have to hurry so much the next time around.

Of course, the picture was hurrahed and heralded by the publicity boys as "a comedy sensation." They claimed it was "the humorous and tragic story of a small-town 'Sarah Bernhardt' so absorbed in her profession that she allows a great love to come into her life and watches it leave unprotestingly." So *that's* what it was about. I thought it was mostly a piece of cheese. (Next week: Elinor Glyn's *It*, starring Clara Bow.)

That chapter, like this, has a surprise ending. One September evening, I was sitting with Jack Pickford and some other friends who were listening to the Gene Tunney-Jack Dempsey championship fight in Philadelphia, on the radio. Not particularly interested, I picked up the late-night newspaper. Sensation! Read all about it! I was being sued by the wife of a scenario writer who'd worked on the picture. Alienation of affection. It struck me that, had it been true, she'd set a bargain price on his feelings, a mere $20,000 in damages.

"Hey," I said, "look at this."

"Hush it," said my gallant companions, used to such interruptions from me, as they focused their ears on the loudspeaker. "And there's a right to the midsection, and another, and another . . ." spake the radio.

"But this is terrible," I said frantically.

"You'll just have to wait," said Jack, reaching out to turn up the volume. "And it's a knockdown," shrieked the announcer. "Boy, what a fight!"

"I AM BEING SUED," I shouted, but they went on listening to the thumping Dempsey was delivering to his challenger.

Tunney and I had to wait for the end of the round.

News that the law had been called in against me brought Big Bobby rushing to Hollywood. Not long after, the unhappy wife canceled the action. "It was," said Big Bobby, "a perfect frame-up."

Nobody could argue with him, least of all me.

CHAPTER NINE

THOROUGHLY MODERN LILLIE

There's nothing like being the toast of two continents when the butter is being applied to you with jam on top. It's *delicious*, though it can make life a little slippery. The jam was usually spread thicker on the American side, however, so that's where I was likely to be, given the least provocation.

Heaven knows, for the next thirteen years I sailed the Atlantic so often that I could have shown the way to any captain if he'd lost it, including the short cut past the second porpoise on the right after you pass the Ambrose Light, inbound.

In more senses than one—oh, let's say at least three —I was all at sea, in a quandary without a paddle. Here was I, variously described as an Englishwoman from Canada or a Canadian woman from England, but a lady, forsooth, in any event, apparently to be permanently employed three thousand miles from home, if that's what one could call Drayton Manor.

I enjoyed living and working in London and I enjoyed working in New York; I still do. American audiences at this time seemed to be a bit quicker off the mark, and American *producers* decidedly so. For years, I'd breeze into London for a vacation or some such thing, crossing my fingers in the hope that one of the local impresarios would want me for a show. Then nothing would happen until the day I was leaving to meet a commitment on the opposite side of the ocean. That would be the day the telephone would ring.

"Bea, I've got a wonderful idea for you . . ."

"Sorry. Must be going. Boat train to catch, you know. Let's talk again next time I'm over." But we seldom did. I dearly love the English—their slower pace, courtesy and traditions. But in business, they were too slow, especially on Tuesdays. People think that having a career on both sides of the Atlantic is all glamor. Believe me it's not. It's hard work!

The family was neatly divided between the two countries. Muriel lived in London. My husband, abandoning Australia, was still looking around for a career. He had taken a fancy to politics and was talking about joining the Labour Party as a shock measure and standing for Parliament. Bobby tried just about everything, but his interest always quickly faded. I sometimes think he should have been an actor.

Certainly, the coal miners of Staffordshire, where he was well known and much liked, would have voted for him to a man. He would have done well in Birmingham, too, where for a while he managed a suburban dance hall, of all things.

"You get more fun out of life if you disregard the conventional," he was fond of saying. He never *did* offer himself to the voters in an election, however.

Little Bobbie and Mother stayed with me at the

house I'd taken in Fairholm Drive, above Laurel Canyon in the Hollywood Hills, after spending that bit of time at the Garden of Allah, the now demolished bungalow hotel which was a kind of oasis for most of the British colony. My son started kindergarten while we were there. He had a new trick now, designed to tease and please me simultaneously. He'd put himself to sleep, after I'd tucked him in bed, by murmuring with a smile in a variety of inflections, "*Yes*, my lady . . . Oh, *no*, my lady . . . Why, *certainly*, my lady . . . Of *course*, my lady . . . Good night, my lady . . ."

Bygone days. Halcyon days. They appeared so calm and peaceful at the time, no matter how many ripples there were on the domestic pool. We all thought, didn't we, that the world had quite recovered from Kaiser Bill's madness, and we were convinced the future stretched endlessly ahead of us into ever sunnier, happier times.

I remember once, after saying good night to Little Bobbie, I walked down the stairs and turned to a friend who was visiting us from New York. "Thank God," I said, "*he* won't have to go away to war." But he did, he did.

After *Exit Smiling*, for all its flaws, the people at MGM had a three-year option on my services. But making more movies would have meant that I had to live indefinitely in Hollywood, and I had engagements to fulfill on the stage. For one thing, I'd signed with Charles Dillingham for my first musical comedy on Broadway. I'm sure there were occasions when he wished I hadn't, though what evolved wasn't any fault of mine.

The title of our falderal was *Oh, Please!* Every other show had an "Oh" in it somewhere. There'd been *Oh,*

Boy! and *Oh, Joy!* and now there was *Oh, Kay!*
which had opened a month earlier with Gertie, Oscar
Shaw and Victor Moore, music and lyrics by the
Gershwins.

A few days before our première, a very agitated Mr.
Dillingham discovered that *Oh, Please!* and *Oh, Kay!*
came perilously close to being twins. Two Frenchmen,
Maurice Hennequin and Pierre Veber, were the au-
thors of a farce called *Madame President* in which
Fanny Ward starred in 1914. It appeared that Gertie's
librettists had turned to that rusty opus for inspiration
in the writing of *Oh, Kay!* So apparently had Anne
Caldwell and Otto Harbach in assembling *Oh, Please!*
As for me, O, for the wings of a dove!

Some last-minute changes were in order, especially
since Gertie had already been playing for a month.
So the old French farce became the dithering frame-
work for what was now billed as a "farce revue." The
young ladies of the show, including one red-haired
basso who smoked cigars backstage, got to parade in
the latest lingerie; Charles Winninger, a darling man
and the costar, got to play the trombone; and I dipped
into the Charlot repertoire to revive *The Girls of the
Old Brigade*. My dress was an exact copy of a traveling gown from Queen Alexandra's trousseau (ah,
memories!) and the chorus was got up in everything from bathing costumes, *circa* 1880, to nippy
skating outfits of the same era.

The plot was *that* one about the clean-living businessman, whose wife is head of the hometown's Purity
League, priding herself on keeping her husband spot-
less in thought, word and deed. She figures that he
isn't receiving the promotion he deserves, so she ups
and offs to New York to see his boss.

No sooner is she out of the house, of course, than in

moves the star of a traveling burlesque company, which has been evicted from the local hotel on the orders of the clean-living businessman. Lily Valli— such was my name in this epic—vamps him out of his mind and he introduces her as his wife when the boss from New York drops in that evening.

Well, there you have it. I had an idea that it would need a Few Lillie Touches contributed to liven it up when we opened. Poor Mr. Dillingham, who'd been personally working us over during a tryout in that show-biz mecca of the day, Atlantic City, wasn't really looking forward to our first night at the Fulton Theatre. Neither, frankly, was I.

The overture sounded fine, and the critics liked the conductor, Charles Previn. One of them wrote the next day that Charles "would never be able to lead if he had his hair bobbed like Miss Lillie's. He led with all his front locks."

After the overture, things tended to run downhill, including the curtain, which tended so to do when it was supposedly heading in the opposite direction.

On Lily Valli's first appearance, the audience decided to enjoy a seventh-inning stretch and applauded for three and a half minutes, as clocked by the stage manager. I shook my finger at them, murmured, "Book, *please*," and that started them off for two minutes more. (Ask the stage manager if you don't believe it!) As the evening unfolded, it proved hard to follow that little gem.

Then the real troubles began. Walter Winchell, who was a theatre critic and not a columnist at the time, poured out his heart for his readers the following morning:

"No star, perhaps, ever received such wretched and abominable support as that which Lady Peel drew last night. When an ensemble maiden wasn't catching her ice skates in the star's frocks, or a youth didn't forget his lines, or a curtain refused to lift, or Conductor Previn didn't muff a music cue, a stage mechanic or two interfered with Miss Lillie's solos before the olio ... This affectionate spectator wept for her."

"Press on!" I told myself, repressing an urge to throw things. Ignoring the knee-and-knuckle dancers swooping down from all sides, taking care to stay clear of the hollyhocks with which the director, Hassard Short, had planted the stage, I did my best. "Miss Lillie's stamina," said one newspaper, "is remarkable."

The other critics, armed to the teeth with adjectives, sounded as if they'd been in attendance at the opening of an ice-cream parlor instead of surveying Lily Valli. Allow me to quote:

"Scrumptious"—Gilbert Gabriel.

"Nourishing"—Alexander Woollcott.

"Bonny"—Burns Mantle.

"Sweet"—George Kaufman.

"Darling"—Robert Benchley.

"Delicious"—Alan Dale.

"Ducky"—E. W. Osborn.

"Splendiferous"—Edward Pidgeon.

"Hotsie-totsie"—John Anderson.

For reasons we hold to be now self-evident, *Oh, Please!* did not so much run as take a stroll on Broadway before it was off, with us in tow, on tour, taking its banalities to Philadelphia, Boston and so forth and soon. Mumsie brought Little Bobbie to see me in Boston, and in Chicago Ashton Stevens wrote his unfailing *chanson d'amour:*

"One word of encouragement from her and I should have broken my engagement to wed the Duncan Sisters and become Mr. Lillie . . . Oh, well! Perhaps she is not so marvelous in the morning." A perceptive man was dear Ashton. I'm fit for nothing until I've had breakfast and read the newspapers.

By this time, Charles Winninger, playing Nicodemus Bliss, the sanitized businessman, had added a new bit of business to milk a laugh or two. Ever so inadvertently, but ever so passionately, he had taken to kicking Lily Valli, to use Ashton's phrase, "where Grandma used to wear yesterday's newspaper."

Strange to say, but as true as I'm standing here, I came across a woman at a party not very much later who was Mrs. Nicodemus Bliss to the life, a crusader against some variety of reputed evil, though I couldn't remember which. Since it was my party, I stopped to chat for a moment and this quickie developed:

"I know I mustn't offer you a cocktail," said I, making small talk. "You're chairman of the Temperance League."

The good lady glared. "I am *not*. I am president of the Anti-Vice Committee."

My service. "I knew there was something we mustn't offer you."

I can't *stand* pompous society!

Before *Oh, Please!* eventually closed, I had finally agreed to appear before a different kind of audience from any I'd played to for years. Not, in fact, since the red-faced night as an extra turn at the Camberwell Palace of Varieties. I was signed to appear in Vaudeville. The experience, I reckoned, would be good for me, and the money would do wonders for the bank account.

The contract contained no fancy clauses except one, which I asked for specially. I'd heard that August was a particularly pleasant time of year to be in San Francisco—cool breezes and all that, you know—and the tour was due to begin that month. At the rate I was going, jumping from one engagement into another, I couldn't see myself getting to San Francisco any other way, so I made sure that I opened there. I didn't regret it; that city is my favorite in all the U.S.A.

My first swim around the Orpheum circuit couldn't be counted as a baptism; it was more like a dunking for the initial week or so. Not yet having put together an act of my own, I was doing the skit which Noël Coward had written for me, *After Dinner Music,* lyrics, music, "business" and all. So a while later, I could truthfully tell a New York audience at the Palace, "This is my first appearance in Vaudeville, me as always 'ad me own 'orses."

Being a headliner at the Orpheum, I imagined, would be a kind of busman's holiday, keeping myself busy until the fall, when Charles Dillingham wanted to stage another Broadway show with yours faithfully once more his leading lady.

Venturing onto the Orpheum's stage in San Francisco, it struck me rather forcefully that if this was a holiday, I'd rather take thirty days in Alcatraz on bread and water. I counted myself fortunate that nothing else struck me, possibly of a vegetable nature.

I had never been so nervous in my life. The customers and I were not communicating. I was tense, and they were mostly silent. I felt that I could do nothing right, and they were inclined to agree.

This kind of theatre performance and I had been strangers far too long. There was no time to warm the audience. I felt that they didn't dig my brand of labor, the accent, the timing. I realized I had a lot to learn, and I'd better be sharp about it before the tour ended.

A woman interviewer enlightened me on one point. "Why don't you take all your bows?" she asked.

She explained that in vaudeville a performer was graded largely on the bows the audience is expecting. "I heard a lot of applause," she said, "but you only took a couple of bows and left the rest unacknowledged."

"They wouldn't want me to keep on rushing out and bowing, now, would they?"

"They would, and they do," she answered. Point taken.

Arriving early at the theatre, I spent all the time I could spare, standing in the wings, watching Diero, "master of the piano accordion"; Dainty Marie, "physical culture expert and professional beauty"; Wiest & Stanton, "a little rhyme and less reason"; and every other act on the bill.

After Dinner Music is a sketch involving an aging prima donna in a garish red wig, a green velour court gown and a mangy feathered fan, who sings a few songs for her guests—her repartee is expensive, she says—while having a mishap or two along the way. I felt certain that Noël would understand what I had to do. He did when he heard about it, as he invariably does, no matter how we've fought to reach the moment of truth.

"Now are you going to shake your finger at me?" I scream.

"*Certainly!*" he screams in return, and within an hour or so, we can be as happy together again as Tristan und Isolde.

To win more response from vaudeville audiences,

After Dinner Music had to be somewhat broadened, and broadened it was at every successive performance. There was no shortage of performances—three a day and four on Sundays.

My *prima's* bedraggled fan was waved so grandly that it shed feathers all over the stage. When she picked up her evening cloak, an end of a tablecloth got caught up, too, and a tableful of china and silverware crashed to the floor. She reached for a high note, and a floor lamp that was part of the sketch lost its shade. She tried again, and the same thing happened. Ever resourceful, she seized the shade and held it fast while she made a final, successful struggle to reach her high "C," at which point, naturally, the light bulb exploded.

She sang about an "old-fashioned girl in an old-fashioned garden, wearing an old-fashioned gown, with her old-fashioned stockings about to fall down." That was followed by a ballad of such sentiment as to dampen every eye—*"The Roses Have Made Me Remember What Any Nice Girl Should Forget."*

She backed into pianos and tripped over chairs. She had to battle her long chiffon handkerchief to extract it from her evening bag, because it got mysteriously entangled in the handle. When she finally disentangled it, she pitched the bag at the piano top, narrowly missing the handsomely tailored accompanist, Hugh Sinclair. Then, after announcing that she was about to retire to change her costume, she emerged from behind the curtain, intact and unaltered, from glittering bandeau to run-over satin shoes. May I whisper that there was a certain amount of caricature of Madame Luci Lillie, the *original* mezzanine soprano?

It was at that point I decided to introduce "March

with Me." I should like to report that the increasing response from the clientele at all performances, now and then amounting to storms of applause, could be attributed solely to the old tried-and-true melody. But I couldn't be positive; there were too many changes to credit any one of them. Maybe it was the handkerchief.

Anyway, the audiences came to life, and so did I. They began to "get" what I was doing, and as always that made me full of the dickens, dreaming up new bits of business to keep the pot on the boil.

Except in Cleveland. There was a banjo player on the bill who joked, "He who laughs last comes from England." Some local patrons of the arts must have saved up their giggles for breakfast the following morning. I understand that they accepted my *prima* getup as something a vaudeville artiste might legitimately regard as stylish.

Two matrons in a loge, to judge by their chatter, couldn't make up their minds whether I was trying to be funny or fighting a heavy cold. When, at the end of the sketch, I appeared in a white dinner dress to sing a straight song or two, one of the dowagers turned to the other with a know-it-all look and declared, "Now if she'd stick to this kind of stuff and leave the other alone, she'd be all right."

Perhaps it was one of them who took the trouble to write to the local newspaper's entertainment editor, George Davis: "Beatrice Lillie is your favorite comedienne, you said last week . . . I can't see that there is anything so funny in backing into a piano or upsetting a chair . . ."

But the cram course in vaudeville, self-taught, worked well enough, and as the act acquired more muscle, I was "held over" for second weeks along the route. When I arrived in Toronto, the band of the Canadian World War Veterans, with pipers, flags and aw', paraded at the railroad station to welcome me. I managed to murmur, "Aren't you mistaking me for Lindbergh?" before I burst into tears. *At last,* a respectable welcome home. Toronto the Good had finally come through in a big way.

As always, however, *Chicago* was the place for the hot news of the tour. I had to change trains there—doesn't everybody?—and at La Salle Street Station I had an item to announce for the society pages. I'd just had the word from Muriel. She and Arthur Weigall had been seeing eye to eye for a long time, and now they were engaged. Then the October skies opened up, and it began to pour. I led the assembled reporters in one brief chorus of "It Ain't Gonna Rain No More," gave them my blessing and darted off to Ernie Byfield's Ambassador East Hotel to wait for my next train.

I was on my way back to New York, to appear one more time in another "farce revue," *She's My Baby,* for the diligent Mr. Dillingham. As usual, he had expended all kinds of money for a flawless production —costumes, sets, lyrics by Lorenz Hart, and eight long-limbed dancers identified as "John Tiller's Lillie Cocktails." He had engaged all kinds of talent, too, from Jack Whiting to a pre-Hollywood Irene Dunne. And the program also listed William Frawley, who later came to television as Lucy's next-door neighbor, and a slip of an Irish girl, playing a bit as a nursemaid, named Geraldine Fitzgerald.

The plot? Aye, *there's* the rub. This was one that predated *Uncle Tom's Cabin,* having to do with the rich, old uncle arriving unexpectedly to meet the imaginary wife and baby that his improvident nephew has been telling him about, so *now* they must be produced somehow at twenty-four hours' notice. Tilly, the maid, is talked into masquerading as the wife, the uncle is persuaded that the baby's been kidnaped and —Oh, you know how it turns out, and you can be sure who was playing Tilly. Clifton Webb, known fondly as "Ding," who was a song-and-dance man with a mauve manner in those days, portrayed a character named Clyde Parker.

Some of the lines had obviously been imported at great expense from the British Museum. "I'm not a menial," says Tilly, "if you know what I menial." She describes herself as a Rotarian—"I only eat meat once a week, and lots of vegetables with vitaphones." Collapse of stout party in the second row.

"Let us ensconce ourselves on the sofa," says Clyde.

"No, I prefer to sit down," responds Tilly, quick as a flash. Five people require first aid in the dress circle.

Let us not linger too long over this doddering joke of a production. Though the critics didn't care for it very much, they were all perfect gentlemen in their references to me. Fortunately, I don't depend entirely on dialogue for what I do, not entirely on stage business performed during the dialogue. It's what I do *after* I say my lines that counts.

Raise an eyebrow? Curl a lip? Flutter the eyelids? Tilt the chin? Someone once kept score of how many responses there might be, but I've forgotten the number he came up with, and I actually don't keep track of such things myself. I leave that to the audience, telling me what to do next. It's a clear case of *osmosis*, doctor.

Believe me, I never calculate a gesture, inflection or movement in advance. If I were consciously aware of what I was doing, I couldn't function at all. Whatever creativity is involved has its origin in this area of spontaneous, uninhibited activity. *Timing* is of great importance. So are articulation of speech and movement. Wit, which I regard as an important element of humor but not the whole, makes a contribution, too, plus an appreciation of the fads and foibles of humanity. Topicality can have value for a fleeting moment, though frankly, nothing dates faster than topical humor.

There! Once and for all time I've tried to be analytical and explain Beatrice Lillie, a bit of what makes her tick, and some of my ideas about what is funny in her. Full stop. Period, Amen.

One raving fan had said, "Her shoulder shrugs are worth a hundred guineas a shrug to the management that employs her." *Managements,* please note. Tax inspector, don't think for a second that I ever made that kind of money, or I'd have shrugged myself from here to High Holborn.

But I need time to work out the "after business," as it's called in the theatre. I sometimes have to ask actors appearing with me and rehearsing with me for the first time to wait for a moment or so after I finish my line before they go on with theirs. There has to be that pause to give me the chance, when we get before the audience, to develop my business. Without it, I'm ruined (and you wouldn't want that to happen, would you)?

I thought I was ruined, anyway, in the fall of that year, tackling my next engagement. This would be the first time I'd been directed by Noël, and it was a miracle that it wasn't the last.

When *She's My Baby* closed, I snatched a few weeks in England, to take a brief intermission and see the young man, not quite eight years of age, who was now in school but finding time to write me such notes as this:

> Dearest Mother,
>
> It has been such a lovely day. And we were out for a walk by the lake. And I have just bought a train. It was all hand made in wood. I like my lessons very much and my school. I have been practicing my piano. I love playing rugby. I hope you are well, Dearest Mother. All my love to you.

He added, as a postscript, a careful pencil drawing of the new train.

There were moments when I wondered whether I'd become too busy a beaver, but I brushed them aside on that trip to London and made my debut at the London Palladium at the same time I started rehearsals for *This Year of Grace*, for which Noël had written book, lyrics and music as well.

I had another companion in a thousand frolics in the person of the Alabama peach, Tallulah Bankhead, who had set London on its ear from the moment she arrived in 1923 to play Maxine in *The Dancers*. We bumped into each other from time to time, but never with greater impact than on a certain evening when I arrived back latish and solitary at the Savoy Hotel, where I often stayed, and went to bed in a healthy state of exhaustion after a long day of rehearsals and a long evening of cabaret.

Blissful sleep was shattered by the telephone. "Beattie, dahling, Tallulah."

"Who?"

"Lulu Ta Birkenhead." She'd picked up the nickname as the result of a well-publicized romance with Lord Birkenhead, the pillar of the British bar (where justice is served, not drink).

"Dahling, you must come to my place right away. We're having a little pahty, and you'll absolutely love it."

"I'm still asleep. I can't."

"Oh, come on, Beattie. I'll send someone to fetch you."

I was too tired to argue. I didn't want to bother dressing up again, but I hadn't the strength to refuse. In her living room at Farm Street, everybody was sipping one or two. I arrived like a sleepwalker, said my hellos and had one stiff drink. Within ten minutes, I slipped away to a quiet guest room, locked the door and laid my head to rest again. As the "little pahty" of roughly eighty livened up, I wasn't missed. Those who vaguely recalled my late arrival thought I'd gone off home.

By the dawn's grim light, Tallulah woke me with thunderous pounding on the door. "Wake up, dahling. Let's go. I'll take you back to the Savoy."

"Think we can make it?" I muttered, generously.

"Don't be so perfectly absurd," said Tallulah, who was feeling no pain whatever. "They always know me at the Savoy. I got you here, and I'll help you home."

After making our way through Berkeley Square to the Hotel Ritz in Piccadilly, we found a taxi. Reaching the Savoy in early sunlight, the special variety that looked just like an early etching, I hopped out, hoping to keep "Lulu" in the cab.

"Thank you," said I. "Be in touch."

No chance. Tallulah poured herself from the taxi. "Nonsense, dahling. I'm going to see you safely in." I half-carried her through the revolving door into the lobby. At the reception desk to the right of the entrance sat a young porter, who recognized both of us. We staggered up to him. In her dark-wine voice, Tallulah said, "Lady Keel's pee."

At that, all activity around us came to an instant halt.

Silence fell. She tried again. Still no response. I focused on the poor porter, thinking I had better help out. "My pee, my good man, if you please." .

Stifling his laughter, he handed over the key to me at last. Now the lobby of the Savoy has a shiny marble floor which is washed in the small hours every morning. The carpets had been rolled up, and two charwomen with buckets were dousing the floor with suds. Into one of the buckets went Lady Keel's left foot. Down I went, clutching Tallulah and pulling her down with me. We slithered together across the marble, our London *derrières* dampened but our spirits high. After a long night's journey into day, "Lulu" had made her point.

The sensation of the moment in London was Aimee Semple McPherson, a Canadian-born farm girl now known as the "Four-Square Gospeller," who had booked the whole Albert Hall for her revival meetings and was packing in half-hysterical crowds for every performance. And "performance" was the word for it. I'd met her when I was in Hollywood, which she made her center of operations after arriving with ten dollars and one tambourine.

I considered her a charmer, with a tangle of bobbed auburn curls, a determined jaw and a nose that even I envied. She was an actress to her fingertips, who could hold an audience for an hour and more while she told them such home truths as, "We want less pie and more piety. . . . To God, oratory doesn't matter.

... Watch out for the cloven hoof of Satan."

A choir of Four-Square Gospellers straight from her Angelos Temple in Hollywood sang her onto the platform, where she popped up dressed in a long white skirt, white stockings and with a white college badge on her blazer.

One of Sister McPherson's fascinated followers was Tallulah. Sister was staying at the Hotel Cecil, which stood in those days a few steps along the Strand from the Savoy. Perhaps it was the day following the trouble with Lady Keel's pee—I don't remember—but Tallulah went to collect the gospeller and bring her to a rehearsal of *This Year of Grace*. Dorothy Dickson, the Kansas City girl who'd been a converted Londoner ever since she starred in *Sally*, came with them; Dorothy's another dear friend of mine.

Sister had never been backstage before. She was fascinated. What caught her fancy especially was "Dance, Little Lady," a big production number danced by Florence Desmond, galvanized until she drops, while Billy Milton scourged the chorus like a demon slave master.

"I'd like to write something like that myself," Sister said knowingly.

This was now Monday afternoon and the final rehearsal to be held in London. I was sailing the next morning in the *Leviathan* for New York, where the show was to open in something less than four weeks. Big Bobby was accompanying me this time, and that evening we caught the boat train at Waterloo Station together, to make the three-hour journey to Southampton and spend the night aboard.

We didn't know it, but we were being followed. Tallulah and Sister were inspired to nip down to Southampton by car to throw a surprise party for us in our stateroom. Sister, as Tallulah said later, had taken a great interest in me—watch it!—and insisted on coming to the dock.

Somewhere along the line, they picked up Gwen Farrar, who had appeared with me in *Pot Luck*, and Audrey Carten, another actress and great friend of Tallulah's. Somewhere along the road, their car broke down.

Rustic Hampshire in the middle of an October night has more farmhouses than filling stations and more cows than telephones. So Sister and her flock got out and pushed and pushed for a mile or two. Cut.

The surprises got under way, a bit delayed, at eight o'clock the next morning when Big Bobby, still in bed, was aroused by rapping on the stateroom door. The girls had arrived. He was livid, but Sister, who had joined in taking a little refreshment en route, was not to be deterred. She used to say, "I see no monkeys growing like men—only men growing like monkeys."

In no time at all, she had fallen on to her knees, with me beside her, offering a few kind words to You-Know-Who on my behalf. The cabin steward eventually broke up the party just before the ship sailed, but Sister left me a souvenir before we said farewell; a black-bound, gilt-edged Bible.

The shipboard reporters cottoned on to the story and telephoned their Fleet Street colleagues, who banged their heads on a wall of silence. But that didn't stop them from running their versions of what had happened all over the front pages.

Audrey said, "I'd rather not say anything. You'd better ask Miss Farrar."

Gwen said, "Well, I don't know anything about it, and I wasn't there."

Tallulah, who didn't get back to Farm Street until two in the afternoon said, "I have nothing to add to anything Mrs. McPherson may have said."

Sister said, "I went to Southampton to give Miss Lillie a Bible." And she did. So *there!* Your witness.

This Year of Grace was imported by our old friend, Archie Selwyn, and produced by C. B. Cochran, a calm, soft-spoken, true gentleman who came within a whisker of shedding his serenity before we had finished preparing the show. "Cockie" had started out as Charlot's press agent when Uncle André was managing director of the Alhambra several years before I showed up there in *Not Likely*. Now Cockie was, if anything, bigger in the business than his former boss, whose stars Cockie often hired. As Charles Graves, the Fleet Street columnist, noted, "Charlot giveth and Cochran taketh away." *This Year of Grace* was the second revue Noël had written for him.

Noël had boundless energy. Besides writing and directing the show, he was going to play in it as a featured member of the cast. Before starting in at the Selwyn on Forty-second Street, we had a week's tryout in Baltimore. "Trial" might be a better word. Or even "ordeal."

For various reasons, some domestic and others due to my insecurity over my material, I was rather overcome by what Cockie called "an inferiority complex." To be blunt, I was bitchy. I was no happier at rehearsals than I'd been the first go-around with Archie Selwyn. I didn't even want to speak to Cochran.

"You're both amateurs, so far as I'm concerned" were the kindest words I could say to either of them. Wasn't I *naughty?*

I insisted that after God knows how many years of

working, I knew what I could do and how I could do it. Cockie stood calmly but resolutely in the way, with different ideas.

Noël remembered years later, "I have never really directed Beatrice Lillie any more than anyone else has. I have guided her, argued with her and, on occasions, squabbled with her, but direction *qua* direction is in her case an academic term. She is not in the least uncooperative. She listens attentively when told when to move and where to move and how to read a certain line, and she tries willingly and earnestly to comply. But the results are short-lived. Her *instincts* take command and her intuitive obedience to them is absolute." So a-ding, a-ding, ding! Noël has also been kind enough to add, "I must say Beattie is *usually* right."

Dearest reader, I hasten to add here that, for once and for all, *I* was entirely to blame. I was inhibited, worried, upset and *wrong*. My material was excellent. My fears were unfounded.

But by the time we reached the final dress rehearsal, Noël was showing signs of strain. Cockie, in fact, insisted that he should take the day off. "If you don't, you're going to have a nervous breakdown," he said. The producer himself conducted what he described as "the most dreadful dress rehearsal I have ever experienced."

At this eleventh hour, Cockie was still cutting and changing scenes in which I appeared, and I would not tolerate it. I fled to my dressing room, and Cochran followed on my heels. War was declared.

"I refuse to go on if you force me to do that number and make all these last-minute changes."

"If you walk out, I shall personally report you to Actors' Equity."

That did it! An overnight cease-fire was called between us out of sheer exhaustion on both our parts, but neither one would talk to the other, and the next day my blood was still gently on the boil.

On the morning of our debut, my husband telephoned C.B. "I have passed a most dreadful night with your leading lady."

"I'm glad *you* had to sleep with her and not I," said C.B. He would talk to Bobby, but not to me until after the performance. Later, he recalled thinking at the time, as he gloomily put on his white tie, "I would not have given a nickel for the show's chances."

But, *ah,* the first entrance, when I played a weary suburban lady waiting for a bus, clutching two shopping bags and three balloons. Howls of delight from the entire house! In Baltimore, yet, where I'd never appeared before. And so it went right through to the final curtain, when the roof shook and the side walls rattled. We had a hit on our hands again, a palpable hit.

Backstage, C.B. and I galloped into each other's arms. "Cockie, dear, you were right, and I was wrong, and I'm so sorry." What else was there to be said?

Well, Noël thought of something. In that strangely effective voice of his, he had been singing one of his songs in the show, *Room With a View,* which he decided should be handled at subsequent performances by Billy Milton.

"I cannot," said Noël, "go on singing those terribly slushy words."

The night after our première at the Selwyn, the third member of the three former Charloteers opened at the Alvin, ten blocks away. Gertie was starring in a new George and Ira Gershwin musical, *Treasure Girl,* with Clifton Webb and Walter Catlett.

ALL THE LUCK IN THE WORLD FOR ANOTHER BIG SUCCESS, DARLING. LOVE—BEA, said one telegram.

ALL MY LOVE FOR A BIG SUCCESS AND HAPPY MEMORIES OF THE CHARLOT REVUE—GERTIE, said another.

The audience and the critics found *Treasure Girl* disappointing. One of the reviewers, remembering my slightly frustrated efforts with the diligent but not very inspired Mr. Dillingham, wrote, "Since their joint *Charlot Revue* days, Miss Lawrence has had all the breaks and Miss Lillie none. But *This Year of Grace* versus *Treasure Girl* evened the score."

I didn't envy Gertie's life, and I doubt if she envied mine. We went separate ways, always in contact, but sometimes not meeting for long periods of time. But whenever we met, we quickly picked up the old friendship so that it seemed as though we had never moved out of Fifty-fourth Street.

CHAPTER TEN

FUNNY GALS, FUNNY GUY, FUNNY MONEY

Was there anybody in the world I envied? I suppose I must bear the bottom of my sentimental heart and confess that yes, there was, in a way. Ed Wynn. So far as I was concerned, he *was* "The Perfect Fool," just as his billing on Broadway, radio and then television used to say. Not that I ever told him so. I figured he might have been as tired of his label as I was of mine, "the funniest woman in the world."

I worshiped him from afar, a touching case of unrequited adoration. Once I caught sight of him on a New York street, a chubby little man with sad eyes, and followed him, undetected, for ten blocks to get a better look at his remarkable face.

For years, the critics fancied they saw a resemblance between us, but I always thought that I had the better chin. As a matter of fact, upon occasion, I seemed to remind the critics of almost everybody. According to one of them, I was "remarkably like Charlie Chaplin in features as well as mannerisms." I was sometimes tempted to grow a mustache to make the illusion complete, but I hadn't a Chaplin walk. Mine was more of a hackney action, a cab horse encountering mud, with a Canadian caper now and then. Certainly, completely original.

Charlie called me "my female counterpart." On rare occasions, at parties, we'd improvise an act together. He'd sing tenor in fluent Spanish against my eloquent French soprano, both of us faking the words but totally intelligible, at least to each other. What a happy partnership! One regret; I *do* wish we'd made just one movie together.

We had Harold Ross, who had just affronted every little old lady in Dubuque, Iowa, by founding *The New Yorker*, rolling on the floor at one performance. But the tables were turned on another occasion, and it was my turn to roll on the floor—of a taxicab in which I was riding with Harold and his wife. We'd been hit in the midsection by a runaway car driven by some college lads on Ninth Avenue. I played *This Year of Grace* for a week or two with a broken rib.

Over the years, I have also been compared by sundry reviewers with Bobby Clark, who for me was the second best stage comedian in the world; with Al Jolson, Elsie Janis, Thurston the magician, Babe Ruth, Herbert Hoover, an Egyptian frieze and a jack-in-the-box. The truth was that I have imitated nobody. I have burlesqued all kinds of people, from Ruth Draper even to Gertie, but I've never consciously been anyone but Beatrice Gladys What's-her-name, whoever she may be.

A woman I wanted not to burlesque but portray in a movie was Fanny Brice. Like so many Hollywood excursions, nothing came of this ambition, and then along came Barbra Streisand—Ah, well! You can't have everything. There occasionally were great plots to make Fanny and me rivals, but we confounded the plotters and finished up firm friends, clutching hands across the sea.

One day she invited me up to her handsome town house on New York's upper West Side for our first social engagement together. We were going to have a little chat, and then reporters would be asked in to witness the monumental encounter of two funny girls. The butler showed me in.

We started off brightly enough. "I don't know what's the matter with me," said Fanny. "Geez, kid, I feel terrible. I woke up this morning with a vertigo, and I—"

"With a what?"

"With a vertigo. I got out of bed and fell on my nose. One of those things. My new nose, too. Can you beat it?"

"Something you ate, perhaps."

"Maybe. I wonder if it could have been that rarebit I had last night before I went to bed."

She asked about Little Bobbie, and I told her he was in a boarding school in England, with my mother keeping both eyes on him. I asked about her Billy, and she said he was miles away in school, too. Suddenly, we began to feel very sorry for ourselves. I showed her my snapshots of Bobbie, and then fished out the latest letter I'd had from him:

Dearest Mother,

You asked me to write to you, and I am. I am writing this in prep. Ha! ha! It isn't long until the end of term, only another day, and then I am home again. How is your stomach-ache now, I hope it is quite better. You know that little place on my leg? Well, Matron says that it is only a little boil, and she pressed it today and lots of blood came out, but it is nothing to worry about, dear. You must come and see me sometime. I have to cut off now as a master is walking round the room. Well, Dear, all my fondest love, from your loving son, Robert. P.S. Come on a Wed. at about half past two. OK? Yes. Ha! ha!

Then Fanny got out her photographs, and we discussed the braces Bobbie wore on his teeth and the terrible cold her Billy had suffered from last winter. Then her eyes began to tear up, and so did mine.

By this time, the reporters had arrived. They took a quick look at us as the butler ushered them in. We were sitting side by side on a sofa, weeping on each other's shoulder. "What goes on?" said one young man in a gray raincoat. "We were supposed to come see the funniest women in the world."

The two of us sobbed, "Geez, kid, take a good look."

Fanny was a wonderful friend. I was forever dropping in on her in New York or staying as a guest at her house in Holmby Hills, California. At the end of an evening's appearance, she'd give her standard welcome.

"Come on, kid, let's go up to my room and put your feet up. Geez, you must be tired, kid." The *boudoir* was always a kind of *salon* (one "o," please). Whoever was in the house would join us ladies, lolling around on the beautiful furniture that she bought, as she thought, wholesale.

Fanny had great talent as an interior decorator, and she kidded herself that she got a discount on everything she picked up for herself or her friends, whose houses she liked to decorate, too. *Not* for free. It was easy to discover what happened when she walked into a store: the price tags were often as not switched on her.

But Fanny didn't really care, so long as she could return triumphant and say, "Geez, kid, I got ten bucks off . . ."

Up in the boudoir, I'd say, "Come on, get the jewels out. Let's see them." If there was horse racing on the radio, you could bet she'd have that program on, "Stop a minute, kid," she'd say. "I got to listen."

Where she hid her jewelry, none of us knew. She'd disappear from the room, then come back in with her hands full of bracelets and necklaces, rings and tiaras, oozing emeralds and diamonds and pearls.

"Put them on, Fanny," I'd say. She'd dress up with as much as she could carry and hang the rest on me. "Geez, that's all right for you. I'd look silly with that on, kid. They'd all laugh if I wore that stuff; they call me Dead End."

Or else she'd come up with, "Kid, it's not right for me. I'd look too Jewish." I'd answer, "Funny, I hadn't noticed," and we'd go into stitches, laughing.

She was forever threatening to give some of her collection away, but she never did. A mink stole, maybe, she'd hand over to a friend, but not her jewels or money. She once lost the lot, however, when a burglar literally unearthed the secret of where she kept her treasures.

In no time at all, the police caught the culprit and brought him around in handcuffs for Fanny's inspection. She was a woman full of admiration for anyone who performed well at what they chose to do, no matter what they chose. She couldn't be angry at being burglarized, because she recognized talent when she saw it, and the man who'd found her jewelry *had* to be talented.

"You're a smart kid," she kept telling the policemen's prisoner. "Geez, how'd you ever figure it? Go on and show me how you did it."

So the luckless burglar went through the whole routine. Fanny had a window box planted with potted flowers outside one of her upstairs windows. That's where she kept her jewels, wrapped in bathroom tissue and hidden in the earth around the pots. When she wanted her ornaments, she simply pushed away the earth and retrieved them. And that's where the greenthumbed crook had found them, in her little garden. We figured he deserved her applause.

Fanny knew both sides of the law. The man she loved, and sang about, was, of course, Nicky Arnstein, the gambler, who had his share of troubles with the police. She told me she loved him mainly because he was always so clean and dapper; she said she especially loved his monogrammed shirts. I saw Nick hanging about in the next room the day Fanny and I wet our handkerchiefs together, but we weren't introduced on that occasion. Too many reporters.

Soon after the two funny girls came to know each other, Fanny somehow received word that the police were looking for Nick, who was suspected of some new misdeed or another. She convinced him that he should present himself at headquarters, rather than have a patrol car come to pick him up.

Fanny drove with him down to the station. They arrived just at the start of an identification parade, when witnesses to another crime were inspecting a line-up to see whether they could spot the criminal. Fanny and Nick found themselves in the room where the parade was in progress. Fanny pulled up a chair, and Nick stood in with the group under inspection. None of the witnesses, of course, chose Nick as the wanted man.

So at the close of the parade, the sergeant in charge said to everyone in general, "Okay, that's it. You can go home now." Which is precisely what Nick and Fanny did.

We are back now, naturally, in the shoot-'em-up days of Prohibition, when Al Capone was King and the Internal Revenuers his nemesis. Jack "Legs" Diamond was almost a folk hero, and J. Edgar Hoover was warming up to gun down Dillinger. According to the strict letter of the law, most of us were criminals who'd go to a place like "Jack and Charlie's," be examined through a slit in the door, then go in and drink all night, if you wanted to.

Fanny was in deeper than that, though. Through Nick she knew half the stars of the *National Police Gazette*, and she reveled in it. I was lunching with her one day at Dinty Moore's on West Forty-sixth Street when a tall young man in a rather prominent pinstripe suit walked over to us.

"Would you like a drink, girls?"

I hastily assembled my "No thank you" look before I got a kick in the shin from Fanny. "Sure," she said. "Pull up a chair."

As he turned away for a moment to bring a chair from another table, Fanny delivered another kick to attract my attention. " 'Legs' Diamond," she whispered.

"Legs? Whose?" I said. I got another kick for that.

I don't think I was allowed to contribute much to the social chatter that began as soon as he'd joined us. Every time I opened my mouth to utter some pleasantry, Fanny kicked me into silence. He struck me as a likable enough fellow. It was a pity that, forty-eight hours later, he was killed in a gang war.

There was another man in Fanny's life whom I have always rated number three in the world's comic sweepstakes, though comedy wasn't his profession. Roger Davis, who still writes to me sometimes from retirement in Los Angeles, was a dancer in one of the *Follies* when we met during a lay-off period. That was in Neuilly, on the outskirts of Paris, where the Dolly Sisters, Rosie and Jennie, had an extraordinary house, decorated in pure Metro-Goldwyn-rococo.

Roger and I, with a lot of other people, were invited there to a party, which was under way when we arrived. Holding forth in the middle of the fantastically furnished room stood Maybelle Webb, a commanding woman, one of the original stage mothers, whose son, Clifton, was making a name for himself on Broadway.

Roger sized up the situation instantly as we walked down the steps into the room. "Folks!" he boomed, and there was sudden silence. "I don't want anybody to touch these things here at all. Leave everything on the set just the way it is. We're going to do the same scene over tomorrow. Oh, and, Maybelle—we won't need you."

I became an instant, fully fledged member of the Roger Davis fan club, of which Fanny, who knew him first, was chief executive officer. A year and more might go by without seeing him, and then he'd pop up again in my path. He came literally dancing down a London street one day beside Noël.

"Hello, hello!" said I.

213

"You'd hardly think you were on a boat at all, would you?" said Roger. "Where's your cabin? What number?"

Fade-out. Years pass. I was gazing into a Fifth Avenue store window when I noticed someone stop behind me. "No, not a cent," said Roger Davis, very loudly. "I'm not going to give you another cent. You've spent everything I've given you, and you ought to be ashamed."

By now, a small crowd of afternoon shoppers was gathering around us. He ignored them and continued his scolding. "What did you do with all that money?" he demanded. "You frittered it away. But no more. Not a cent." Whinnying happily, I had to pull him around the corner.

More years pass. Playing in Chicago, I took a morning stroll along the promenade that runs alongside Lake Michigan not far from the Ambassador East Hotel. On a bench sat Roger, contemplating the wind-whipped waves. He glanced up for a second when I called his name, but instantly returned to studying the water.

"I don't know whether to buy this thing or not," he said.

The fan club was constantly growing. "Hizzoner" Jimmy Walker was a charter member. Roger traveled everywhere with him for a while, even to Rome, where Roger spotted a crowd of tourists of various nationalities as well as many citizens of Rome milling about in the Piazza del Populo. The plot hastily assembled itself in his nimble mind.

He nipped into their hotel, which fronted on the Piazza, though its entrance was just around the corner. Outside Jimmy's bedroom window, there was a balcony, and balconies, for some reason, hold an equal attraction for comedians and dictators. Roger improvised a costume from a bed sheet and towels, and somehow contrived to make a headpiece that looked enough like a biretta.

Out through the french windows he went with measured steps. At the rail, he raised both arms in a gesture unchanged with the centuries and began blessing the crowd below in mock Latin, knowing not a word of the language.

"Horam novarum bicyclorum domani spumani instanta infanta benny bella. *Bagarinaggio!*"

The crowd moved in closer. Heads turned and fingers pointed. Roger gave them a performance to remember. Then with a final "Pax vobiscum," Il Papa Davis retired to the sanctuary of Jimmy's hotel suite with the cheers of the crowd ringing in his ears. Roger once was specially flown to Palm Beach, Florida, and delivered, gaudily wrapped, as a surprise Christmas present for the children of friends. Roger is everyone's Santa, without the bother of all that hair.

One of the soul-destroying burdens of having a reputation for being very funny is that you're constantly expected to live up to it. This expectation, of course, is apt to destroy every bit of humor within you at any given moment. "Here's Bea Lillie, the funniest woman in the world," is an introduction with a 50,000-mile warranty of turning me into a very sour pickle. Roger has just the same response. He's supremely funny only off stage at a time and place of his own choice. How right he is!

Our host at one London party had heard of Roger's reputation and, before he arrived, went sidling around the room, whispering in every guest's ear, "Roger

Davis is coming. He's just about the funniest guy alive. Everybody sit down and listen to him when he gets here."

As soon as Roger walked in, our host called for silence and introduced him to the assembly. "I think we've all heard about you, Rog, and everybody's looking forward to meeting one of the funniest men in the world."

"Yes," said Roger, "I just got in from New York." Picking a comfortable chair, he sat down. That was all he said all evening. To everyone who came up to him, he repeated with an overly polite smile, "Yes, I just got in from New York." And to think there were those who wondered why we loved him and still do!

Now skip to Hollywood. The three of us, Fanny, Roger and I, were sitting in her living room, reading the afternoon newspapers while the radio was playing. Nobody seemed to be paying particular attention to the program, on which Uncle Wiggily or some such treacle-toned character was conducting a children's show. Let's call it "The Itty-Bitty Hour."

In the course of it, Uncle Wiggily had a special offer to make to the itty-bitty audience. "Right here in the studio, boys and girls, I've got a beautiful itty-bitty kitten. He's got beautiful eyes and a beautiful tail and he's black all over. Tell your mummy that you'd like him for your very own, and the very first one of you who calls the Itty-Bitty Hour number can have this lovely itty-bitty pussycat . . ."

Roger, who had been intent on his reading, put down his newspaper, went to the telephone and dialed the I.-B.H. number. In a shrill falsetto, he asked, "Is this the Itty-Bitty Hour where they have an itty-bitty puthy tat?" It was.

"Is it a *dood* little puthy tat?"

Yes. Just right for a good little boy. Are you a good little boy?

"Oh, yeth, very dood. I'd take real dood care of him, I would. Has he got beautiful black ears?"

Yes. He certainly had.

"*Oh,* and has he got lovely big round *eyes?*" squeaked Roger.

Why, yes, of course.

"And a lovely, long black *tail?*" Fanny and I were all ears ourselves by now.

The itty-bitty kitten clearly had just that kind of beautiful tail.

Roger lowered his voice to a baritone boom. "And does he have two big black *balls?*" He hung up and went right back to reading his newspaper, while Fanny and I collapsed.

We thanked the Lord for Roger. He lightened the load a lot, and when it counted. *On* stage, he simply couldn't turn it on, so he didn't try to. If only some others, with not half his talent, would just quit trying to be funny.

I saw a lot of Fanny when I went to Hollywood again, in 1929, to make another stab at the movies, though once again it was a movie that stabbed me. *Are You There?* was described by Fox-Movietone as a "musical farce." Farcical it was. I played Shirley Travis, a lady detective who, in a series of capers, later to be known in televisionland as the "I Love Lucy" style, is transformed into an acrobat, a nurse, a masseuse, an intrepid horsewoman and a big-game hunter. The script, assuming that there was one, called for the last transfiguration to take place at a Scottish castle, into which was imported a complete menagerie. I performed opposite an ostrich, a gorilla and George Grossmith, an idol of the British theatre, appearing as a nobleman called the Duke of St. Pancras.

"G.G.," who owned theatres of his own in London, had been acting for nearly forty years. He wandered around the studios, elevating his celebrated eyebrows in horror, complaining, "My dear fellow, it is not *done*. It just is not *done* like that, I assure you."

The British were rather fashionable with American producers of the day because British voices, with their crisp, clear pronunciation and enunciation, registered well on the crude sound systems of the early "talkies." The first time I heard the lady detective speak, overly amplified through a bawling loudspeaker in a cutting room between takes, I had to wrestle down the impulse to dash for cover.

That was the least of my troubles. Much of the time, I was black and blue. The whimsies of the plot called for jumping into haystacks, dancing wild adagios and slipping into bathtubs. I was battered as an acrobat and bruised as the masseuse.

I tottered to a party that the William K. Howards —he was a big-time producer—were giving in Brentwood. It was a shower given for Bebe Daniels before her marriage to Ben Lyon. Carey Wilson, the screenwriter, was there, carefully explaining the wonderful ways of Hollywood with a girl like me. (I couldn't help thinking, "Here we go again. Better watch him.")

I needn't have worried, though, since his caustic wit demolished the studio: "Fox knows *exactly* how to take advantage of her kind of subtle humor. Somebody says something to her and, being notoriously quick on the comeback, she splashes the somebody with water. And since she's made a name as a mono-logist, they have her do a slapstick adagio." I thanked him very nicely for those few kind words.

To stay with Fanny was usually good for your soul. She could build you up if you needed building up, and knock you down, too, if that's what she thought the prescription called for. Making movies was hard work, lasting sometimes until seven or eight in the evening, then starting in again bright and early *before* dawn the next day. On another occasion, I'd origi-nally intended to stay at the Beverly Hills Hotel, but Fanny wouldn't hear of it.

"I have to get up at six in the morning, with all these things to do," I explained to her. "It won't be any fun for you since I have many social commit-ments. I'll stay at the hotel."

"Ah, the best of legs must part. I've never been so insulted," she replied. "You come and stay with me. I insist."

She had other guests in the house, including Dor-othy Dickson, and space was running short. I slept in the same room with Fanny's daughter, Frances, who is now Mrs. Ray Stark. Besides making the movie, I was also doing a radio broadcast now and again, which did not really sweeten my disposition. After one live broadcast, I arrived home at Fanny's house quite late, weary and a bit dissatisfied with my perfor-mance.

Fanny and the rest of her guests had been listen-ing to the program. I went into the living room with a slightly forced smile, anticipating the customary rather insipid comments of friends, no matter how your performance goes, along the lines of "Darling, you were absolutely *wonderful*."

I wanted to get upstairs and rest, but I knew I had to mix in and chat. That's one of the things I *hate* about being a houseguest, even of dear friends, when I'm working. Give me a *quiet hotel* any time. Also, I never enjoy sharing a room except during wartime or under *field* conditions, if you'll forgive this expression.

When I entered, nobody said a word. Fanny and the others looked up at me, then looked at each other in a deadly silence. Smile fades fast.

I said, "What's the matter?"

"Kid," said Fanny, "you know what you were? Just Lady Peel. You were being Lady Peel on the radio show."

It was really very late, and I was very tired. I drew myself up to the full sixty-three inches and said, "I *am* Lady Peel." Then I ran to the room I shared with Frances, locked myself in and her out, and, since luckily it was a Friday night, refused to emerge for roughly forty-eight hours. I believe they pushed a few crumbs under the door from time to time to keep me from starving.

That radio show, by the way, was a Bing Crosby hour which won the National Broadcasters Award as the year's best musical variety. One never knows, does one?

Whatever they fed me, it *couldn't* have contained garlic. Otherwise, I'd have been happy to shuffle off this mortal coil rather than eat it. I don't just *hate* garlic; I'm totally allergic to it. It makes me deathly ill, the smell, the taste, even the suspicion of it. When I stayed with Fanny, I was haunted by the thought of confronting the evil bulb, because I knew she had a weakness for it. I could always detect *something* at the dinner table, though she strenuously denied its presence. And I began what became a daily exchange.

One evening, doubt became certainty. "Ah, don't pull that, kid, don't pull that," said the hostess. "There's no garlic tonight."

"There *is* garlic here," said I. "I know."

"Geez, you're imagining things."

"There is garlic, and I cannot stay at the table."

"Okay, fine," Fanny said. "Okay, Lady Peel, Lady Peel."

"Oh, God," I said, wrinkling the nose with which God endowed me. "It *is* garlic." Game, set and match.

I suppose I might have known that Fanny, who had a will of iron, would try to prove to herself and to me that a root as beneficial to mankind as garlic could not *possibly* have any adverse effect on anybody. The test she devised came a few days later, when we were nibbling a sort of brunch-early tea, served on trays in the newly decorated living room, which was heavily scented with hyacinths, tuberoses and gardenias.

By now, the entire household was avoiding mention of garlic; in an attempt to ease the situation, it was referred to only as "the big G." On one restless night, I even dreamed about it: there was Fanny, eating breakfast cereal, smacking her lips over every mouthful she took from the bowl which she had just liberally sprinkled with big G, poured from a sugar shaker. Ugh!

Meanwhile, back to reality. While I took in my watercress sandwich with some soup on the side, Fanny was tucking into some delicatessen items and happily chewing on what appeared to be gigantic green olives, served on a separate plate.

"Bea, kid," she said, "try one of these. They're really great."

"What's the big white spot at the end of each of them?"

"Just a stuffed almond. Go ahead. Have one."

One of the few rules I have for living is, *Be pleased with what is intended to please*. What follows illustrates perfectly a basic weakness in this otherwise fantastic motto! I believed that Fanny intended to please, so I trustingly took a prime specimen from her plate and popped it, whole, into my mouth. The odor of flowers must have hidden the smell. My tongue and mouth and throat told me the truth—the olives were stuffed with *garlic*.

Within seconds there came the horrible, inevitable consequence. I couldn't even utter the word to give fair warning. A little of Fanny and a great deal of her beautiful room were decorated with a sample of my own work. That did it. Fanny evermore showed a little respect on the subject of big G and me. I was thereafter known as "The Lotus Flower of the Far East"; famous for my carpet decoration!

Generally, we had a lot in common, especially the subject of our children. Fanny was a good audience for my bulletins about how Little Bobbie was getting along with his lessons or how plans were going for Mother to bring him over to see me again. He was starting to grow up, and grow up the way I'd planned on more or less, which made the working life of the busy Bea worth while.

In keeping with Peel tradition, he'd been entered for Harrow, the school his father and grandfathers had attended. Now he was writing me letters like this:

Dearest Mother,

It will soon be the holidays now, but no *you*. Do you think you could possibly tell the housemaster to give me some money for my holidays? Say about £5 a week for films and shows and entertainment for my friends. I know I am asking rather a big thing of you, but you have never disappointed me yet, so please try and do this for me. I am having great reports from various masters, and I am getting along great. Well, my dearest, I am longing to see you again. All my love from your loving son, Robert.

During the busy, busy years, I fitted in cabaret, too. In the 1937-38 season I appeared in the brand-new Rainbow Room high up on top of New York's Rockefeller Center, "doubling" after my regular performances in *The Show Is On* at the Winter Garden Theatre. One night, up came a friendly gentleman who had heard about Little Bobbie's educational program, though our friend's knowledge of England may have been a bit limited on other subjects.

"You couldn't send him to a finer place," he assured me. "I've always held that Harrods is the best school in your country for a growing boy."

Somewhere along the line, I was asked by a Chicago newspaper to contribute a thought or two, if I could spare them, to a series of interviews, which called for comment on a statement made on his eighty-second birthday by Thomas Edison. "Happiness," he declared, "is a myth. There is no happy man."

Who would want to go that far? Certainly not Julius Rosenwald, the millionaire philanthropist, who led off our responses by saying flatly, "I am the happiest man in the world. I have more enjoyment and fun out of life than anyone I know."

My own reflections were a trifle more complicated. This is how they came out in the newspaper: "I think most people are happy in normal satisfactions. Happiness for the average person may be said to flow largely from common sense—adapting oneself to circumstances—*and* a sense of humor."

Who was the happiest person I knew? "My son, Bobbie, because he is a boy."

Big Bobby's searches for happiness had taken a new turn. *Now* he was the leader of a seven-piece orchestra, the Staffordshire Miners and Unemployed Workers' Jazz Band: piano, violin, saxophone, trumpet, sousaphone, banjo and drums. My husband handled the singing, and received some very good notices for his handling of "Sonny Boy." Gertie, Jack Buchanan and I had appeared with the group once or twice, when possible, to help with the publicity, and they made some professional appearances, raising money for the unemployed, of whom there were many in Staffordshire.

Drayton Manor did not exist any more either as a home or even as a monument to "Parsley" Peel's wit or wealth. Because of unpayable mortgages entered into by my father-in-law, the mansion in which Queen Victoria had once slept was dismantled for its bricks and mortar. What had once been the deer park was converted by Bobby into a playground primarily for the people of Tamworth and the community around there, including working folk from Birmingham.

The distance between Beverly Hills and Tamworth is, I suppose, six thousand miles, as the crow flies, though I never saw a single crow trying to make it. That is literally a great many miles, and emotionally a great many more if you start thinking about them. I'd begin to write a letter, then consider how long it would take to arrive. So I'd give up the attempt; a good part of what I wanted to say might be out of date by the time it was delivered; no jets, remember, just trains and ships!

I'd pick up the telephone, certain that I shouldn't be able to hear a word, because I never can. But when I stay up late, I'm overcome by the telephone craze. Then the bills would come in and—zap! I've contributed a few thousand "hellos" at a dollar or so a word to the transatlantic traffic in my time, mostly in the small hours of the morning because of differences in time zones.

The only *real* way to keep in touch was to bring Little Bobbie over to visit whenever I could, in Mother's company. He grew to be such a familiar sight in Hollywood that MGM wanted him to play young David Copperfield when they turned the Dickens novel into a movie. But his mother said No, and a lad named Freddie Bartholomew got off to a flying start in his acting career.

Muriel and her new husband came over. We put on a party for them at Leo Carrillo's ranch in Santa Monica Canyon, where Bobbie spent a slightly bored afternoon skipping stones across the water of Leo's lake, and Mother starred in a duet with "Fatty" Arbuckle. Arthur Weigall had his own audience for his account of the opening of Tutankhaman's tomb.

"We found a mysterious vase of oil," he said, "which we imagined must play a part in the embalming ceremonies. Finally, when we had it analyzed, it turned out to be common castor oil, probably put there in case of royal indigestion in the other world."

During these years between engagements in the United States, I'd sail to England, to see as much of Little Bobbie as I could. Occasionally, we'd get the lines crossed, or maybe Mumsie misunderstood all my telephoned "hellos," and I'd turn up in London to find she'd taken him to Montreux, Switzerland, where he was now enrolled in a well-known private school for assorted reluctant students; princes, princelings and what-have-yez. I remember one wild ride when Bobbie drove me from Montreux to Cannes in his small two-seater sports car. He was determined to break his previous time record for the journey. I gamely endured rally speeds and conditions throughout the mountainous route in order to assure him success. Arriving numb and a bit lightheaded at Cannes, I remember only congratulating him on his driving ability, fluency in French and bloody great luck. On other occasions, we'd compromise and arrange to assemble on the Riviera, which he enjoyed, though it struck me as an exotic road to rapid boredom, except for the joy of being with him.

Deauville was the hub of that strange little universe, with its enormous cream-colored casino haunted by the likes of the Aga Khan, Lord Derby, the two Dolly Sisters, Harry Pilcer and the Syndicate led by a weary, coffee-tinted Greek named Nicolas Zographos. There it was that I backed accidentally into gambling and won a nice little pile without even trying.

Alec Woollcott was with me as we stood watching other people lose their money at baccarat. I was suddenly taken with an attack of hiccups, which the croupier interpreted as an indication that I was betting. Every *hic*, half-lost in the general din, sounded to him like *banco*, and I couldn't stop the *hics* to explain. After he pushed 100,000 francs at me, I reflected that I shouldn't confuse him by returning it. As Alec said later, quoting Robert E. Sherwood, "None but the brave *chemin de fer*."

Along the coast lay the new and exceedingly *chic* little places, like Juan-les-Pins, Eden Roc and Cap d'Antibes, which Bobbie much preferred, and so did I. You could find Noël there usually, Somerset Maugham and Michael Arlen, who tried to make amends for Hollywood's use of the Lillie talents by writing a movie short for me entitled *Why Light Women Float Best*. Unhappily, it never left the quayside.

Elsa Maxwell, whom I regarded as thirty-nine of my most intimate friends, was often in sight, up to her habitual larks as a professional hostess. Bernard Shaw showed up one year in white beard and pink sunburn, but I didn't know at the time what troubles *he* was going to bring to my young life. I remember my "relative" breast-stroking through the water in high old style, wearing a floppy straw hat that made him look like some variety of pale water bug with a white tail. We made a cute pair, *not kid I you.*

It was a relief to be away from movie-making, which just didn't bring out the best in me. Endless retakes weren't for me. I needed an audience to coax into its first laugh. Once I had that, I could build it into further laughter, and the louder it grew, the more blithely I could improvise the next bit of comedy. No laughter, no wind in sails and therefore much harder to find my way to a satisfying result. The inspiration of live-audience reactions stimulates my creative juices and establishes a subconscious bond between us.

Actually, a kind of osmosis takes place between me and my audience. It stores up somewhere—in my subconscious—and later pops out as inspiration. Whee!

In the theatre, I've found that, in general, reaction and laughter come easier at an evening performance, when the audience is more inclined to forget its troubles. Matinee customers must enter the theatre in a more matter-of-fact frame of mind, hanging on tightly before they let themselves go. Making movies was like playing to people when they've just climbed out of bed, without having enjoyed so much as a cup of coffee—which is pretty much what happened, in fact.

Hollywood meant lawyers, not laughter, to me. I ran into my second legal bout when I sued Warner Brothers. They had signed me for what turned out to be a boring pastiche called *The Show of Shows*, shot in primeval Technicolor, which in those early days came out in brick-red and slimy green. This was one of the very earliest uses of color on what had been the "silver screen." The stars ranged from H. B. Warner, who had played Christ, to Rin-Tin-Tin, who usually played Rin-Tin-Tin. The sets consisted of endless stairways of imitation marble, peopled with zillions of chorus girls.

The star of stars in *The Show of Shows* was John Barrymore, who stalked off with most of the honors wearing black armor and a make-up like Dr. Jekyll's alter ego, reciting the soliloquy from *Henry VI* ("I'll make my heaven to dream upon the crown"). I was booked to do a comedy sketch with Louise Fazenda. The more perceptive critics noticed that she somehow managed to thrust me into the background. As one of them wrote, "You are presented with the amazing spectacle of Louise Fazenda trying to do a Lillie of her own." Maybe it was true that she *was* under long-term contract to the Warners, which would explain the curious editing of the movie.

Subsequently, when the studio *extracte*d that scene to be shown as a separate two-reeler, I felt that it had gone far too far. The Irish dander of the Lillies was roused. My lawyers filed suit against Warner Brothers Pictures, the Vitaphone Corporation and Darryl F.

Zanuck, too, "for presenting our client to the world as a cheap and inconsequential performer." Hear! Hear!

For reasons we hold to be self-evident, I chose playing in vaudeville any day, week or year to working in Hollywood. During the next couple of seasons, I criss-crossed North America, topping bills made up of acts like Marc Nathal ("The Man Monkey"), Buster Shaver and his Tiny Town Revue, the Three Midnite Steppers, wire walkers and clowns. New York's Palace Theatre was second home; I was there the day a brilliant young man with a mouthful of teeth made his Broadway debut as master of ceremonies on my bill, and I *do* mean Milton Berle. He was a bit cheeky at first, but he quickly got the word, and we've been pals since then.

He and I fall about with laughter now, but at the time I was just a bit ruthless. When he breezily asked, "Miss Lillie, is it true you are really Lady Peel?" "You're God-damned right," I said. The audience loved it. I should have left this line in every performance but I was still too touchy about allowing "every *other* inch" on stage.

I was making so much money in vaudeville that it terrified me. When I first appeared at the Palace, I was booked to appear for two weeks. Toward the end of the second week, Edward Darling, the manager, came unheralded into my dressing room. That annoyed me for two reasons. For one thing, the room was so small you couldn't swing a mouse in it. And for another, I was in my customary state of nerves before going out onto the stage; I've always made a point of never seeing *anyone* just before a performance; short of matters of life and death.

Up to that moment, my plans were clear, in the back of my head. I was earning a fantastic $6500 a week. I'd received wonderful press notices. And I thought, "I'm not going to kill that kind of reception. I'll go while the welcome's still hot."

"I'd like you to stay on for another week," said Edward Darling.

"I can't do it. I've got to go back to England."

"Well, let's change the terms. I'll give you $10,000 a week."

That scared the pants off me. For two shows a day, $10,000? I glared into the mirror, fixing my face for the performance. He was making me more nervous by the minute.

"No, no, *no*," I declared. "I've too many things to do in England. Can't do it. It's impossible."

"Tell you what," said the manager. "I think I'll be able to get you $15,000."

Imagine, $15,000! "Get out of this room," I yelled, scared stiff. "I'm trying to dress and everything, and I can hardly put my make-up on. Don't you keep worrying me."

"Now be reasonable—"

I was really terrified now. "Get out! Get out! How can I do my work while you're here talking to me? You leave this room at once, do you hear?" To speed him on his way, I threw a shoe at him.

And that is why, dear listener, Auntie Bea never earned $15,000 a week playing the Palace. . . .

CHAPTER ELEVEN

LIFE STYLE OF A QUEEN BEA

Travel is one of the handful of subjects in which I lay claim to a modest *expertise,* as the result of a life spent journeying hither, thither and dither over a fair-sized portion of this planet. Travel, they say, broadens the mind but in my experience it is the other end of the anatomy that feels the effect, when all one has is a seat in a jet, with an occasional skip to the loo.

In my case, getting about has sometimes presented additional difficulties. I combine a certain restlessness with an uncertain sense of direction. Friends have known me, when visiting their houses, to head for the bathroom and arrive in the kitchen as sober as a woman magistrate. The kitchen is where I invariably end up, too, when I'm leaving any unfamiliar restaurant, looking for the way out.

I also tend to become stuck in places. I'll go to London, meaning to stay one week but linger on for six. I once went to take an overnight look at Las Vegas and spent more than a month there, acquiring a new station wagon in the process. Invited to Los Angeles

231

to do a television show with Dinah Shore, I was gone for three months before I came home again. Not too long ago I flew to Hawaii for a week and remained for two months. Why not? If the place suits, bear it!

Even without the Palace Theatre's $15,000 a week, the jam was spread thicker in America. Since the overheads of keeping the family in groceries on both sides of the Atlantic were going up all the time, it probably made sense to find a little *pied-à-terre* and set up housekeeping again in New York, halfway between London and Hollywood, the two other places where I was likely to be working.

After my initial shock, New York appealed to me. This was the city where anything could happen and, as often as not, did. One stage-door admirer tipped his hat and wondered if I'd mind autographing his wooden leg. Why not? It was off, signed and back in place in a flash.

New York was a place where, one winter's day, a sweet-looking old lady on a streetcar nagged me so hard about being out without my galoshes that, for the sake of peace and quiet, I had to get off and trudge for blocks in the snow.

Maybe the city lacked a little of Chicago's gaudy color—a man *there* once dashed out of a barbershop with his throat cut and turned back to apologize for bumping into me. But New York had a host of friends, Sixth Avenue shooting galleries, Dinty Moore's for delicious corned beef and cabbage, and Sardi's, which made its debut on West Forty-fourth Street just after I'd made mine on West Forty-second Street.

It was time to go house-hunting. The mood came over me when I returned from London and another show for Uncle André, the first for five years. He had come over to New York to see me, still smoking fancy cigars and eating too much, and we sailed for Southampton together in the *Homeric*. He'd given up the struggle to find oddly original titles. *Charlot's Masquerade* was what he called his new revue, due to open the brand-new theatre, the Cambridge, that Bertie Meyer had built in the Seven Dials, a raffish corner of London where the daytime streets were filled with Cockney costermongers.

The book was written by Ronald Jeans, but I had a few Lillie Touches to contribute—an Irish jig performed in a pair of five-year-old wedgies I'd bought in the United States when I fancied I had a weak ankle; a clog dance in galoshes; and a sketch about Hollywood that expressed some of my feelings about that earthly paradise.

In the sketch's opening half, we displayed Hollywood as people in those days pictured it, a den of drink, dope and dissipation. Curtain. "Now we will show you Hollywood as it really is," said I, and when the curtain rose again we did the whole sketch exactly as before, line for line, gesture for gesture.

My first glimpse of the plushy little theatre, with posh, soft lighting behind every seat for reading programs by, made me suspect that audiences would either doze off in such comfort as theatregoers scarcely enountered or else spend so much time switching their cute little lights on and off that they'd miss what we were doing on the stage. I also had a secret notion that, after all my years of absence, the patrons would be sitting there with looks of "So this is the girl who's made so much money" on their faces.

Were such misgivings justified? Well, I'd say that a roundup of the reviews the next morning would have shown that 100 per cent of the critics admired the theatre, while three-quarters of them rated Charlot's entertainment like the curate's egg in an old *Punch* cartoon—"good in parts." To a man, they had nice things to say about the principal herself, and some more nice things for Flo Desmond, formerly of *This Year of Grace*, who gave a startling impersonation of Tallulah Bankhead. Unfortunately, Tallulah in person arrived too late to see it on opening night, though she eventually caught up with it.

That most charming gentleman, Bertie Meyer, when audiences grew a little thin, had one or two ideas for stirring up the customers. At a party given by Gordon Selfridge, the American-born tycoon, who was forever playing host on the upper floors of his Oxford Street department store, Bertie had been introduced to "Aussie," a boxing kangaroo. Pursuing him to Glasgow, Mr. Meyer booked him as an extra added attraction for *Charlot's Masquerade*. Get *that!*

As for myself, I was urged to reintroduce one song from the repertoire to the show every week, starting with "Michigan." I was already a woman with a past. Then it was all ashore that's going ashore, and I was over the bounding main again to keep some appointments in New York, notably with real-estate agents.

I'd stayed in London in Ivor Novello's flat, relishing its views of church spires and rooftops and those same red buses chugging along between Fleet Street and the Strand. This was a kind of trade; Ivor would stay in my place the next time he came to New York, assuming I could find one.

He had a landscape of rooftops; the one I found looked out on the East River from the windows of the apartment Helen Hayes steered me into. She and her husband, Charles MacArthur, were among the first tenants of the brand-new building on lower East End Avenue, and I was among the second. Runners-up included Gladys Swarthout and Rudy Vallee. There were tugboats and barges to watch on the river and pigeons cooing on the window sills or once in a while taking a turn round the ceiling. (Any messages?)

Aside from the fact that I took to sleeping with cotton in my ears to deaden the din of waterfront living, I liked my new home. I must have done; I'm still a tenant.

Moving in marked some kind of a turning point, maybe. I had become what may be described as a bachelor lady, with a long-distance son to care for. For a while now, rumor had been in hot pursuit, centering on the leading question, "Is everything all right at home?" or "Whatever became of *him?*" or something along those lines.

One intrepid interviewer in Hollywood went so far as to ask whether Big Bobby and I were separated "by something more substantially impassable than the Atlantic." How utterly quaint, I thought.

In that era, I enjoyed the support of a secretary-dresser-companion-chatelaine-and-scrapbookkeeper in the stern but kindly person of Sadie Walsh, known as "Walshie" and, alas, just, no longer with us. I let her handle that interviewer's thrust.

"Getting a divorce in London," she said obliquely, "is comparable to signing your own death warrant. And we did so enjoy the interview . . ." In all too little time, the question lost its relevance, as you will soon learn.

Everyone rallied round to make the East End apartment a happy home. Harold Ross sent books by the dozen as a housewarming gift, after insisting I install bookshelves along one whole wall of the living room. The MacArthurs, who lived on the same floor as I, supplied laughter. They were great friends of Alec

Woollcott; Charles, in fact, once shared the ownership of a car with him. Get them!

Alec lived downstream a piece from us, in a cooperative apartment at 450 East Fifty-second Street, which Dorothy Parker christened "Wit's End." He also rented a villa with built-in butler at Antibes, and the same flood of people poured into both establishments: Noël, the MacArthurs, Gertie, Harpo Marx, Elsa Maxwell, Marc Connelly, Lady Mendl, the knights and attendant ladies of the now dismantled Round Table, and—on the Riviera—Bernard Shaw (that man *again*).

To Alec, I was "Toronto's nightingale" or "The Canadian catastrophe." There were parties where the nightingale joined Gertie and Noël and anybody else in town in singing until the larks got up to take over from there.

As a neighbor, Charley MacArthur had some of the marks of an amiable madman, remorselessly given to playing practical jokes on Helen, who bore them with the patience of a saint. He once strewed their apartment with crumbled female lingerie for her to find when she returned from a tour. He'd take me down to the studio sometimes when she was on the radio. We'd sneak into the audience and make faces at her, praying that she'd look up and miss a cue. But little Helen, calm and resolute, never did. She was a hard nut to crack.

Helen considered radio to be "the nuttiest business I ever encountered" without any help from us. When my turn came to go on the air for a year or two, I thought she'd expressed herself mildly, to say the least.

From their windows and from mine, we could see Welfare Island, to be reached by a little ferry crossing the East River. So one gorgeous sunny day, the three of us decided to make the trip and explore. Mingling with the crowd, we boarded the boat at the Seventy-eighth Street pier without any fuss and landed with no trouble. After an hour, or so, touring the island, enjoying fresh air and ice cream, we joined the line of visitors, waiting to be ferried back to Manhattan.

"Passes, please. Where's your pass?" said the uniformed guard when I reached the head of the line.

"I haven't got one," I reported.

"You couldn't be on the island without a pass."

"Well, I *am*, and I haven't got a pass."

"Next, please." He beckoned me away.

Charley was next. He went through the same dialogue with the iron-faced attendant. "But I *am* here, without any pass—" Charley had to step aside.

Helen's turn. There was a gleam of determination in her gray eyes. "I have no pass, but I should like to board this boat." Good old Helen, I thought. We'll get aboard with *her*.

"You can't get on Welfare Island without a pass. Therefore, you can't get off Welfare Island without a pass. Next, please."

When we tried for another hearing of our case, all we got was, "You'll have to stand at the end of the line." Slowly, slowly we worked our way up for yet another confrontation.

"Now, look here," said Lady Peel. "I am Beatrice Lillie, this is Helen Hayes and that's Charles MacArthur. Seriously, we'd like to get off this island."

The guard was now bored with us. "So would a lot of other people."

I recited the whole speech again. "I *am* Beatrice Lillie, this is—"

"Look," said the guard. "We've got three Bea Lillies, four Helen Hayes and a couple what's-his-names here right now, locked up inside. Now go away and don't bother me or you'll join them."

As dusk was falling, we asked to see the resident medical officer. That was grudgingly allowed. At my request, he telephoned my own doctor, Mortimer Rodgers, brother of composer Richard. Morty had a word or two with me, then spoke with the island's sawbones, telling him I was me. No dice. Morty had to come over in person to identify me—*and* be sure that he carried his own means of identification.

And so, as the sun sank over the Jersey Meadows, we finally bade *aloha* to Welfare Island, swearing that never again would we return.

Apart from all this, I hadn't really been feeling in tiptop form for a while, though I couldn't figure out why. I put it down to indigestion at first and went on rehearsing for a show I'd signed to do. Then I was afraid it might be appendicitis, but I pressed on through the week until Sunday came. Late that night, Morty Rodgers made the decision and I was carted into Lenox Hill Hospital. Appendicitis would have been preferable. I really wasn't very well at all after the operation. Blood was called for. Wow!

Charley and a long list of friends volunteered. I thanked them very kindly but thought it best to decline. "I might be handicapped for the rest of my life," I told them, "if I went around with my veins full of dry martinis."

When I emerged from the ether, I was told it had been fairly serious gynecological knife-and-fork work; but *not* the works, girls! Thank heaven, I was soon on the mend and enjoying the first long rest in years.

We must pause here for a moment or two to consider a producer named Earl Carroll, who to be candid was to Charlot and Cochran what salami is to *châteaubriand*. Where Cockie and Uncle André offered their audiences wit and style, Mr. Carroll in his *Vanities* relied on busty blondes and towering redheads. I had met him in Pittsburgh, during the tour of *She's My Baby*.

He was trying then to sign contracts for a new revue which would star Al Jolson, W. C. Fields, the Metropolitan tenor Richard Crooks and, for some reason best known to the producer, Jack Dempsey. Oh, and me. A something-for-everyone type offering.

After the performance, Earl Carroll and I adjourned to the hotel apartment of Clifton Webb, bearing bacon, eggs and spinach, the ingredients for a midnight omelet which Clifton was to cook. Unknown to Clifton or me, Mr. Carroll's sense of humor had prompted him to place a telephone call to Luke Barnett, a resident of Pittsburgh, described later by the producer in a memoir as "the international practical joker who occupies a unique niche as the highest-priced fun maker of his kind in the world."

Clifton was ready to crack the eggs into a skillet when it was announced on the house telephone that a "Dr. Caroki of Actors' Equity" was in the lobby, demanding to see Miss Lillie on a matter of immediate concern.

Once in the room, "Dr. Caroki" informed me in a heavy-weight accent that Equity had authorized my immediate deportation from the United States as an alien actress because so many American performers were unemployed. An officer of the Immigration and Naturalization Service, said our visitor, was waiting downstairs to carry out the deportation order.

I accepted what was said. "Isn't there some way to

work this thing out?" I asked. "Won't you sit down so that we can discuss—"

"No," bellowed the intruder. "I have my dear wife waiting for me at home, and anyway I refuse to associate with chorus girls."

I could feel my *hauteur* rising, but I doubted if *that* would do much good. "Dr. Caroki" went to the door and let in another member of the plot, who flashed a badge to identify himself as the immigration official. He immediately made himself so objectionable that I felt obliged to tell him that as soon as I got back to New York, I should report him to the U. S. Department of Justice, which conducts immigration affairs.

Then the whole scene exploded. "Dr. Caroki" dressed down his colleague for discourtesy. Their argument turned into a fight, and the "doctor" floored the other. Earl Carroll rushed our first visitor into another room—to hide their laughter—and I went to render first aid to the second caller, sponging his forehead and taking back my promise to report him.

Thus Earl Carroll found me when he returned to the room to introduce the "doctor" as Luke Barnett, "the highest-priced fun maker of his kind in the world," and the other man as another Barnett, his brother. Without noticeable delay, I was then asked if I wouldn't like to sign a contract to appear in the show he was dreaming up.

"I'm afraid I couldn't," I answered. "Suppose you had Luke Barnett sign it for you. I shouldn't know then if it was supposed to be a joke or not, would I?"

But Earl Carroll wasn't to be rebuffed so easily. Time passes. While I was in the hospital, recuperating, the star of his current *Vanities* production, Dorothy Knapp, announced that she intended to give it all up and enter a convent. Mr. Carroll announced that he was coming to Lenox Hill Hospital to tempt me into replacing her. A writer for *The New Yorker,* Henry F. Pringle, has related what happened next:

"With the assistance of the nurse and hurried calls upon a costumer, Beatrice prepared for the producer's visit. When he came in, on tiptoe as befitted a sick chamber, he saw the figure of a nun prone on the bed, her hands folded decorously on her breast. It does not *sound* very funny, but it was. Carroll was definitely annoyed. He had planned a stunt of his own to entertain the patient and had brought elaborate properties with him. Two weeks later no one could remember it. They were attempting to describe a Bea Lillie quirk of the eyebrows underneath a nun's headdress."*

I certainly couldn't remember what those "elaborate properties" were that he brought with him. Possibly the brothers Barnett, in aspic?

If, as Ed Wynn used to say, a comic doesn't attain full growth until the age of forty, I still had a little time left, but the days grow short when you reach September. It was a case of out with the stitches, on with the motley. I galloped into rehearsals for *The Third Little Show,* for which S. J. Perelman, Marc Connelly and half a dozen others wrote sketches, though Noël turned up trumps with something written for me, having to do with the noontime habits of deranged canines and the English. With solar topee, tropical whites and rickshaw, please, a soupçon:

In the Philippines there are lovely screens
To protect you from the glare.

* Reprinted by permission of *The New Yorker.*

In the Malay States there are hats like plates,
Which the Britishers won't wear.
At twelve noon the natives swoon
And no further work is done.
But mad dogs and Englishmen
Go out in the midday sun. . . . *

With a shawl over my head, I also did my Ruth Draper sketch, "A Railway Station on the Western Plains," which Marc had written: "In this little sketch, ladies and gentlemen, I want you to imagine *far* too much—"

The Music Box Theatre packed 'em in again, even when they had to pay $5.50 for a seat in the orchestra, which was a great deal of money in the depths of the Depression *and* at the height of a sizzling New York summer, when air conditioning hadn't yet been invented. Those were the days when a hostess had to be careful to keep any Wall Street guests as far away from the windows as possible if she lived above the fourth floor.

Eventually, in best theatrical tradition, we toured with the show, and since all tours had to go to Chicago, I continued my nodding acquaintance with another aspect of those distant days by nodding at Mr. Alphonse Capone as he sprawled in his chair in a courtroom there, nabbed at last for defrauding the Internal Revenue Service, which considered that thirty-two years in the cooler would be a fair price for him to pay as restitution. He snubbed me, of course.

I'd gone to the courthouse on an idle afternoon with Robert McGonigle, a writer friend and adviser

---

* "Mad Dogs and Englishmen" (Coward) Copyright © 1931 by Harms, Inc. Copyright Renewed. Used by permission of Warner Bros. Music. All Rights Reserved.

at the time, who many years later sensibly retreated to a Trappist monastery. The "world's worst criminal," as witnesses had called Alphonse, didn't much care for the looks of either one of us.

"Who's the guy with her?" he asked in a stage whisper that could have been heard in Winnipeg. It should be hastily explained that Robert, known fondly as "Doc," is a Harvard man, a rugged type, a talented playwright, an intellectual.

"Hell," grunted the beer baron. "I thought he was a bootlegger."

He swiveled around in his chair and threw me a wink of such dimensions it was like lowering a shade in a Gimbels store window. What to do but wink right back? When the court adjourned that afternoon, one reporter brought me a sketch of yours truly and not a bad likeness at that. The artist? Alphonse himself.

Mr. George Bernard Shaw and I did *not* wink at each other on the one occasion I saw him close up, on dry land. He was sunbathing on the Riviera, and both his eyes remained closed. I hadn't the heart to disturb him. But he later caused me many a sleepless night, wrestling to remember his lines with a memory that sometimes has resisted recording *every* jot and tittle of a line or lyric.

The Theatre Guild, no less, was smitten with the idea that I could and should play Sweetie the Nurse in *Too True to be Good*, thereby making my debut in which might be called the *field of drama*. I was to take myself seriously and be all dressed up like the grown folks of the legitimate theaytah, but according to one commentator, "No one would have been in the least surprised to have heard that Jimmy Durante and

Harpo Marx had also been added to the cast of characters."

Venturing on ice as thin as a tax collector's smile, I felt that this work of the Irish master was more of a discussion than a play, covering his opinions on vegetables, war, inoculation and the British Army. As Brooks Atkinson said, "It sounds like the conversation of an elderly gentleman feeling comfortable on the veranda after a carnivorous dinner."

Rehearsals began soon after the *Third Little Show* post-Broadway tour came to a rather abrupt end in Philadelphia after ten weeks on the road. Continuing to cherish the belief that the devil finds work for idle hands, I was simultaneously doing two shows a day at the good old Palace, two cabaret shows a night at the Sutton Club and spending any spare moment available learning my lines for the Shaw play.

The timetable made interesting reading whenever I had a moment to set down. Rehearsals ran from ten in the morning until two in the afternoon. Half an hour later, I had to be in my Palace dressing room. At five o'clock, I left the Palace, with a whole thirty minutes for dining before rehearsals resumed. At eight I had to be back at the Palace, and at eleven-thirty I started my first performance of the night in cabaret. It was nothing, really.

Learning lines was only part of the problem. I hadn't the faintest notion what they meant. In this I was not alone; the rest of the illustrious cast seemed just as much in the dark. I was afraid that I'd end up vaguely like Sarah Bernhardt, who by Alec's account, played Ophelia for one hundred performances, never knowing how *Hamlet* came out.

I kept the script under my pillow for four weeks, lugging it out when I flopped into bed after the Sutton Club had closed for the night, or shall we say for the morning? I'd study a few pages, then turn out the light to recite the speeches to myself in the dark. Useless. I frantically took up a memory course known as Pelmanism, whose secret is supposedly to concentrate on key words. That only made things worse— now I found I couldn't remember the key words, much less the lines, save only one or two, such as: Sergeant: I'm in a mess. Nurse: Of course; you're in the sergeant's mess. (*House in uproar; police called.*) The method which finally proved successful, and has been used often since with dialogue, is to work out every one of my lines in longhand. I covered (and still do) miles of odd bits of scrap paper, shirt cardboards, old love notes, bills and hundreds of unanswered gilt-edged invitation cards.

When interviewers asked what was the point of the play, I could only refer them to Mr. Shaw. I assumed he might know. When they speculated that he had written the part for me, I answered, "God knows. I hope not." I was always hoping that Noël, who was in New York at the time, would do something in the writing line on my behalf, but he didn't, drat him.

The longest conversation I'd had with G.B.S. had consisted of his telling me about a movie short in which he'd just starred, and he rated himself terrific in it. I told him about *my* movie, *Why Light Women Float Best,* which I thought was just swell. Our meeting didn't exactly amount to a dramatic encounter on the Field of the Cloth of Gold.

Thank the Lord that Marc Connelly was lurking in the wings, providing a little comic relief to preserve my sanity. I felt that I could make a modicum of sense of the last act, when I had the chance to sit down in comfort and deliver my lines. Being able to settle into a chair on stage and continue to keep an audience laughing has always struck me as something to look forward to in paradise.

"You do the best lounging act of the season," Marc assured me. "You're even better than Alec Woollcott in *Brief Moment*." This was the Sam Behrman play which Alec, who insisted on being billed merely as "A Gentleman of Quality," stole for 129 New York performances. He spent every moment on stage sprawling on a sofa, "proud of his tonnage," as Percy Hammond wrote.

We tried out *Too True to be Good* in Boston, opening there on a rare occasion February 29. Marc Connelly pursued his policy of bringing cheer into our confused lives by telephoning every night after the show and keeping me awake until dawn broke over the Public Gardens. (Or is it *Pubic* Gardens? Never was much on foliage.)

At last, I discovered a way to break Marc of the habit. An hour or so after he'd hung up, I'd call him back to ruin *his* sleep.

We all needed his words of good cheer, however. Boston audiences didn't appear to be making too much of Mr. Shaw's dissertations on Holy Writ, the sex urge and the League of Nations. What to do?

As I've said the play, as a production of the Theatre Guild, was destined to open in New York at the Guild Theatre. I was certain that Theresa Helburn and her colleagues in council assembled had experienced some heart searching, and maybe some heartburn, before they decided to engage a comedienne to appear in a work by the venerable gentleman who was regarded by many a Guild subscriber as a seer and prophet.

Our director, Leslie Banks, was a veteran actor who

had played almost everything from *Major Barbara* to *Peter Pan,* and he wasn't in a mood to be trifled with, not that anyone wanted to trifle him. Perhaps we were all taking the play too seriously. I knew that I was. The process of being Guilded was making me a decidedly twitchy Lillie.

So a series of diplomatic cablegrams went ticking across the Atlantic. Would Mr. Shaw agree to change a line or two for better effect, "Go to sleep," for instance, being replaced by "Go to hell!" Could certain horseplay as specified be introduced to hide the infirmities of the script? No, we didn't actually *say* that about his play, but that's what we had in mind. Let's face it—*TTBG* just wasn't the best thing Cousin George had ever written.

We all buckled to: Hugh Sinclair, who played The Burglar; Claude Rains, who was The Elder; Leo G. Carroll, who appeared as Private Meek; Ernest Cossart, in the role of Colonel Tallboys; and yours sincerely as a *Nervous Wreck.*

Marc continued to play Little Mary Sunshine when we moved into New York. To my understudy, Ethel Borden, he addressed an opening night telegram: YOU WERE MAGNIFICENT. She hadn't had the chance to appear at *any* performance.

When I made my first entrance as The Nurse, the audience began to giggle. I swear on a stack of pancakes that I did nothing to encourage them. The scene is a sickroom, where The Patient, played by Hope Williams, soon launches some snide remarks at The Nurse. In a matter of minutes, Hope and I were rolling around on the floor, skirts up and legs in the air, slugging each other.

"All the first-nighters roared at it," wrote one reporter, "with the exception of Mr. Noël Coward, who seemed to be regarding it as a theft from his *Private Lives.*"

Then when I threw in my new line, "Go to hell!" the patrons' joy was complete. (Remember, please, that *hell* was a bit of a shocker in the *American theatre* as recently as the thirsty thirties.)

Noël was waiting backstage after the final curtain. "Beattie, dear, how are you?" he said. "Where have you been all this time? I haven't seen you for *ages.*"

The critics were generous, as usual. The *Herald Tribune* went so far as to say, "The Guild subscribers and the Shavians speak of it with proper respect, but unregenerate outsiders called it Beatrice Lillie's show." So far as I was concerned, the Shavians could have had it.

Drama wasn't for me, not as written in this piece by G.B.S. I felt restricted by his lines, and I missed the chance to ad-lib fresh bits of business. The strain was killing, but I suffered nobly through the engagement. What I wanted next was a good revue. Unless, of course, Noël would write a play for me.

"I'd rather have a part in a show by him than anything else in the world," I told Lucius Beebe at the time. "I'd accept it without reading a line of the script." Noël didn't get the message until years later, but I did find a pretty good revue—at least, *I* thought so—in something called *Walk a Little Faster*. I wasn't sure that the title applied to me, when I was already running so hard my friends used to wonder whether I had ambitions for the Kentucky Derby. Work, I found, kept one's mind off other subjects, until the taxman took his bite.

The nicest thing to be said about *Walk a Little Faster* is that it provided the opportunity to appear with one of my idols, Bobby Clark, with his painted-on spectacles, and his partner, Paul McCullough, so why don't we leave it at that?

After 119 performances, it was time to pack again and listen for those steamboat whistles calling. I felt as if I hadn't seen my son since the close of the Stone Age. There were some other chores, to attend to at the other end of my commuting run. It turned out that there were many more than could be counted on. Two seasons went by before Broadway and I exchanged regards again. And in the long interval, oh, so much happened that neither one of us was ever the same.

I think this was one of the voyages when Sam Walsh, my accompanist sailed with me. This was gentle, bald-headed Sam, who'd been part of Ethel Barrymore's plot to add "There Are Fairies at the Bottom of Our Garden" to the repertoire. I've lost track of how many crossings we made together, but they lasted almost until the outbreak of the Second World War.

In the early days of the London blackout, Sam—no relation to Sadie, my secretary-dresser-scrapbookkeeper—was strolling around Piccadilly, quite well-known in his way. The Wolfenden Act hadn't been thought of, and the ladies of the evening were plying their trade. One of them called after Sam, flicking the beam of her torch on his face, which was a custom that wartime necessities had produced: "Come on, lovey, want some fun?"

"Oh, Gawd," she said when she recognized him, "it's *you*, Sam! Let's go and have a cup of tea." Sam knew them all, like a father-confessor.

The war had ended when he and I sailed together for Southampton for the last time. Among my hand baggage was an urn containing the ashes of Sam Walsh, put into my hands by his closest friends. Sam had loved the sea, and he wanted to be buried somewhere in midstream.

Two or three days out, I arranged for a small, solemn farewell party to be held in the suite I occupied, which had a little sitting room forward opening into a bedroom aft. The weather was warm, so the steward had unfastened the portholes in both rooms.

At the conclusion of our modest wake, I climbed up onto a chair with the urn in my hand and committed Sam's ashes to the waves and the wind. None of us had calculated what the wind would do. My suite was on the weather side. The remains of dear Sam, scattered out of one porthole, blew mostly in through another and landed on the counterpane. I thought as I sneezed, "How Sam would have laughed." It was his last and best gag. Could anybody top this? Not on your bing-bang.

Nobody returns to describe the face of death, which wears so many masks—shock, relief, doubt, despair. And, strangely enough, even hope. My father, in his old age, went back to the corner of the world where his life began, County Down. I doubt whether London ever seemed like home to him. He'd take his daily walk to St. John's Wood Churchyard across from Lord's Cricket Ground and sit by the hour on a favorite bench. I'm sure he couldn't really make out what had happened to his "perwerse" little daughter. I remember taking him once to see my name in lights outside a theatre, and he shook his head in a kind of disbelief.

I used to visit him from time to time at the house bought for him at Corcreevy, near Hillsborough, sharing in his pleasure that on the way, so help us, there

is a sign standing at a crossroads in the middle of nowhere in particular that identifies the spot as "Lillie
Corners."

In London that summer, we received the news that
he was seriously ill at the home of a friend in Duncairn
Gardens, Belfast. The only hope of reaching there in
a hurry was to charter a plane. André Charlot drove
"Doc" McGonigle, Muriel and me helter-skelter
through the streets of London, up through the northern suburbs to Hendon airfield. A chartered plane
was waiting for us, with the engine warming up.

The weather was foul, and every other pilot but
ours decided to stay on the ground. But we wrapped
ourselves in scarves and climbed into the little ma-
chine. Somewhere over the Irish Sea, it looked as if
we'd have to turn back. We were boring into head
winds and enough air pockets to keep us all pale
green, in spite of an occasional nip from the brandy
bottle that "Doc" had brought along. The winds made
us run short of fuel, and we were forced to land on the
Isle of Man. With extra gas in the tank, we took off,
and then miraculously, the winds changed and began
pushing us, whistling round the edges of the plane's
mica windows. Not long before we landed, there was
a sound like the wail of a banshee.

We knew what it meant. "Pa's dead," I said.

We landed in a rough field, filled with sheep. Muriel
ran off to look for somebody with a car, to convince
him that we had to get to Hillsborough. But we arrived half an hour too late. My father had died not
long before we'd landed, while the wind wailed like
a banshee.

John Lillie was always a careful man in matters he
regarded as important, so he had written a will. In it,
he returned to me virtually every penny I had ever

pressed on him. His wants were always simple and un-complicated, which made them not too difficult to achieve. He was buried from the Moravian Church at Lillie Corners and lies in Hillsborough Parish Church-yard with a view, far away, of the Mountains of Mourne, which go down to the sea.

A few months later, I opened at the Savoy Theatre in the last show I did for Charlot. Dion Titheradge and Doc had combined forces to write, *Please*. In his first-night curtain speech, Uncle André was pleased to call me his "prodigal daughter," returned to the fold after three years away. We both waxed a touch sentimental over that.

Skipping ahead for a moment, to 1954, I was ap-pearing at the Biltmore, in Los Angeles, in *An Eve-ning With Beatrice Lillie* when I saw him for our last meetings over the teacups in his home at North Havenhurst Drive, Hollywood. He had decided to try to make a new life there as a film actor when his ca-reer as a producer, so brilliant in his heyday, petered out in London. I asked him, "Why not write a book, Dada?"

He said, "Oh, that takes money. You need a secre-tary, you know, and you have many expenses before you find a publisher."

Trying to find a pretext, I took the approach that there may have been money I owed him, on old royalties or something like that. I knew he would be reluctant to take a cent from me, so I thought I'd write him a note to this effect, enclosing a very siz-able check and give it to him in an envelope. I had it ready for our next meeting one week later, another in-vitation to tea at his home.

"What's this for?" he wanted to know, as we were leaving.

"Something I owe you. It's towards your book."

He opened the envelope and read the letter, puzzled, yet seemingly charmed. I'd forgotten to put the check inside! (It had to, and *did*, follow, on the next day.)

Charlot laughed, "Beattie, God bless you, you haven't changed a bit."

I was delighted that Uncle André saw the prodigal daughter in her own production three times; once from a place of honor in the stage box, twice from his favorite spot, standing backstage in the wings.

I shall never regret bringing him to San Francisco several weeks later, to stay nearby my suite at the Fairmont for a week while he and my personal representative, John Philip, poured over some of Charlot's best material for a proposed new show.

It was Uncle André's first flight in a big airplane. I saw him happily board the plane for Los Angeles with a fresh check, which we'd forced on him, in his brief case. Alas, the proposed show never came about. I never saw Dada again.

CHAPTER TWELVE

GROWING PAINS AND PLEASURES

I hadn't stayed so long in London for ten years. Here it was spring again, with tulips and daffodils blooming in the Embankment Gardens outside the River Entrance of the Savoy Hotel, which had again become home to me. My father had been gone for eight months now. My son was "Little Bobbie" by pet name only. Every indication was that he would soon stand nearly as tall as his father. Big Bobby and I seldom saw each other. Going his own way, he had taken a house in Penhurst, Kent, and led a separate, unobtrusive life there.

"Knocking about the world broadens a man's mind," he once said, "and I have done a good deal of knocking about." True, too true; at least he was honest about it.

For the umpteenth time, I'd been appearing at the Café de Paris, made popular by the Prince of Wales, where the lights were soft and the music sweet for dancing. I was getting to know the town again after a long absence.

One April day, two telegrams came to me at the hotel, both from the Lonsdale Nursing Home in Tunbridge Wells, not far from Penhurst. My husband had gone in there for an appendicitis operation. The first telegram said that he had developed peritonitis following surgery. The second said that he was dead. It was the eve of his thirty-sixth birthday, fourteen years after our marriage. Little Bobbie was now Sir Robert Peel, the sixth baronet, the only treasure my husband had to bequeath.

It was all too late, but I drove to the nursing home immediately.

Nearly three thousand people came to the hamlet of Drayton Bassett to take final leave of Big Bobby, on foot, by car, in dozens of chartered motor coaches. They overflowed the tiny parish church, St. Peter's, and packed the churchyard. We sat, my son and I, Muriel and Mumsie, facing the plain oak coffin, which six sturdy farmhands, from the estate that was a Peel's no longer, carried from the chapel to the family vault beside the church's south door. Most of the flowers were daffodils. The sky was filled with gray clouds.

The vicar of Tamworth spoke the final words. "I am not going to make him out a saint, but we all know that handsome figure, that cheery nature, possessed an exceptionally kind heart."

There was a parting thought. "I ask you to pray that his son may catch some of the inspiration of those who have gone before him. I ask you to pray that Lady Peel may be guided to bring up her son in the steps of his illustrious ancestors." I privately vowed to do the very best I could, but I prayed that he would take after the earlier generations of Peels, not the later.

Big Bobby had been as improvident as his father and his father's father. He died, as a friend once said, "leaving a thirteen-year-old son and £1640." And debts of nearly ten times that much.

I was too shaken to allow myself to be idle very long. In May, I went back to work at the Café de Paris and from there to appear once again in vaude-ville, which the British call "variety," at the London Palladium. Sometimes, it's nice to forget, and some things are best forgotten. But for this funny life of mine to be understood, it is necessary to touch, just for a moment, on a story the London newspapers reported one year later.

A woman I had met before, but not to know well, chose to sue a firm of New Bond Street dressmakers for the return of two ermine coats. She appeared in court wearing a diamond eternity ring. In the course of evidence, it developed that she had been known in some quarters as Lady Peel. She spoke afterward to a reporter from the *Daily Express* and to another from the *Daily Mail*.

She told the first, "I don't care about the conse-quences. I can live with memories now. People who throw mud just don't understand the circumstances. We loved each other. After he was separated from Lady Peel and my own marriage proved unsuccessful, we met again. Each of us was tied. I mothered him. When he was very hard pressed financially, I gave him my jewels. I know he would have done the same for me. Then he died."[*]

To the *Daily Mail*, she said, "I went to stay with him in Westfield, his house at Penhurst, and it was there that I found happiness. We lived the simple life

[*] Reprinted by permission of the London *Daily Express*.

amid gardens of flowers. . . . At night, Sir Robert would sit with me, making colored rugs, while I crocheted tea cloths."*

It was she who had called the ambulance that took him, after a sudden attack of appendicitis, to the Tunbridge Wells nursing home. It was I who took her to the nursing home, because no other member of the Peel family felt that it was a proper thing to do.

Looking back with the perfect hindsight that time gives us all, I can see that the distance that grew between Big Bobby and me was a sad necessity—on my part. I couldn't endure a life of social nonsense as Lady Peel. I was confused by the fact that I had fallen in love originally with the dashing, charming *Mr.* Robert Peel, without thinking of the problems that would possibly develop when he became *Sir* Robert.

I literally *had* to make a living, and a good one, because careless spending by the Peels, together with death duties, had drastically eroded Old "Parsley's" fortune. Big Bobby's problem essentially was that he couldn't make people believe that he desperately needed to work, the more so because I was kept so busy and won so much recognition. It is a familiar tale, with an added twist; personal achievement *vs.* marriage compounded by the nobility.

God knows, he tried hard, but he could never completely overcome his inborn pride and channel his energies toward a single goal, instead of striking out to seek so many. Perhaps it was the old, old story of what happens when a man is married to a woman with a career of her own and he has no fixed work or business to fulfill his need for acceptance, self-expression and self-respect.

* Reprinted by permission of the London *Daily Mail.*

In the end, my husband felt that he *had* to be on his own, and off he went. Together, we might have been able to work things out, but I doubt it somehow. So now the whole situation had resolved itself. I felt stunned and truly sorry.

Something else had to be done before the last threads with Drayton were broken. In the summer of the year following my husband's death, I went back to unveil a memorial tablet to the man who had so greatly changed the course of my life, as perhaps I had changed his. I have been back only a few times since.

Now my son needed more time and thought than I'd been able to give him before. "Harrods" still seemed to be the best place in England for him to be educated, but he would spend every possible holiday with me. That meant my refusing an offer from MGM of a seven-year contract. I should have been able to spend only three months of each year with Bobbie, and we had to see more of each other than that. Considering how Hollywood and I got along, I probably shouldn't have amounted to too much at Metro, anyway.

So when the London producers, true to form, hemmed and hawed, and in New York the Shuberts wanted me for a new musical show they were planning, Bobbie had to become a kind of commuter like me on the transatlantic run, sailing over in Mumsie's care whenever Harrow was on holiday.

Inevitably, I suppose, he grew up to be a rather worldly young man, soon to be so tall that he could hold out his arms and I could walk under them without ruffling a hair of my head. In New York, his friends were Fanny's son, Billy—ice hockey and elephant rides in Central Park—and beautiful young

Cobina Wright, Jr., named for her mother, and squired by her two adolescent admirers to skating parties and most of the shows on Broadway.

In London, and the south of France, a little later, Bobbie had another rival for the attentions of Miss Wright. Prince Philip of Greece, the son of the refugee King, was for a while a schoolmate of Bobbie's and the two were pals. The future Duke of Edinburgh, who used to call Cobina, Sr., *"madre,"* had an eye for her daughter; so did Bobbie. Philip slept occasionally on the sofa in the living room of my London flat—I'm still in the same building—in Park Lane. He accepted similar sleeping arrangements over many a weekend at a place I (years later) took for the summer, Chetwode, at Burchetts Green, just outside Maidenhead, Berkshire.

Years later, for old times' sake and out of admiration for him; before a tour matinee, I whiled away a contented hour and more in a crowd on a street corner, in Liverpool, to wait for him to pass by in an open carriage with Queen Elizabeth, on their way to some ceremonial occasion. He clearly pays attention to the faces in a crowd. When I waved to him, I received what in the theatre is called "double take," a wink and a grin. I've seen Philip socially over the years in London and New York. I love his humor and keen wit.

For Bobbie, I used to hope that he would find a girl to marry who was not too much in love with him. Too much in love, and the boy and the girl were almost fated to walk the road to disillusion. But he wasn't to have the chance to marry anyone.

He was still very much a schoolboy when I worked for the Shuberts in *At Home Abroad*. He'd grown accustomed to having an actress for a mother and had long since lost his resentment of people who laughed at me. We used to dream about his studying for the law in dressing-room talks at the Winter Garden Theatre, where he was fast becoming something of a stage-door Johnny, waiting for me just as his father had done.

I remember we went one day to lunch at what was now called "The 21 Club," having retained its popularity and lost its identification as "Jack and Charlie's" with repeal of Prohibition. Bobbie carried in his pocket a Mexican horned toad, sent to me for unfathomable motives by an unknown admirer. The toad made a getaway and qualified as the all-time champion tablehopper hours after we'd left. One of the Kriendler brothers—was it Jack or Charlie?—cornered the creature and kept it for Bobbie until our next visit.

There were all kinds of contributions that made a hit of *At Home Abroad*. We had the latest thing in tap dancers in Eleanor Powell, a long-legged, statuesque girl who, as Ashton Stevens used to say, "looked as if she had a mother." Ethel Waters invariably stopped the show with a Jamaican plantation number which, in these much altered times, would probably bring out a picket line. Mrs. Blodgen Blagg introduced her troubles in buying "two dozen doubledamask dinner napkins." I also pretended to perform on one set of bagpipes, while backstage another set was blown by a real piper. After the dress rehearsal, he found himself locked in the stage manager's office and had to give a lonesome performance of "The Flowers of the Forest" to attract the night porter's attention.

And I had brought over from London a new leading man, Reginald Gardiner, who began by doing brilliantly original imitations of wallpaper and went on from there to imitate everything from record-changers to a ship's engine room. We regarded each other as rather funny in a deranged sort of way. Who but an inspired loon could reduce an audience to helpless laughter by sounding exactly like a swinging door, empty shoes, trains or fog settling over Flushing flats? A complete original, Reggie, *and* a darling man.

The reviewers came up with the, by now, usual kind words about "the funniest woman in the world," which was a tribute to something or other, because I didn't feel especially funny at the time. Robert Garland wrote a line that struck me as hitting the nail rather smartly on the head: "As is the case with olives, Ed Wynn and Philadelphia, you like her or you don't like her, and that's all there is to it."

Reggie Gardiner said something nice, too: "I believe she could make people laugh in a dark room, and do this by the inflection of her voice." I wouldn't dare try. (Rudolph, where *is* that watch?)

It might be tantamount to looking for laughs by reading a telephone directory, which is supposedly the test of every comedian and, so far as I'm concerned, the cliché of all time. I think Ed Wynn came closer to the truth when he said anybody reading the Yellow Pages to him would reduce him to tears.

But it was a generous thought on Reggie's part, and who could help liking a man of such kindness? During the long run, we saw something of Manhattan together, and, for long stretches, we appeared each night to entertain at the New Montmartre, a supper club that had most conveniently been opened on the roof of the Winter Garden Theatre.

It's great to be laughed at, but just think, if only my nose had been a quarter of an inch *shorter* I could have been a *femme fatale*. Ah, well!

Parties were the order of the day and night, when

your hostess and mine was as often as not Elsa Maxwell. She could have thrown a pajama party during a North Pole blizzard and made it a wow. The closest she came to such an undertaking was giving a skating party on the then new rink in Rockefeller Plaza. Unfortunately, it was raining rather than snowing at the time. The affair was called for 9 P.M., I was there at ten, Elsa dropped by at eleven, most everyone else came straight over from the Metropolitan Opera at midnight, and the ice arrived three days later.

On another occasion, due to overwhelming popular demand, with my evening skirt bundled up to my knees, I skated three times round Rockefeller rink until I came to my doom and a forced landing in the lap of Prometheus.

All for Elsa! She gave one soirée, and announced it as such, "for the coming out of Cole Porter's legs," which had been crushed in a riding accident. Just out of the hospital, he came in a wheel chair, wearing two enormous plaster casts, and watched us play musical chairs. I made sure of winning by carrying my chair clasped firmly to my nadir. All for Elsa.

Cole Porter wrote "Mrs. Lowsborough-Goodby" for your correspondent, and I sang it for Elsa's sake at a Waldorf party that lasted until dawn broke like an ostrich egg over the Brooklyn Bridge. At five o'clock Barbara Hutton, wearing an amber crown bedecked with diamonds, was still dancing with Serge Obolensky. George Gershwin, Lawrence Tibbett and a few hundred others had stayed on, too. Tallulah's diamond necklace had a hard time competing with the diamond-and-emerald earrings of a usually imperturbable lady, Mrs. William Goodby-Loew, known fondly as "Queenie." Her pendants swung to her shoulders. (Watch it now!)

She did her best to take it as I sang Cole's lyric about the disastrous weekend parties for which Mrs. Lowsborough-Goodby was renowned—but before I had finished, Mrs. Goodby-Loew's face was scarlet, her pendants were heaving nicely and her chandelier earrings were swinging like ship's lanterns in a gale.

Once, I played an ever-so-modest burlesque chorine, for Elsa, with a chorus in which she was included, along with one professional peeler, a girl named Della Carroll. Reggie, William Gargan and Bert Lahr made up the rest of the line, but they were not, I think, among the sponsors of the affair, each of whom had contributed several hundred dollars to one of Elsa's charities.

When the lights were lowered and the blue spotlights glowed, we started to do our stuff. A certain amount of argument broke out in the audience. Some cried, "More! More!" Others, sorely tried, shouted, "Less! Less!" Then, without warning, every light in the room blacked out, the band stopped and our show was suddenly over.

Elsa explained why. "Of course, I had them turned out instantly when the one professional in our act started to be herself. I would never permit such a thing at a party of mine. Nothing is so ugly as undraped flesh."

I accepted an invitation to a different kind of party at which I set out to be serious for a change, but it didn't work out that way. The powers that be at the Metropolitan Opera House decided to put on an affair to say farewell to Guilio Gatti-Casazza, who was retiring after twenty-seven years as general manager.

Would I graciously consent to sing the role of Carmen as the guest *artiste* in an excerpt from Bizet's opera?

Apprehension was acute. For a start, I'd been too busy working all my life to have seen *Carmen,* or heard it, except bits on the radio. I had a general picture of stilettos, shawls and cigarettes. I'd be playing on a stage as big as Grand Central Station when I always thought I was best in slightly more intimate surroundings (not *too* intimate, mind you). I should be the only *theatrical* in the house, appearing on the same program as Lily Pons, Gladys Swarthout, Helen Jepson and the other stars of the Met, before an audience of opera lovers.

Taking everything into consideration, I agreed to appear. I wanted to be good, and I wanted to be straight; an irrational ambition that I've frequently had but seldom been able to achieve. So I bought a record album and played it all day long for a month. I was set on being word perfect for once, and the little gray cells, as always, found it hard to remember, prepositions, conjunctions and such trivia.

As the days went by, with the record-player wearing its heart out, and the Sunday night of the performance drew near, the panic increased. I'd been nervous often enough before, but now I was truly terrified. When I walked through the stage door on The Night, I was thinking quite calmly, "I hope I slip here and break a leg. I hope I suddenly collapse with pneumonia. Dear God, I don't want to do *Carmen.*"

There had been only one rehearsal—that afternoon —and I was as helpless as ever in rehearsal.

I put on the long, ruffled dress, the mantilla, the trailing shawl, with not a line of the libretto remaining in my head. I most sincerely did not want the audience to laugh at me. I wished and willed myself to be *straight* or fall dead in the attempt.

To make my entrance, I had to climb a ladder, then emerge at the top of a flight of perhaps a dozen steps, trailing my scarf along the balustrade. I licked my lips, parted my jaws and began to sing in a shrill scream, with one hand on the painted wood bannister, descending the stairs slowly. Applause. Then my shawl caught on a nail and slowly parted from me as I continued my descent.

If you will be good enough to stack the Bibles over there, I am prepared again to swear that it was an *accident*. As I felt the shawl tugging at my shoulders, I took a quick look around and climbed back up the stairs to retrieve it, shrieking my head off in French gibberish.

The whole house screamed. The chandeliers, I'm sure jangled, and the maestro fumbled with his baton. It was all that was needed to throw the switch. The wand was on. "Well, all right," I said to myself, "you might just as well let go now." The panic was over. I tore into the arias and amazed myself by remembering most of the moves and lyrics.

Crazed with relief, I abandoned the mantilla. Now it was singing, singing all the way, so I started carrying on with the prompter, trilling to him my SOS calls for help. "Qu'est-ce que la next line, s'il vous plaît, monsieur? . . . C'est impossible pour moi to remember, et je cannot hear quoi vous parlez." I finished lying on the stage, peering into his little box, flirting with him shamelessly while Georges Bizet, perhaps, revolved *adagio* in his grave.

Paul Althouse sang the role of Don José in one brief scene, and I yelled right back to him. "Excuse me," I asked when the final curtain had come down and the audience had composed itself for another bout, "do you speak French?"

In the course of the evening, Lawrence Tibbett walked around on his hands in a footballer's version of *Pagliacci*; Mesdames Pons, Swarthout and Jepson rendered "Minnie the Moocher," to the music of Chick Webb's orchestra; Lauritz Melchior and Miss Pons, both in tights of shocking pink, performed some acrobatics with the help of wire ropes; the entire company plus one wilted Lillie joined in a finale entitled "Putting the Rah in Opera"; and a forthcoming attraction was announced via slide projection on a screen—*Salome, Tomboy of the Nile,* featuring a new smash-hit aria, "What's Godunoff for Boris is Godunoff for Me."

And so we bade *bon voyage* to Signor Gatti-Gasazza, who sat in a box, struggling to hide his tears behind his beard, and we prepared the way for his successor, Mr. Herbert Witherspoon. If nothing else, this excruciating experience should have taught me how utterly futile it is for me to aspire to theatrical matters non-comedic. It appears that I'm a natural-born fool and I guess I'd better stay that way.

I have neglected to mention that while all these goings on were going on, I was also on the radio. Not in the sense of a goldfish bowl placed on a doily on the Victrola, but as a real, live, presumed entertainer on a weekly, coast-to-coast hookup, with meelyuns listening to you, and you mustn't be the least bit nervous.

Everybody who was anybody was on the radio. The world, especially the United States, was hypnotized by what Signor Marconi had wrought. The networks—red, white, blue and various other colors of the spectrum—were beetling around signing up All and Sundry, and several other vocal groups. It was to be precisely the same in the early days of television.

Helen Hayes was on radio, and she shook like a leaf for ten minutes after her first performance. Ethel Barrymore confronted a microphone, and it took her years to be herself again. Babe Ruth went on the air, and you could hear his script rattle. Claudette Colbert made her debut on CBS, and after each of her two songs, she boke down and wept.

I'd had a stab or two at guest appearances before being asked to jump in the deep end with a network contact. If I remember rightly, my very first time was on the Rudy Vallee show. He asked if I wouldn't mind making my time his time by introducing him to Noël, a man whose every word Rudy would be hanging on, by Rudy's account.

After some persuasion, Noël agreed to be introduced to Rudy—who proceeded to monopolize the conversation by talking to us about his favorite subject, which just happened to be a curly-headed Yale man, band leader and radio sensation whose name you have but one chance to guess. Noël sulked for weeks.

If you have come thus far in the story, you'll need no prompting to speculate on the headline which one magazine put on the account of our three-corner meeting. Yes, it was, "Lillie and the Vallee," so help me.

My broadcasting career may best be described as *fluid*. The greater part of it was spent contributing to the sales of Borden's Evaporated Milk and a somewhat harder liquid, Red Cap Ale. I thought that either one was better than singing for Ex-Lax, as some people did.

My initial performance for Borden's was not unaccompanied by the customary cursed attack of the trembles. Not to be compared with the great Metropolitan Opera House neurosis, but troublesome, nevertheless. How could I pull the first laugh from a radio audience, and if I did, how would I know they were laughing and telling me what to do next? I'd have to trust to experience, the script writers and the comfort of being paid $25,000 for thirteen weeks of jollity.

For the first Friday night, I wore a red evening dress for mental support and included "Dinner Napkins" on the menu. In advance, I had received fatherly advice from Alec Woollcott, Charles Winninger, Ed Wynn and Eddie Cantor, plus some sisterly words of cheer from Helen Hayes and Fanny Brice, one of the few women in the universe to know that a comedian and an audience draw on each other.

If fish was served that first Friday, it was *sole bonne femme*, and I felt extremely sole. Instead of a floor model, a suspended microphone was provided so that I could make the habitual gestures à la Harry Rich. But I had no more than started when I took a smart pace forward, banged my forehead on the mike, turned pale and almost lost my balance. The inner voice said, "Be calm. Never despair."

A fast glance at the sound-effects man, fresh in from Chicago, produced such results that he sent a gush from the Seltzer bottle, which he had been toying with for later use, down the neck of the saxophone player, who was sitting next to him. The program nearly ended there.

Yet, miraculously, bolstered by screams of audience laughter, we survived with no serious impediments to the end of our allotted half-hour. It struck me as being a bit like Reggie's idea of making people laugh in a dark room, but at least I hadn't run into such dire trouble as Alec on his maiden mission before a microphone, when his *savoir-faire* took to its heels and he finished in a cold sweat with a mouth as dry as a Pharaoh's tomb.

Laboring on the Blue Network treadmill, I found, was as wearing as toiling at the Hollywood salt mines. Perhaps slightly more wearisome because, as a creature of habit, I was simultaneously putting in two performances, eight o'clock and midnight, at the Rainbow Room, which virtually doubled the number of doubloons forthcoming every payday.

At East End Avenue, the day customarily commenced at 7 A.M., when a tribe of jolly truckmen heralded the dawn by bouncing cast-iron radiators onto the sidewalk from a riverfront warehouse close by the apartment. Occasionally, I would retaliate by throwing things at them from my bedroom window, until one morning, staggering half-asleep, I tossed out a vase I'd grown rather fond of. That did it. Never more!

I'd made up my mind that Beatrice Borden was going to favor caviare rather than sauerkraut, so I shunned the waiting legions of radio script-writers, eager to thrust gag number 2197 into my hands. I was vain enough to believe that I could do better standing on my ear. So three inspired beginners worked on the words for me—Doc McGonigle, Peter Sharpe and Nancy Hamilton, a pretty young actress from Pittsburgh whom I'd met when I went backstage to congratulate her on a burlesque she did of me. At one period, when she wrestled with scripts by day and played Miss Bingley in *Pride and Prejudice* at the Plymouth Theatre by night, her life got almost as complicated as mine.

After every Friday evening broadcast, we looked forward to a weekend of rest. Then in the car, going back to my apartment, somebody would say, "Well, what are we going to do next Friday?" Farewell to the weekend of relaxation.

On Saturdays, we'd gather to talk all day. On Sundays, out came the scribbling pads. By Tuesday, the script would be drafted, with rehearsals beginning on Wednesday. Every Thursday, there was a dress rehearsal with Lee Perrin's band getting its licks in, the Revellers murmuring their harmonies and our announcer, Ben Grauer, adding his tributes to evaporated milk.

By this time, of course, I was good and tired of the jokes we'd been kicking around for the past four days, so we'd try to whip up a new batch. On Friday afternoon, there was another dress rehearsal, and it was there that I stumbled on how to find the audience. I played to everybody in the studio, from the bandsmen to the gnomes in the control room.

When the orchestra was having such a good old time that it forgot to come in on cue, or the poker-faced men at their poker-faced dials lost sight of their stop watches, then we stood a chance of putting on a worth-while show. (Quiet, *please!*)

Friday evening again. "Hello, hello, and so on from the sweetheart of show biz." Strange to say, Beatrice Borden was a success almost from the minute she went on the air. "Perhaps radio's finest job of clowning," in the opinion of one girl reporter. (She *would* have to say "perhaps.")

Enough of the forty million people who listened to radio in those days sent fan letters for them to be a monumental nuisance. A nurse in Montreal wrote, for instance, that "after hearing Miss Lillie, my patient enjoyed a normal night's sleep, for the first time in months, which greatly improved her mental condition."

An irate Bostonian saw fit to report, on the other hand, that "your program was so bad that not only will we never drink that particular brand of milk, but I am urging my entire family of nine to stop drinking milk entirely."

That was more in the spirit of things. I held that no cows, not even the sponsor's herd, should be sacred, and he didn't object to my unburdening myself of such lines as, "Let's pour a can of milk over Junior and see if he will evaporate, too."

Such innocent pleasantries—well, and a few other jabs—gave us the reputation of concocting the most daring comedy ever transmitted through the sweet, unpolluted air. We ran into censor trouble and accusations of turning the Blue Network a shade more azure. It's almost impossible to recall how guileless the standards were in the days of early network radio, but if you are curious (blue) to taste the fruit that was forbidden to us, well, here goes. . . .

When I wanted to sing Cole Porter's "Miss Otis Regrets," I was ordered to omit the line, "Down lover's lane **she** strayed."

At the end of one sketch, playing a hostess covered with spilled milk, I said to my stiff and starchy butler, "Parker, I am ruined." He was not allowed to answer, "Very good, madam."

The Blue Network's blue pencil prohibited me from saying, "Stop biting that announcer—you'll get chilblains." I was gagged when I tried to explain, "She would take up oriental dancing, but she has no stomach for that sort of thing." Likewise, "She was wrestling with her conscience when she fell."

But there's a way around everything, as the actress said to the bishop. I developed a stutter now and again in front of the microphone. "Son of a b-b-b-b-achelor!" I'd murmur, sweet as pie. Or, with an eye cocked toward the sponsor's booth, "That's a h-h-h-hole lot of sh-sh-shortening." Sometimes on the air, there'd be a slip of the tongue and—oh, hell, the next day Jack Benny and the rest of the senior comedians would march on their respective studios, raising cain: "If she gets away with it, why can't we?" Pity, but you see, they were never ladies.

For my part, I felt more like an ostrich, perched on my padded stool, clucking at the mike. It was like having my head in the sand. Nobody could *see* me, with my silver Thermos bottle and water in a paper cup.

However, I firmly resolved to be kind to my throat, start the day right, keep Kool, ask the man who owns one, see my dentist twice a year, look for the date on the can, lose that fat and taste the difference. Tune in again next week, same time same station.

Thus 'did the busy little Bea improve the shining network hours. When I toured with a show, I checked in at the local radio station to do the weekly broadcast program by remote pickup. Once again, the reviewers discovered fresh comparisons to make. I reminded them, they said, of Fred Allen, Jack Benny, Eddie Cantor and Joe Penner (or was it his duck, which he was forever trying to sell?). At the other extreme, one gentleman caller with notebook in hand, sighting me in the throes of rehearsal, concluded that I looked "like any bookkeeper's assistant from the accounts department." Me, as 'ad me own 'orses!

The fan mail flooded us, in envelopes of every shape, shade and fragrance, bearing tidings on a generous range of subjects, from acne to zoology. "I have seen your picture and think you look funny. Do you look that way on purpose or are you really beautiful under it all?—Curious Kate."

What to answer? "Dear Curious Kate: My face is twisted into funny angles to give the definite appearance of a comic hoping to keep the radio job until they invent television. Sincerely, Auntie Bea." It wouldn't do at all.

Then there were the missives that ended with the plea to send an autographed picture. They presented a bigger problem. Which picture to send? Something to scare the daylights out of Junior? A print suitable for framing, to decorate the walls of the local Elks Club? Or Baby Beatrice on a bearskin rug?

Dismissing all prejudice, I realized there was only one reply to make in most cases, and that was to send no reply whatever except the photograph. For those epistles that merited more conventional responses, I toyed with the idea of having a form letter printed, to read:

"Miss Lillie thanks you for your charming letter and hopes that you will write again and again. Signed, Lady Northcliffe, Secretary to the Secretary of Miss Beatrice Gladys Lillie."

Without unduly straining the imagination, it may safely be concluded that when an invitation came along to play in a new musical under the direction again of Vincente Minelli, who handled *At Home Abroad*, I set off at a fast trot for c-o-c-ktails (radio had also taught me to spell, rather than say, possibly embarrassing words!) at his studio, Reggie Gardiner was invited, and so was Bert Lahr, completing the trio wanted by the producers, Lee and J. J. Shubert.

"Musicals," Reggie has observed, "are popular delusions shared by normally sane and rational people who become hysterical at the very mention of musical." Brilliant!

By the time Reggie arrived, I'd almost given up trying to control an attack of delirium brought on by the prospect of getting back onto a stage again. Vincente's gentle salesmanship may have done it—perhaps he picked up the technique when he worked for Marshall Field's Chicago department store. Or it may have been the sight of a stack of gold-lamé, panne-velvet and glass-cloth costume plates—I was a bit of a fashion plate myself in those days.

Bert was the last arrival, wearing his habitual look of profound misgiving. He was the only performer I knew in my life who was jumpier than I at rehearsals. He used to fidget with his buttons while he fussed with his lines, with never a smile on his mournful jowls. "Yeah," he'd say, at any gag, "but I don't think it'll do." Or in the middle of a sketch, he'd interrupt to ask the time, then mutter, "Excuse me, I've got to call my lawyer." Needless to say, I adored him; a kindred spirit.

As soon as Bert had settled himself uncomfortably in a chair, Vincente began. "Of course you understand that this is an informal meeting of old friends. We were all together in *At Home Abroad,* and I thought it would be jolly to meet here today. There is absolutely nothing definite yet, despite rumors that a musical is being planned."

"Yowsuh, Uncle Tom," Bert moaned, inexplicably.

"Make it double yowsuh, Uncle Tom," said I.

"Then it's all settled," exclaimed Vincente. *"The show is on."*

He was a bit premature. He'd sold the Shuberts the idea of staging a "very cockeyed and very wonderful" revue spanning the years between the Gay Nineties and the Grouchy Thirties. "It's practically my life ambition," he told them, "to see Beatrice Lillie and Bert Lahr on the same stage."

With their consent, he put out the call for lyrics, sketches and songs, which began to be delivered by the carload, while Minelli, a twenty-eight-year-old wonder, personally designed sets and costumes. The day we started rehearsing, nobody had laid eyes on a complete book. One week before we were due to try out in Boston, someone claimed to have seen part of the scenery for one set, and we jeered at him.

Bert was in seventh heaven. His torn-off buttons littered the backstage and rehearsal rooms. Seventy-two hours before our appointment at the Shubert Theatre in the Athens of America, the first half dozen of our five-hundred costumes showed up. A good omen, we thought.

Boston could have witnessed a reunion of three musketeers if it had been paying attention. Gertie and Noël were playing at the Colonial in *Tonight at Eight-Thirty*. Noël made it his business to drop in at the Shubert for our last rehearsal. Afterward he sauntered into Bert's dressing room and caught him in the act of taking off a jock strap. A Frère Jacques strap (for you delicate types!).

"Hmm, bags of fun," murmured Noël, leaving a highly colored Bert, who had never met the master before, to finish dressing.

The Show Is On appealed to every Bostonian, proper or otherwise, who came to see us; it was as popular with the local citizenry as a bucket of steamers on a Fourth of July clambake. But Vincente, the quiet perfectionist, wasn't satisfied. He made changes in Boston, changes in Philadelphia, changes along each of the two thousand miles we traipsed up and down the Eastern seaboard before we limped into Pennsylvania Station, red-eyed but wrapped up in red ribbon, for our Christmas-night opening at the Winter Garden Theatre.

Of the cast of thousands—well, I actually counted one hundred and twenty-five—I may have been the most frantic. Bobbie was due over *in* the *Aquitania* for the première and the holidays. The Atlantic breezes, however, were blowing up a hurricane.

Would Bobbie and ten thousand bags of mail dock in time for Christmas? Would the ship sink? Would our show be a success on Broadway? Would the Duke of Windsor, who had just abdicated, find happiness with Wallis? We may just as well relax, I guess. They all made it.

Bert and I had come to an agreement. No matter what Vincente did to the book, the two B.L.s would have exactly the same number of songs and sketches. When Broadway flocked to see what was pretty much acknowledged to be the best revue for years, audiences raved about his "Song of the Woodman," which gave every baritone pause for thought ever after, and something I did called "Buy Yourself a Balloon."

The song had been written by Herman Hupfeld (about whom more to come!), the sensitive, somber-looking little man who had also worked on *At Home Abroad*. It was planned as a song to put an end to all other "moon-June" melodies. (Unfortunately, it didn't, but it had its points.)

> Some nice day in June
> Buy yourself a balloon,
> Take a trip to the moon,

Then go ahead and croon.
Teach the stars to spoon
With a popular tune. . . .

To deliver this item required the services of a steel crane that weighed a ton and a half; a sturdy prop moon that swung out over the audience as far as the fourth row of the orchestra; six property men clutching ropes to control the swinging; me, sitting on the moon, wearing a rather insecure safety belt (which the management considered advisable, though I disagreed) and an air of supreme nonchalance.

The nonchalance had seen me through one traumatic rehearsal, when a stagehand fumbled one of the ropes, and the moon and I collided with one of the upper boxes. The effect was so hilarious that, by my special request, we kept this bit of improvisation in future swingings.

During one performance, a stately dowager I knew socially sat at the front of the box as I chirruped my way toward the ceiling. When I approached, she reached out and shook hands, almost pulling me off my perch.

"Bea, darling, what are you doing for luncheon on Thursday?"

Hurriedly, I asked her to phone me and carried on with the number.

I was costumed like an Edwardian belle in a saucy pink silk dress with a froufrou skirt and lace-up boots. From the comparative safety of my moon, I tossed three pink garters a night down on the audience, aiming, if I could, for bald men with the pinkest pates. On opening night, one grasping customer couldn't wait until I got my first garter off. He stretched up and tried to tug it from my ankle, and almost got more than he bargained for. Don't misunderstand, please; I very nearly fell on his face and into the orchestra pit.

Those blooming garters became a sort of door prize flourished all over town. I flung them at Noël and Gertie when they paid us a visit, at Bob Hope and Irving Berlin, to whom I owed *something* for "When I Lost You" and countless auditions long ago. I couldn't go into a restaurant or a nightclub without someone standing up and waving a pink garter at me. Since there were more of them on display than I could have handed out in ten years, I concluded that bootleggers were busy behind the scenes.

Bobbie, understandably, had some reservations about the whole act.

Though we ran for almost a year, *The Show Is On* came off sooner than it should because two or three of us had new movie contracts to fulfill. With my son nearing the end of his school days, I was going to test myself yet again in Hollywood. Once more onto the beach! If I could make reasonably good pictures, I'd be content to settle in California on a temporary basis, so that he and I could share more time together.

I'd flown overnight to Los Angeles and back—yes, in a plane—to sign with a producer who, characteristically of his kind, had more ambition than money. His first project, for a musical called *English Derby,* came to nought at a gallop. Now he was taking an O. Henry short story, *The Badge of Policeman O'Roon,* and transforming it into a Bing Crosby vehicle entitled *Dr. Rhythm.* O. Henry might have been surprised if not positively dumfounded to learn that I was to appear as an eccentric socialite, a Mrs. Lorelei Dodge-Blodgett, and among other things do the "Dinner Napkins" dialogue, rights to which I'd purchased, with Franklyn Pangborn as an hilariously *zee daintie* counter salesman. Der Bingle himself made a very good comic, joining me in a lavish operetta, *Only A Gypsy Knows*.

Tout ça change and all that, but sadly, Hollywood was *la même chose*, only more so. At an early press interview, I asked a reporter if he'd seen either of my first two movies, perchance. He said, "No." I breathed, "Thanks."

The Lillie hairdo, I thought, was something close to a trademark, so I was taken aback a bit when I reported for work and spent days in Make-up under a succession of wigs. At first I looked remarkably like Gloria Swanson, then like Norma Shearer's second cousin and finally like King Kong's inamorata, Fay Wray. Reluctantly, the idea was dropped, and I was allowed to wear my own head.

This time I was one guest at Fanny Brice's California home, and André Charlot was another. Fanny's marriage with Billy Rose was running into trouble and the newspapers printed stories that she wanted to talk with me before deciding what to do about it. But the decision was hers, of course.

"I wouldn't give anyone advice about a divorce," I said for publication. "What do I know about divorce? I've never had one."

Something else was printed in a trade paper, which was believable, if not true, to anyone who saw the confusion over *Dr. Rhythm*, including its title, which had begun as *On the Sentimental Side*, before what were known as "variations" were introduced by two additional writers.

"Gossipy Hollywood," said *Motion Picture Daily*, "cherishes a report that when Paramount liquidated

Emmanuel Cohen's production contract he delivered the negative of this picture in takes without the script and the studio had to fit it together like a jigsaw puzzle."

I waited to read what the critics wrote when *Dr. Rhythm* was released before I made up my mind about what Bobbie and I should do next. Those reviewers who I respected, mostly sweet as pie about me, poured vinegar on the movie. This was getting to be a habit and just a wee bit of a bore.

"The presence of a Beatrice Lillie is not to be slipped in among soothing Crosby croonings without a certain sense of monstrous contrast," said Archer Winsten in the New York *Post*. Frank Nugent in the New York *Times* was more pungent, and funnier: "Bing Crosby, Bea Lillie and Company are wooing the comic muse as though they had a $5 bet on its surrender. Maybe a $3 bet. Nothing quite so grim as their pursuit of the elfin guffaw has been seen in these parts since Martha Raye fell down the incinerator chute."

Would someone please tell me when the next train leaves for New York? Oh, and while you're at it, check the sailings for Southampton!

CHAPTER THIRTEEN

MADLY KEEN, AND
A REMEMBRANCE OR TWO

Time goes so fast sometimes that it frightens me and thee, but not to worry. Let's take hands and press on. Now we're back in London for what seems, in retrospect, to have been no more than a minute, in another revue for Charles B. Cochran. *Happy Returns* was its name, which was supposed to have opened on Friday the thirteenth of May, but I'm superstitious enough to be unhappy about such dates. To improve our luck, Cockie agreed to wait six more days. But it didn't really make any difference in the long run to fate or destiny or whatever you like to call it.

What else to remember about that show? I did a burlesque of Evelyn Laye playing Helen of Troy, and she coached me in the part. I repaid her later by trying to make scrambled eggs and toast in her kitchen and accidentally cut the cord of the toaster. I did another ride, this time on a British property moon, again tossing out garters. And my adorable costars, Bud Flanagan and Chesney Allen, looking like two overworked bookmakers, had even more trouble than I in learning the lines, which they tried to memorize in the back of the car that whisked them, during rehearsals, between twice-a-night performances at two London music halls.

Personally, I was moonlighting at only one other place, doing a forty-five-minute non-stop appearance at nine o'clock and midnight at the Café de Paris. Mr. Chamberlain and his umbrella were having problems with Hitler and his Nazis, but most of us imagined everything would be worked out somehow, and the Café de Paris seemed secure as the Rock of Gibraltar, as indeed did the "Tight Little Isle" itself. . . .

Leaving the hotel in which I was staying, I overheard a bellboy whisper, "Ain't her ladyship a *nib?*" Weren't I, though?

One year later, with the beginning of war again in Europe only a matter of weeks away now, I was back at the Café de Paris, thinking mostly about Bobbie, who was now old enough to have an MG sports car. At about this time, he was bringing it singlehanded from Switzerland to London. Not too many optimists were left who thought that peace would last much longer (but German tanks were made of plywood, and if the boys had to go, they'd be home by Christmas). Little did we know, and thank the Lord we didn't.

Where had the past year fled so quickly? Much of it back in New York, on another commuter run, this time playing in one more Noël Coward revue. What is there to remember about *Set to Music?* That Noël wanted me to be discovered in bed when the curtain rose, but I thought that was dull. Noëly asked me what else I had in mind, so I persuaded him to let me sit astride a white horse as Brünnhilde. We bor-

rowed Dobbin from the Met, where he was appearing
simultaneously. He was rushed back there every night
immediately I dismounted. *Set to Music* deserved to
run a lot longer, and could have, but 1939 was a very
queasy year for everybody, especially for us British.
As soon as my contract permitted, which was in late
spring, I made off for England to keep an eye on my
son, Mumsie and Muriel.

I can't believe that anybody felt more inadequate
than I did when the war began. It has always seemed
to me that most of us make a great deal out of very
little. The little I had couldn't mean much, I felt,
when the world was trying to destroy itself again. I
was so panic-stricken half the time that I didn't know
what to do for the best except stay home in England,
help in whatever way I could, and see whether audiences, large or small, servicemen or civilians, would
still consider me to be a funny woman.

I was sure that the Luftwaffe would never bomb
St. John's Wood, where I had taken a super-modern
house in Hamilton Terrace, because too many Germans were living around there. But I've got more
newsboys for you. The big raids had scarcely begun
before a bomb fell smack at the bottom of our garden.

At first, we had no air-raid shelter, nothing more
than a trench, hastily dug, in which my mother and I
took shelter when the sirens wailed out their warn-
ings. I used to keep my head down, but Mumsie, for
the sake of comfort, sat in an armchair, which kept
her head well-above ground level. I tried to convert
her to safer habits but nothing doing. As always, she
did it her way and never received a scratch.

It was the job of Civil Defense wardens to take a
kind of poll of every household to see what we all
might do to help defend the country if the Germans

invaded, which appeared to be their plan as soon as they'd flattened London. A little man in a steel helmet, dutifully carrying his gas mask, came around one day and as luck insisted on having it, I answered the door.

"Excuse me, madam, but what will you be willing to do if anything happens?"

He looked so solemn that I tried to make a little joke about it. "What did you have in mind?" No soap. He didn't read me. "Well, I could do some washing." He dutifully and very carefully entered me as a volunteer washerwoman in his little black book. I thought, "It's for free. . . ."

We all do strange things in wartime, to keep ourselves sane, I guess. As the air raids continued, we gave up the idea of going to a shelter. I slept beside Mumsie in the hall of the St. John's Wood house or in bed at the flat in Park Lane.

One night I was dining at the Savoy when the sirens started to moan and the anti-aircraft guns began pounding away. The party of us abandoned our table by the blacked-out windows and made off for an inside room, where we lay flat on the floor, with bombs falling not so far away. But we hadn't a thought to spare for the blitz.

"You've got my drink," I said to one companion.

"I didn't touch your silly drink," he said. "This is mine."

"It is not. Anyway, if that's yours, where's mine?" And so we whiled away another social evening while Hitler raved that he'd bring London to her knees. Strewth! If only he could have seen us, even *he* might never have dared to try.

Laugh? The English could be counted on to do that, even if they nearly died, and I love them for that. One morning after an especially bad raid, I took my daily walk and came across a brand-new scar, a great big hole with a little water trickling into the debris. Some wit had hung a cardboard sign on the barricade around the crater: "No Fishing Today." I was alone, so I stood and laughed all by myself, until one by one a crowd collected and joined in.

It wasn't always funny. Once, when that very peculiar whistling sounded in the sky, I threw myself into a ditch in time to escape any damage, but a woman across the street wasn't so lucky. I hurried over to see if I could help her as she lay on the pavement, wounded by bomb fragments.

"Are you trained in first aid?" asked another passerby, a man with an intimidating glare. I shook my head.

"Don't touch her then!" he ordered. The sense of inadequacy was very strong just then. Was I only good for entertaining? And just what good was entertaining in times like these?

I'd started attempting to cope about a month after that early September morning when the church bells, the first alert (which was a false alarm) and the radio voice of Neville Chamberlain declaring war, all sounded at about the same time. I was in a hurry to get going, and I particularly wanted to sing to the Navy for personal reasons.

My son wanted to enlist. His school days were over, and he'd no desire to enter a university in wartime. He'd finished growing upward, topping out at nearly six feet five, and was filling out very nicely, a handsome fellow, with a finely shaped head, shining eyes and a sensitive mouth. He had a glorious sense of humor, great timing and considerable charm. He promised to be quite a ladies' man, but like most of the world's best young men he wanted to be off to join the fighting, and his heart was set on the Royal Navy.

Bobbie refused to waste time in officers' training; he wanted to go to sea as soon as possible as an ordinary sailor. His problem was that he was a long way short of being twenty-one. Would I give my permission and sign the necessary paper?

I had tried never to refuse him anything; to give him whatever he desired, short of spoiling him. It was no time, I reasoned, to deny him now. So, after much pressuring, I signed him up for the Navy, and he was delighted, as he stood by to go.

I boarded a warship long before he did—I sang at Scapa Flow, the naval base off the northern tip of Scotland, facing the cold, gray North Sea, icy-cold even in October and cheerless, one imagined, even in June. I was the only woman in the little chilblained company of entertainers, and I wasn't supposed to be there, but strings had been pulled on my behalf by someone in the Admiralty, since this was *very* early on; long before it became *chic* to entertain the forces!

The males in our troupe including Tommy Trinder, a very funny man indeed, stayed aboard ship while I was billeted ashore with a family of amiable but dour Scots. They had a five-year-old son named Ian, who was the dourest of the lot. That night and almost every night the German bombers came droning over to attack Scapa Flow. So every evening, we'd say to each other, "Well, eight o'clock, sheltertime." Down we'd go into a damp, sandbagged retreat in the garden, with our wee laddie wearing my steel helmet.

After my initiation into this way of life, the night grew utterly silent. Not a sound anywhere, except the breathing of my host, hostess and their son, all sound asleep. I peeked out the door. The silence was terrifying. Then away in the distance came the scarcely heard drone of the bombers and the soft thud of ackack shells bursting above the clouds. I ducked back in plenty of time before the gentle noises turned into the thunder of bombs.

The raid lasted a comparatively short time, so I was told. Eventually the frightening silence returned, and I settled down to try to nap. "Bang! Aaang! *Wheesh! BOOM!*" I nearly collapsed from heart failure. It was the little laddie, rehearsing his new-found sound effects. How easily they learn. . . .

Back indoors before breakfast, I found that he'd taken my rouge and the one lipstick I'd brought with me from my handbag. He was having a fine time with them decorating the bedroom wall.

"Ian, give those back to me this instant," I demanded, unforgiving for his predawn *booming*.

"*Git oot' a ma hoose!*" the wee Scot replied.

Our opening concert was given on the deck of the *Ark Royal,* a vessel which, for years, "Lord Haw-Haw," the British renegade who broadcast propaganda for Hitler, sank many a time before she was, in fact, torpedoed later in the war. Among the ships riding at anchor was the French warship, the *Richelieu,* which intrigued the seamen operating the tender that took me to our floating concert hall.

"Why don't your ladyship go over and give 'em a Free-French Kiss?" said one fresh-faced sailor. I rather liked his nerve and, more than that, his *verve.*

I stood with a microphone on top of a canvas-covered something or other, singing. The audience in navy blue reef coats faced in, the guns in steely gray faced out. I'd finished my opening number and was halfway through "Love Walked In" when the sirens shrieked and two thousand sailors stood up and marched out to their duty stations. Very creditable performance on their part, I thought. I went on singing. False alarm.

The alarms got less and less false as the blitz stepped up and the bombs rained down. In London one night I was invited to dine with a good family friend, Reggie Rychek, who lived in a section of the old Richmond Palace. We'd put on our best for the occasion—very grand long dresses and baubles, dinner jackets—the lot. But we had to top off our finery with proper tin hats, provided by the butler, when the sirens howled. The first bomb landed in the middle of the fish—or was it the Spam? It was too close for comfort. Plaster fell from the ceiling, dusting our helmets with vintage dandruff. The second bomb finished the job. When I collected myself, I was in the downstairs powder room, picking bits of fruit salad from my décolletage.

There was a song I did in those days—nobody dared to stop me—that summed up the situation rather well. Muriel supplied the catchy music. Part of the lyric goes like this:

> I'm madly keen to entertain the troops.
> I don't mind if it's singly or in groups.
> I'll entertain in barracks or even a large
> marquee.
> I'll give them swing, or Wagner's *Ring*,
> Or selections from *Rose Marie*. . . .

Service hospitals were also big on my list. Whenever the chance came, I used to go around the wards where the wounded lay, exchanging a few words and a joke. If I could think of one. I'd say something along the lines of, "This is a wonderful thing for me, seeing you, and I'd rather be with you than anywhere else. We owe you so very, very much. Suppose I just move in with you?"

I'd spent an hour or so in one ward, wondering to myself why every patient had an odd look in his eyes and why he laughed so hard at the "Suppose I move in" line. As I left, I said to the medical officer at the door, "They're all so wonderful, these poor men. They've sacrificed so much for us. What ward is this?"

"Venereal diseases," he said, coolly. Blackout!

A place I stayed away from one night was my old haunt, the Café de Paris. I'd promised to attend a party there, but Bobbie was home on leave, soon to ship out in a troopship for oceans unknown. Ordinary Seaman Peel had distinguished himself in training to the point where he'd been instructed to sit entrance examinations preliminary to taking an officer's course. I used to pray every night, and not only then, that he would pass, that he would be kept ashore for at least a few more months. It all seemed so quick.

But he failed, and I couldn't understand why. Now there was a full-blown war on, with Germans and Italians and, very soon, the Japanese to fight, and it wasn't going any better for us. I took what consolation there was to be found in the thought that I shouldn't be the only woman weeping to see her son set sail for unknown ends of the earth. A strange mood of foreboding overtook me. For the first time I strongly regretted giving permission for my only son to volunteer.

Before he sailed, not too surprisingly, Bobbie wanted to be married; my permission would be needed for that, too. I knew the girl, and, because of the spirit of wartime urgency that dominated the situation, I had some doubt about this being a lasting relationship. I needed time to think about it. On the night I was supposed to be at the Café de Paris, Bobbie and I argued long and hard. It got to be so late that I was ashamed to turn up at the party. That was the night the Café de Paris, which we all thought was as safe as an air-raid shelter, received a direct hit, and forty people died in the rubble. Who says one shouldn't be a fatalist?

Bobbie shipped out from Liverpool, a bachelor. Years later, I learned that he joined an R.N. draft of some 200 men, which embarked on January 10, 1942, in the converted troopship *Letitia*, joining a large troop convoy. After dodging German reconnaissance planes, they arrived at Freetown, South Africa, two weeks later. After another fortnight, the enlarged convoy rounded the Cape and was divided in two. The *Letitia* went to Durban, arriving on February 14 for a week's stay. Bobbie was then transferred to a troopship bound for Colombo, Ceylon, and he must have arrived there by early March.

South Africa was apparently a kind of paradise to these young men who had been raised in the Depression of the nineteen-thirties and who had just endured over two dark years of danger and privation in Britain. I am thankful that my son and so many others were able to enjoy, however briefly, a few happy days of what seemed a bit like peace.

At about the time Japan entered the war, Charles Cochran had asked me to do another show for him. I eventually agreed. Bobbie had been gone for months, by then, and for much of the time I'd heard nothing from him. I had no idea where he was; letters to and from an unknown warship could say little else but "I love you—keep safe."

Cockie's new revue, *Big Top*, opened in Manchester on Easter Monday, April 6, 1942. It was a gay, ambitious effort in those hard times, when every clothes coupon for the costumes had to be eked out of a ration book. I had one number that became the hit of the show, to be counted on for laughs from any audience. If you'll allow me to, I'd like to quote from it, though you'll have to imagine the moody piano playing quite softly to begin with, so you're not really certain what's to follow.

> The night is black, and the icy rain
> Keeps beating against my window pane,
> Trickling down like my lonely tears,
> While the sound of the wind is all one hears,
> The wind that moans with a doleful wail
> While the stars and the moon and the earth
>   turn pale
> And the trees complain with a mournful
>   whine—
> But what is their anguish compared with
>   mine?*

The song, of course, is a burlesque, which I still sing, but only on festive occasions. There's a kind of recitative, developed over the years, that goes with it:

> Oh, I was just a sentimental fool, but I trusted you. I trusted you as any fool would do. Love was blind. So was I. And now when I think of you, I don't know whether to laugh or cry. Ah, well; it's all over and done with. Let's forget the

* "Wind Round My Heart." Copyright © 1942 by Chappell & Co., Ltd. Copyright renewed. Used by permission of Chappell & Co., Inc.

past. The love affair that is ended was much too sweet to last. Now I must learn to smile and be gay whatever comes along. I'll laugh with you, I'll sing with you. Yes, I'll face life with a song. . . .

So now I wear this painted face to hide an aching heart. The heart of a fool who loved you from the start. I've tried to laugh, I've tried to cry. I don't know what to do. But every time I think of you, there's gas—*wind*—round my heart for you.

I was in my room at the Midland Hotel, relaxing over a game of "I spy with my little eye" with a few cast members after the Tuesday evening performance, when Mumsie telephoned from London and read me the Admiralty telegram opened by her in my absence. It said: RESULT JAPANESE AIR RAID COLOMBO HARBOUR EARLY EASTER SUNDAY MORNING . . . REGRET TO INFORM YOU . . . SON BELIEVED MISSING. Those were the words. That's how they wrote it.

I thought, "What should I do?" I thought, "How can he be *missing?* Why don't they know? He has to be somewhere." I couldn't think what to do, but do you know what I really did? I put on some lipstick.

Then I called Cockie, and he came to see me. When I told him what I'd heard, he said, without a second thought, "We'll close the show tomorrow, for as long as you need."

"Oh no," I said. "Don't do that. That would be terrible. I'll play the show. There are so many other women, the cast, the audience. You can't do that."

Then I told him what I'd been telling myself, silently, all the time. "Anyway, it says he's believed missing. Just *missing.*"

292

I wrote out a notice that my dresser, Daisy Flanagan, pinned up on the board by the stage door: "I know how you all feel. Don't lets talk about it. Bless you. Now, let's get on with our work."

That's what we did. Nobody said a word to me. I went through two shows, our first Wednesday matinee, and the regular evening performance. Only once, in the middle of my new song, I came off and started to cry. "Get out of that, Lillie," I said. "There are worse things. Think of your son. Don't think of yourself. He isn't the only one. Neither are you." But he was; to me.

I was certain he would come back. He must be in a hospital somewhere, I said. Maybe he lost his memory. Bobbie's bound to turn up if I keep looking for him. *Missing* meant that he had to be found.

I was so bright and gay *in public*. There was no giving way that night or for the nights to come—hundreds and hundreds of them—because I existed with the knowledge that I'd find him again. That certainly lasted through all the run of *Big Top* and for months or maybe years after that.

You just go on. I did a lot of work in a lot of places, at home and overseas. I did my best to entertain the troops anywhere, at any time, at home and abroad. And I kept looking. I'd be on a stage someplace, it didn't matter where, and instead of thinking about what I was singing, the thought would be in my mind, "Supposing I look in the wings. What should I do if Bobbie's standing in the wings?" All kinds of things circled round in my head.

There were so many other women with missing sons. They wrote to me, and I often talked with them. "Don't worry," I used to say. "You may as well cheer up. You have to, you know, because—well, they're *missing*, and that doesn't mean they're killed. There still is hope. Get that into your head. Press on and hope and pray."

When I arrived back in London after the tryout road tour, I received another Admiralty telegram: PRESUMED DEAD . . . but I didn't believe it. I kept looking, and I kept hoping, heavily encouraged by family and friends. In retrospect, the constant hoping and searching seems wrong, though, at the time, it sustained me.

I was still looking as the year ended and another began and we were off to Gibraltar again. I'd been there before, trouping with John Gielgud and others. This time our ENSA tour took us clear around the Mediterranean to the Middle East, putting on shows in Alexandria, Carthage, Tripoli. Every sailor I saw, swinging along in his navy blue and whites, might have been or seen or known Bobbie. I was a terrible pest, buttonholing every one of them. This was particularly excruciating torture for me, but I had to keep up hope and explore every possibility.

From the varied impressions I remember of the trip, it was both rugged and, funnily enough, rather social. In Carthage, there was a special message waiting from King George VI. General Eisenhower gave us a party in his villa in Algiers. I remember he showed me how to fall forward stiff as a board, breaking the fall with his forearms and hands. ("Like him; likes me, I hear," says my clandestine wartime diary.) "Us" included Dorothy Dickson, who was happy to be my touring roommate much of the time, and I badly needed a roommate. There was Vivian Leigh, who was happy to attract the most attention, but I was rated the best-dressed—I'd had my uniform tailored by Hartnell, Molyneux or Beaton—there were so many who had designs on me.

Other tour members were Dickie Haydn, whom I'd brought to the United States to appear in *Set to Music;* Leslie Banks, overflowing with health, energy and good humor. Our stage manager was one of the early casualties—he had to be taken to the hospital, suffering from infected mosquito bites, in danger of losing an arm. Then, Kay Hammond, much admired by one of the generals, fell prey to the trouble that sooner or later affected most of our party. We called it the Tripoli Trots. (A great revue title!) I stayed with her when her fever mounted, trying to give her a bed bath, which proved to be a trickier job than I'd anticipated. Once, when the sirens wailed, I had to give up before I'd finished, leaving her half-way laundered. I went back to finish the job after the all clear. Nurse Doodah, that was me.

We were top-brassed at luncheons and dinners from one end of the Mediterranean to the other. Admiral Cunningham, Generals Alexander, Briggs, Doolittle, Brian Robertson, Spaatz, Vandenburg, to list some of them in alphabetical order in case of professional jealousy—you name 'em, we met 'em.

Speaking of generals, I spent one night in a bed which had been captured, along with his villa, from General von Arnim by the Desert Rats. General Montgomery came backstage to tell us we were a "very important, battle-winning factor in the war." "Very flattered," says the diary in which I scribbled every night, contrary to all the rules, which said diary-keeping was prohibited.

In Cairo, an Air Vice Marshal told me devotedly that he'd been in love with me from afar for several years and still was. ("Think he meant it" says the entry for that day; "very confusing.")

For weeks on end, we bounced around in planes of all shapes, sizes and condition. We jounced about in trucks and lorries, with and without springs, playing rain or shine, wherever there was an audience wanting to see us, in the sizzling heat of the day or the chill of the night. It was good to keep busy. We gave impromptu shows even when there wasn't a piano within a hundred miles.

Seventeen thousand men, in two sittings, saw our show in an amphitheatre, ruined by time, somewhere in the desert. Dickie Haydn was awe-struck by the experience. "How wonderful it must have been in Caesar's day!" he said. "Just think of it. And now, instead of the Romans, there's our lot of dreary, tatty actors."

We turned up one night at what had been announced as a big party given in our honor by General Patton. But when we arrived, our host, his fellow officers and every blessed soldier on the place had vanished. Only then were we told that at that very hour they were starting the invasion of Sicily. Our troupe had been part of the camouflage to keep the secret. I did my act, anyway, to an audience made up of one Arab cook and three Italian prisoners of war serving as waiters. They couldn't understand a word, but who cared? They blew kisses and *brava fantasticas*.

> When the soldiers are off duty for a moment,
> I feel they need a bit of boop-a-doops.
> It's my duty to the nation
> To stay well in circulation.
> Oh, I'm madly keen to entertain the troops!
> (*whee!*)

I used to leave behind as souvenirs the little beanie skullcaps that have been a trademark of mine longer than I remember. Besides keeping the hair neat, it turned out that they made very comfortable liners for steel helmets. They also tended to make trouble among the *fellaheen*. The Arabs were apt to fancy that I was copying their headgear and poking fun at their faith. Even with only one eye showing behind their yaskmaks, they looked sometimes as if they were shooting daggers at me.

What was the overall impression of those days; the one thing that sticks in the mind like a key word in Pelmanism? I think it's *sleeplessness*. More often than not sleep was impossible. Sometimes bedbugs would force us to move from room to room, or else try cat napping on a balcony. Occasionally, the mosquito nets would be missing, and I'd lie awake until the sun came up, listening for the whining of some lethal winged creature. Or there'd be beetles, so the light would have to stay on all night.

Most of the time, I experienced the joys of a local ailment, also lightly known as "Gyppy tummy," presumably named for Egypt, but apparently unavoidable wherever our caravan had rested and a second cousin, twice removed, of that other staple of the desert, the "TT's"! One of the symptoms was an unnatural craving for toilet tissue. Doctors along the route were forever prescribing a few days in hospital, but I was terrified of being left behind. (Oops, *sorry!*)

Once in a while, at a party, I would prescribe myself a nip of two of gin—quite nourishing with pineapple juice—but since I have a deserved reputation of being able to fly at the mere sniff of a cork, I'd usually wake with such disastrous headaches that I'd swear off the stuff for days thereafter.

Beer sat better with me, and that was medically approved, because the doctor said I had to put on some weight. For days at a time, I'd survive on nothing but tea, lemonade and the sandpaperlike toilet tissue, followed by seven pills the size of golf balls administered every four hours, ("Never felt so ill in my life," says the faithful diary; "was looked after by the French cook.")

None of the treatment had a lasting effect, so I'd be off to bed on many a night right after our final performance, hoping that the little creeping people wouldn't invade the sheets to nibble on me, trying to recite myself to sleep. *Mouse, mouse, come out of your house . . . You shall sit on a tuft of hay, I will frighten the cats away . . . Mouse, mouse, when you've gone to bed, I shall give you a large loaf of bread . . .*

But during one night of "Gyppy tummy," the mouse emerged as a rat, and he brought his family with him, one of them wearing glasses.

I missed seeing King George VI at a party that lasted until after two in the morning—that's when he sent a message back to me with one of our girls—but I did manage to stay on my feet long enough to watch him review his troops in Tripoli.

And I dragged myself along to do a show aboard H.M.S. *Indomitable.* In the audience I found Dennis Hawks, of the British Navy, who had known Bobbie as a close friend. With four other sailors, he had the job of presenting flowers to all us girls. ("Also presented me with a kiss, so the rest of the boys followed suit. Very, very sweet.")

Afterward, he and I sat talking by the hour, but he

had no more news of Bobbie than I had already heard. I saw so much of Dennis in that short time that I felt I'd known him all his life.

At the end of our tour, the medical officer said I wasn't fit enough to leave Gibraltar with the rest of the company. But I didn't really want to be left alone in an armed forces hospital, swallowing my seven golf balls every four hours. I braced myself, stuck out my chin, packed my bag and checked out with the rest of them.

Where my son was concerned, I felt that everything remained in its same state of uncertainty, and uncertainty meant hope. I'd learned nothing more from anyone I'd questioned. He was still missing, no more than that, when I thought of him.

It is not possible to name the day when that changed. Like grains of sand trickling through an hourglass, the words of the second Admiralty telegram, ever at the back of my mind, slowly grew heavier and heavier and more significant. Bobbie wasn't missing at all. He was dead. Well-meaning family and friends had encouraged my optimism far too long and now, in the face of ever-increasing evidence, I had to begin to admit the truth.

During this period I spent a lot of time with the girl known then, as now, in the secret language we shared as "B.F.," meaning "Best Friend" Mary Lynn, who was a dancer in the 1925 *Charlot's Revue* in London, and is now Mrs. Bernard Gordon.

She recalls that in England we lived mostly on rabbit stew which she cooked because meat of more distinguished cuts was scarce in wartime. My appetite was very skimpy. She says I dreamed one night that Bobbie appeared, explaining that he had suffered a severe wound of the head and should no longer be considered only as missing. I accepted that, she says, and wept for some time, but I really do not remember those details.

This is what happened to Bobbie. It took a long time to piece it together—not before Easter Week, 1954, in fact—and even longer to accept it as true. But I don't question it any more. He had just been transferred to the newly refitted escort frigate. H.M.S. *Tenedos*, serving in the Indian Ocean. Singapore had just fallen to the Japanese who saw themselves as the future rulers of Asia, and they had now reached the furthest extremity of their conquest.

On the morning of Easter Sunday, April 5, 1942, the *Tenedos* rode at anchor some fifty yards off the end of the jetty of Walter & Sons Limited in the harbor of Colombo, in Ceylon. Just before eight o'clock, the Japanese bombers flew in from the sea.

The ship was almost fully refitted, and new crew members like Bobbie were not yet quartered aboard her but were living in billets in Colombo, within a short distance of the harbor. A Japanese attack had been expected for days. So it was no surprise when the sirens began to wail. Not having been assigned duties or a battle station, my son was *not* required to race down from the hotel where he was billeted to join his shipmates, but that's what he chose to do.

Once aboard, all the "new men" were ordered forward so they would not congest those deck areas where most of the guns were concentrated. Bobbie ignored this order. He went aft to the stern guns and volunteered to carry ammunition to them from below deck.

The Royal Air Force hadn't the planes capable of

dealing with the Japanese Zero fighter-bombers, which had little difficulty in breaking through the flimsy air defenses and the ship's gunfire to attack the harbor. The *Tenedos* took a direct hit aft from a 500-pound bomb. The whole stern was torn off. The frigate went down very quickly.

Young Sir Robert Peel, sixth and last baronet. Ordinary Seaman, Royal Navy, was one of fifteen men who died at that moment. It was the consequence of his own decision. Those who were amidships and forward, where the "new men" were supposed to be, went unharmed and had no trouble reaching the bomb-torn jetty.

The lost were reported as missing until the wreckage of H.M.S. *Tenedos* could be raised from the shallow harbor bed and the difficult task of identification accomplished. Only then were the fifteen dead buried in a single ceremony with full military honors.

For years after I learned to live with the truth of the second telegram which the Admiralty sent to me, it was hard to celebrate Easter Sunday as a day of gladness. It will never be easy for me, but I have tried hard over the years and have at last achieved a sort of resigned peace of mind. I am helped by the belief that "those whom God cherishes are called at Eastertime;" a time to encourage and bolster even those of limited faith.

I have also found solace, apart from my work, in an expanding relationship with young people, from newborn babies to those of any age. I also like little old ladies and little old men, as well as those in between. Liking *people* helps.

I discovered someone who knew my son at the end —or, more truthfully, someone discovered me. During Easter week, in early April of 1954, a cockney waiter at the Carriage Court of the Palace Hotel in San Francisco got to talking one lunchtime with John Philip, who had become my personal representative and remains so today after twenty-three years.

He introduced himself to John as Albert Taylor, an ex-chief petty officer of the Royal Navy who said, quite for no reason, while taking the luncheon order, that he had served for a spell in the Indian Ocean during the war. It turned out that he had been one of Bobbie's instructors at Portsmouth, had been a member of the crew of the *Tenedos* and had been in charge of the funeral details of his shipmates in Colombo.

In my dressing room at the Curran Theatre, after a Saturday matinee, Albert Taylor said, "I've been meaning to look you up for years, Milady, but I never had the heart."

I asked him, once I had heard most of the details of the story, how Bobbie had failed to pass his exams to be an officer. It had been a surprise to me, I said, when I knew him to be so bright and quick, once he was interested in learning.

"He dipped 'em, ma'am, which in the Navy means he didn't want to pass. Your son could have been an officer if he'd tried, but he didn't want to. He told me he couldn't spare the time. He wanted action. He had to go to sea."

I cried a little bit, then I kissed Albert Taylor. The following morning would be Easter Sunday; twelve years to the day, since the senseless infamy. That was when I made up my mind to go to Colombo to say my own *au revoir*.

I set out for Ceylon with John Philip when *An Eve-*

ning With closed after a yearlong tour of the United States. We flew there by way of Tokyo, where I spent a little time visiting service hospitals, trying to cheer up the wounded of yet another war, this one in Korea. Then on to Hongkong and Bangkok, and I remember all too clearly that on the way we peered down at what looked for all the world like a brown-and-green relief map, which John said was a little country called Vietnam.

Each passenger on arrival at Katunayake Airport is handed a cup of Ceylon tea, with the compliments of the National Tea Board. We drove for an hour or so from there through a landscape of hibiscus, orchids and temple trees with their scented, creamy flowers. The little Sinhalese smiled as we passed, and carrion crows flapped up and away from the car.

Later, from my room in the Galle Face Hotel, I could stand and watch the warm, equatorial sea and the girls in soft-toned saris walking on the seafront promenade. A fan circled quietly in the ceiling during the steamy heat of the day, but at night a blanket was a comfort.

I didn't want any fuss made, so I'd told no one that I was coming. This was to be a very personal and private journey. But the news had spread in advance, and the local newspapers carried a story or two before I'd gone on my way again.

The first place to see was the Kanetta cemetery. I insisted on being taken there straightaway, before going to the Galle Face. Its style is British Victorian, a quiet, peaceful place of massive shade trees and gravel walks that crunch under your shoes. The graves of British servicemen lay in a far corner near the Cro-Flite golf course. When I got there, little bare-footed men in sarongs had removed the wooden crosses which had until then served as markers and the next morning, helping John Philip in the early daylight, they propped up, temporarily, the marble memorials that had been sent to replace the wood. The scent of the flowers I brought that afternoon was strong in the heat. I stood there, tears streaming down my face, clutching for any straw.

My only son was not alone. He shared the earth with another seaman, next to the mass grave of the others who had died when their ship exploded.

A futile waste, if ever there was.

John and I stayed in Colombo for a week, getting to know "Jeeves," the room servant who slept in the corridor outside my door; nibbling cautiously on the spicy food; gratefully sipping the cooling juices of limes and pineapple; avoiding the drinking water for fear of whatever they called "Gyppy tummy" in these parts; picking my way through the pensioned-off double-decker buses from London that plied the streets next to rickshaws and bullock carts; nosing around the pettals, where customers haggled with storekeepers over Kandyan silver and inlaid brass, Galle tortoise shell and carved elephants.

Two surprises came my way. An official of the venerable firm of Walker & Sons, Ltd., ships' outfitters, happened to be staying at the hotel *for only a few days,* awaiting his ship home to Britain after completing thirty years of duty in Ceylon. He presented me with a souvenir of H.M.S. *Tenedos,* the ship's crest, which had been blown against a wall of their office building by the force of the exploding bombs.

And when I went shopping for a remembrance of my own, Mrs. Nestle, the owner of the noted jewelry shop with swinging doors, looked closely and asked me my name. I told her, and she straightaway hurried to the back of the store, bringing back a crumpled copy of *The Tatler*, which had chronicled my career over dozens of issues and at least as many years. This particular issue had carried five Cecil Beaton photographs of your ladyship.

"Your son came shopping here, too," she said. "He saw this actual copy of the magazine with your pictures in it. He looked very surprised, and he said, 'That's my mother.' He asked me for one of the pictures, and I cut it out for him. Look, you can see where it was." She gave me the magazine to keep.

So that's where Bobbie had found the emerald, ruby and diamond brooch he had sent me via a naval officer friend. As a memento, I bought a diamond-and-sapphire ring. Bobbie's emerald, you see, was gone. It was stolen in a burglary at the Park Lane flat during the war, and the police were never able to recover it.

CHAPTER FOURTEEN

BLACKOUTS TO BROADWAY

Imagine, if you will be so kind, a theatre full of
dressed-up patrons of the arts, all eager to be seen
and to see, including some who even were interested
in seeing what was about to happen on stage. In the
orchestra seats, at twenty-four dollars a head, dinner
jackets and aftershave lotion alternate with white furs
—very stylish in December 1944—and an aura of
Chanel, Guerlain, Schiaparelli, Martini & Rossi.

Our genial producer and host is Billy Rose, married
now for some four years to Eleanor Holm, and no
expense has been spared to mark this occasion tonight. A face-lift has been performed on the Ziegfeld
Theatre. Paintings by Salvador Dali adorn the freshly
painted walls of the newly carpeted lounges, where
free champagne flows like—well, like New York State
champagne.

There in the front row sits Hope Hampton—hi,
Hope!—and the Robert Sherwoods and why, if it
isn't the William Rhinelander Stewarts. Look, Pat
and Alfred Hitchcock just behind Moss Hart. Isn't

that Oscar Hammerstein and Ben Hecht and George Kaufman? And there's who else but Elsa; she's promised to have a little supper served later for a few hundred people at the Waldorf.

Maestro, if you please. Let's hear the overture of the brand-new Cole Porter score. House lights dim, curtain begins to rise.

In a few days more it's going to be Christmas. The war is still on, buzz bombs and rockets are raining on London, but at the moment, to me, both London and the war exist, if at all, on some other planet. I hadn't appeared on Broadway for five years. Various invitations had come along to the Park Lane flat during that interval, but I thought my place was home in England, where the war was, so I'd refused them, one and all.

I'm loyal always, particularly in wartime, but *why* can't I live where I please in peacetime? I always return to England in wartime.

Now here we were in New York for *Seven Lively Arts*, and I must allow that the audience forgot itself when I made my entrance. Five minutes is a lifetime when you stand on stage, listening to such cheering that it was almost impossible to continue with the show. I'd been almost a war away from Broadway. And now I know that people cared and had missed me. Gratifying, to say the least. I shall never forget it.

I wouldn't have been there at all if plans had worked out for another play. Robert Morley had written a comedy entitled *Staff Dance*, in which we were to appear together. I was in a North London nursing home recovering from a large, economy-size case of influenza when rehearsals began, while Robert was in the London Clinic suffering from jaundice. Mary Lynn Gordon, who was—and still is—a very fine stage and "house" manager, would collect me from my bed at nine-thirty in the mornings, to arrive an hour later at the basement of the Clinic, gaily known as "The Morgue," where rehearsing was performed in an odor of disinfectant and ether.

Our director was Jack Minster, fondly nicknamed "Laughing Jack," because he was permanently attired in a look of haunting gloom and a large overcoat. It was he who later re-directed *Auntie Mame* in London. "I don't think that's funny," was his customary comment on anything I or Robert, with pink eyes set in a bright-yellow flabby face, ventured to attempt.

Since Robert was the playwright as well as costar, my chances of getting equal time with him could be regarded as slim. He was asked, in the course of these days, why he always gave himself the longest speeches.

"Because I can't stand to hear another actor talking on the stage," he replied.

I had one scene where perverse little Bea would work in a few laughs and a line or two. As Frieda, the wife, I received a telephone call from my Italian lover, while Sam, the husband, remained in the room. This entailed my hiding behind a sofa, carrying on in organ-grinder's Italian. One night, it seemed appropriate to disappear up the chimney with the telephone.

"Who was that?" Sam asks suspiciously at the end of the call.

"Selfridge's," Frieda replies.

"Where are you going, Frieda?" is his final line in the scene.

The response is the act's curtain line and something I modestly take credit for, though, as you know, I can get lost on the way to powder my nose. "Really, Sam! Is *nothing* sacred?"

What with imbibing cold cures and other medications, I'd been remiss again in learning my lines. We were to open a pre-London tour in Oxford; on the train from St. Pancras Station to that university town, an attack of cold feet turned into what seemed to me to be genuine paralysis of the jaw. Mary Gordon was with me.

Through clenched teeth that I couldn't pry apart, I told her, "I can't go on. Impossible."

"It will be all right, darling. You're going to be fine, you see."

I don't know whether influential nervous lockjaw is medically recognized, but that was my personal diagnosis. In the dressing room, I couldn't get the hinges working enough to be able to say, *Be calm.* This would be a night, I thought, when Robert could be perfectly content at last that in our scenes together, he'd be the only actor talking.

Yet minutes later, with the curtain up and your memoirist on, there was a spontaneous cure. People said I was really rather super. But Robert's play didn't reach the West End of London. After carefully counting the laughs and conferring with the producer, that fox of good fellows, Binky Beaumont, darling Bob, our non-equal opportunity author, decided to fold his tent in Brighton.

By this time, I had put in quite a bit more of service, madly entertaining the troops, either quick Sunday trips from London bumping to and fro in a camouflaged khaki truck or longer jaunts at home or abroad. In retrospect, I seem to have been mostly chilled to the bones, because, as usual, we had some bone-chilling weather; or lonesome, because I'd be the only woman on the set, and not much of a drinker at that.

I remember one isolated place where the commanding officer was forever saying, "Come on have a drink," and I forever answered, "But I don't drink." Eventually, to terminate this boring dialogue, I said one evening, "If a raid starts in the next ten minutes, if the bombers come, I'll have a drink with you."

Sure enough, within five minutes, the sirens performed their symphony. Within ten seconds, a noggin of brandy had been poured for me. I couldn't go back on my word, so down went on neat brandy. Another? Why not? To the tune of perhaps four.

"How wonderful I feel!" sez I to myself that night as I climbed into my fur coat to go to bed.

"How *stupid* you are!" I sez when reveille and what was clearly my death knell sounded at five-thirty the following morning. The crack of doom. . . .

I had no fear that I was about to die. I thought, "Well, here I am, dead. But where are the flowers? Nobody sent flowers. Ah, well, that's show business."

In the Second World War I learned that men drink heavily, especially in wartime, so as to awake in so numb and bloody-minded a state that they can, by rote, face up more easily to the terrible things they have to both do and endure. Me? I'd much rather face tomorrow soberly and with a clear head—and heart. . . .

Long after reveille, I was still assembling myself in the sanctuary of my fur coat, certain that flesh would melt and the oceans boil before I could face this day. But I got up, so help me, and climbed into a truck for a little drive through the snow. Me (do I mean "I"?) who usually sleep (is it "sleeps"?) until the crack of noon.

In places like this, there was usually no mess hall or canteen large enough to accommodate everybody at one time. The act, therefore, had to be repeated in one

Nissen hut after another, playing to audiences of two or three dozen men at a time, sometimes as many as ten shows between breakfast and bedtime.

On this gray morning, we got to quite a large hut at last. (Oh, God, I shall never drink again.) I peeked out front and saw two enormous cannon pointing in one direction and a cluster of German captives peering in the opposite direction, which is to say at the door and me.

Nevertheless, the show must go on, as somebody has said (was it Lee Shubert?). I was warming up in song and dance when the sobbing of the sirens sounded in the sky. Off went *ours*, and there outside the door, stood what had been *theirs*.

Nobody had mentioned to me where to find the air-raid shelter. So I was alone, with a hangover, no piano and a score or so of German prisoners under guard. "Shall I sing over their heads, because they're Germans, or sing to them because they're my audience?" I asked myself, without missing a note. It was some song about how everything was going to turn out fine, ho, ho, ho!

"Look at them," I said to myself. "Germans. The enemy. The foe. Men who want either to kill us or make us Hitler's slaves. But they are *people*, you know. Just because there's a war—"

I went on singing, and believe me, we enjoyed each other's company. They seemed human too! I couldn't help thinking: "How odd of God to make Nazis."

Life goes on, as somebody else has said (was it J. J. Shubert?), and I continued to spend most of my days in my eighth-floor flat at No. 55 Park Lane, with its view of rooftops and pigeons on the window sills. We held open house on quite a few evenings, among those present being Prince Philip; the Marquis of

Milford Haven; Quentin Reynolds; my New York neighbor, Charley MacArthur; Eddie *Duryea* Dowling, now a United States Army major, who had followed "Doc" McGonigle in the role of my business advisor; Bob Goldstein, head of Twentieth Century-Fox in London then; Clark Gable, regarded by Bob Goldstein as a suitable husband for the widowed Lady Peel, et cetera.

I had a great deal of sympathy for Clark Gable, but no time for anything like *that*. Carole Lombard, Mrs. Gable, as we all know, had been killed in a plane crash. His argument, presented rather forcefully in the course of one evening went along the lines of, "You lost your son, I lost my wife. Why don't we get married?" I didn't see the logic, to be perfectly frank.

He fell asleep on the settee in the living room. I took myself off to bed, ignoring all else. I didn't think that we should get intense about it, and by the time the night had gone, so had he. I did remember hearing him battering away at my locked bedroom door. Such a lovely man, too. My fault. Pity!

Flying bombs, which we called "doodlebugs" with a slightly panicky sense of humor, did little to add gaiety to life. As a matter of fact, they got to be somewhat repulsive, and I jumped at an invitation to spend two weeks of peace and quiet at an old farmhouse in Surrey with Mary Gordon. The house itself was over four hundred years old, but the anti-aircraft guns we found installed in a field at the bottom of our garden were considerably newer, having been put there to shoot down the doodlebugs before they reached London on their flights through the clouds.

One night, we counted twenty-seven of these buzz bombs chugging along overhead in a space of forty minutes. On such a night as this, we all snuggled down in some shallow trenches which had been hastily dug on the edge of the field. One other inhabitant of the field was a Jersey calf with inch-long eyelashes, which I named "Garbo." I had a great deal of sympathy for her, too. I *love* cows!

Our little band of seekers after peace and quiet consisted of Mary; the housekeeper; the housekeeper's housekeeper, who was a refugee from the perils of the big city; nine dogs; six cats and me. Mary and I rolled ourselves up in horse blankets and assorted animals to keep out the cold, then slept fitfully at the bottom of the trench. The two housekeepers had never heard of such a thing, so they enthroned themselves in deck chairs and slept higher and drier, heads up, with a good, uninterrupted view of the terrain around them. Just like Mother.

As a haven from the storm, it was slightly unsuitable, but I felt safe enough. Somewhere along the way, I had picked up a steel helmet, size eight, which sat so comfortably on my size six-and-a-quarter head that whenever I turned my neck, my hat stayed where it was, facing forward in best music hall tradition. To soothe my own jangled nerves, and maybe raise a laugh from the company, I used to recite a few lines from "She's resting in the gutter, and she loves it. . . ." *We* liked it!

In trying to cope and get about in London, I was in permanent, desperate need of taxis. Who wasn't? I got to know two ever-faithful cabbies, Bert Jenkins and his brother Arthur. Bert drove me more often, but between the two of them, I was never stuck for transport. They drove me while sirens shrieked and bombs fell. They brightened the blacked-out hours and renewed my hope when almost nobody else could. We celebrated the war's end at a champagne dinner I gave at the Savoy, and we've been buddies ever since then.

But that's getting along too far. Before the war ended, but when the end appeared to be in sight at last, I felt that I'd like to go to New York to do *Seven Lively Arts* and get another look at a city where the lights still glowed after dark in the "brown-out," and death and doodlebugs seemed far away. But I wasn't entirely sorry when we closed for the last time, and I could slip off back to London, and, this time, into my new pale beige Bergdorf USO uniform, so much admired, for some more troop shows, this time for American Combat Forces only. In early July 1945, in Paris, I sat down and started to write thus to B.F.

Darling Mary,

Well, as you know, I left 55 Park Lane at twelve-fifteen, went to St. James's Palace, signed more papers, weighed everything again, left there at two o'clock, took off at three-thirty from Croydon Airport, arrived here around five o'clock and off to the Ritz Hotel. Since then, have done bugger all.

Wandered into tea here at the Ritz, where there were lots of women in peculiar hats, acting as if nothing had happened. Marlene Dietrich joined us in a skullcap, which she said she designed, exactly the same as the ones I used to throw away to the natives.

All the Hollywood ten-star generals are here, including Harry Cohn, who gave me a lipstick and a bobby pin and asked for my body in return. I retorted, "What, that old thing?" and people could be heard for miles, yelling, "She's just as funny off as on!"

Darryl Zanuck arrived in the dining room with six polo ponies, and everyone had a good meal for once. Had a long visit with Bob Hope. I adore him and wish we could work together.

We are off to Germany in the morning. Should have gone today, but there were Weather Conditions.

Went for a long walk with Reggie Gardiner to Nôtre Dame cathedral. Got caught up in a funeral. Bought a scarf. You can't buy *anything* here unless you pay five hundred pounds. Paris is very sad. The Americans have really taken over, if you know what I mean—and I *know* you do!

Went mad in the PX, but have already given away nearly all the soap and cigarettes.

General Patton in the room below me has just used the four-letter word twice. Can't sleep, not because of the four-letter word but on account of the loud speaking. Not hot-water bottle, but I've got my soap to keep me warm.

Eight A.M. next day. Have just wangled a pitcher of hot water and a cup of coffee. Paid two pieces of soap and two packs of cigarettes. I will do without it tomorrow. But as you know, I hate having to get up for breakfast. . . .

This was a letter that never really ended. It turned into a kind of diary, scribbled on odd bits of paper and the backs of telegram forms and envelopes. (You should not be surprised by this time to learn that though I can be trusted to keep a secret, I can't be depended on to keep a diary.)

I scribbled away when we left Paris and moved into Germany, a blighted country then, doing shows for Allied servicemen by day and night. ("To Berchtesgaden, where the weather was clear enough to see the ruins of this monumental idiocy; we start back late, with fears of peanut-butter sandwiches!") We went from Stuttgart to Heidelberg; Munich to death-stenched Augsburg. And too many other battle areas in Germany.

Six weeks later, we were back in Paris, just in time for V-J Day, trying to remember what the world had been like for me and everyone else six years previously. An impossible task, best not attempted.

There were people who thought that I'd changed, but I didn't think it showed too much. I was a little older and, perhaps, a little wiser, and certainly much thinner. I had rather more trouble falling asleep at nights. I resented *now* more than ever being known as "the funniest woman alive," but making people laugh remained the most important thing I could do. And let's have none of that "Laugh, clown, laugh" routine, if you don't mind. I'd never buy it.

For years, Dame Fortune, wreathed in smiles, had waved her wand over me. I had such a run of good shows and good luck, in one way or another, that brooding was out of the question.

There was Lillie "as superb, as bright and vital as ever, as much loved in Manchester as in Chicago" (huh?), clowning in *Better Late* on the top right-hand side of the Atlantic. One critic's comment struck me as sharp: he decided that whatever ability I possess "is based on a talent for incurring the hostility of furniture."

There was Lillie flying over to the left-hand side of the ocean for *Inside U.S.A.*, a revue bearing an extremely faint resemblance to John Gunther's best-seller. With Jack Haley costarring, we opened in the Century Theatre, New York, then ran there so long and toured so long afterward that it got to be a way of life. I was "irreplaceable," according to one reviewer, which is always good to hear, "immortal," according to another, which left room for doubt, but then flattery will get you anything, dear.

In Chicago, where they loved me at least as much as in Manchester, things happened, as usual. After thirteen years' absence, I was making a temporary home in a suite in the Ambassador East. Ernie Byfield had glamorized the main restaurant, the Pump Room, by serving most entrees, including an occasional waiter's thumb, *aux flambeaux.*

Some *flambeaux* broke out from a faulty light cord and plug in my sitting room one night. When I opened my bedroom door to investigate, I breathed in enough smoke to put me in hospital for a few days, after I'd managed to grab a telephone and choke out, "Fire!" sounding uncannily like Marlene Dietrich. Luckily, when I fainted it was on the inner hall floor, just by the front door. Enough fresh air came in under the door to keep body and soul together until the night porter arrived to rescue me. Bless him!

When I was released and restored to a suite on another floor, I had a small bone to pick with Ernie Byfield. "Don't you think you're carrying your flaming-sword policy too far?"

Inside U.S.A. was where I made the one notable scientific discovery of my life, having to do with the centrifugal effect of a rope of swinging pearls. (The patent has been applied for.) Given a long enough strand and enough rotation of the head, the pearls can usually be counted on to swing themselves clear down past your what-not. The effect is much more spectacular than hoola-hooping, and I find the exercise invigorating, though there's always a certain risk, when getting started, of loosening your front teeth. Sounds intriguing, doesn't it? *Do* come.

I haven't tried it with what I used to refer to as the "Peel poils" in the days when I carried them loose in my handbag. They are too massive for the job and deserve more considerate treatment, having led a distinctly checkered career both before and after they came into my possession. Mumsie was one of the ladies who had charge of them from time to time. They now live in retirement in a safe-deposit box, in the custody of the delightful and venerable Bank of New York.

On a rare occasion when I was giving them an outing at a rather fancy party, a rather bitchy witch doubted my word that they were the genuine article. "Well, I simply don't believe you," she said sniffily. "Just let me have them for a minute. I'll tell you."

"My dear," I said, "you, above all, should know that you can't test real pearls with *false* teeth."

One of my best pupils in pearl-swinging was Princess Margaret, who at one informal party soon had my long string of them whirling about her ears like helicopter rotors. This I found gratifying, me who's likely to be fidgety in the presence of royalty. At our first introduction, I was wandering alone around the Café de Paris, trying to find my escort, who was one of the Peel cousins. As I joined him, he'd just lit a nervous cigarette when I saw Princess Margaret coming up to me.

Now protocol says that you don't smoke in the presence of the Royal Family until permission has been given. So, anxious to do the right thing, I popped his lighted cigarette down my cleavage and hoped neither one of us would notice it smoldering. She was very sweet, and I suffered nothing more than a scorched brassiere and a slightly blistered bazoom. Nothing, really.

My wardrobe seemed to be rather steadily jeopardized when I mixed in regal circles. At one early, glittering dinner party at Buckingham Palace, the trembling hand of a nervous waiter spilled a spoonful of decidedly hot soup down my neck.

How could I manage to ease his mind and turn his embarrassed apologies into a smile, except to put on a pretended frown and say, without thinking: "Never darken my Dior again!"

I don't want to give anyone the impression that I popped in and out of the Palace as casually as the milkman makes his deliveries to the servants' entrance. An invitation has always been something to make me want to jump to my feet and salute. Truly. I insist on being counted among the most loyal subjects of Her Majesty Queen Elizabeth, whom I first met when she was a girl, sitting on the floor next to Princess Margaret, while I rattled off a number or two.

I was doing two shows a night in a London cabaret at the time. On an idle afternoon at home with Dorothy Dickson, who was staying with me, the telephone rang. It was she who answered, then said quite casually, "Buckingham Palace wants to speak to you."

Knowing her wry sense of fun, I merely said, "Oh, belt up!"

"No, really."

"Oh, come on, now."

"Will you *please* talk to them?"

She handed me the telephone. I said briskly, "Hello, dere."

The man's voice was terribly respectable, "Lady Peel? This is Sir Piers Legh. I can't talk to you on the 'phone. Can you possibly come to the Palace to see me at four o'clock, shall we say?"

I felt instant anxiety overtaking me. What terrible crime had I committed? Was this the way they had for deporting people? And if I were to be deported, where could I go? After all, I *was* a loyal subject, and, for decades, I'd paid right royal taxes in Britain and America for the privilege. What was wrong?

In his rather bare office, Sir Piers was reassuring. Would I be kind enough to entertain at a party *they* were giving for Queen Juliana of Holland? *They* all wanted only me. I said I would love to. Charmed. Truly.

On the appointed night, I left the Café de Paris after my early show, hoping to be able to leave the royal party in time to return for my second show. Arriving at the Palace, I was shown first to a room where I was relieved of my fur coat, then to a long hall outside the ballroom, where an orchestra was playing "Mad Dogs and Englishmen." Wee Bea was as jittery as a Toronto belle on her first sleigh ride, alone on a settee, clasping props—long string of pearls, one fan (ostrich feather), another fan (ivory).

Suddenly, the ballroom doors opened, and out popped the King. He welcomed me with a kiss, sat beside me, lit a cigarette after offering me one and momentarily banished my jitters by asking, "Bea, whatever became of Billy Leonard?"

Billy, I should explain, was a British comedian of no small talent who appeared with me in *Oh, Joy!*—and *that* was in 1919. "I haven't a clue," I said, instantly as relaxed as a jellyfish.

My host and I had a chuckle over that one and went on to chat about the Charlot shows, all of which he'd apparently seen as the young Duke of York.

"You're my special surprise for tonight, Bea," said the King. "Shall we go in?" He handed my little collection of props to a footman and let me into the ballroom and into our first dance together.

The two young princesses and guests of their own age all sat plunk on the floor when the time came for your obedient servant to scintillate. So far as my dazzled eyes could see, the King and Queen were entertaining more royalty than may be found in a canasta deck.

The invitations said, and I quote, "A *small* dinner party." Right you are. *Very small.* About two hundred and fifty people. At the sight of them, I wondered once again whether some way might be found of backing out of this particular performance. Then I spotted Noël, standing imperially at the back of the group, doing his best to break me up.

"All right," I told myself. "That's torn it. You just *have* to get on with it now."

I did two or three numbers and then, by popular request, one or two more. The wand was on. Now this was *fun.* Someone asked for "The Lesson with the Fan," which begins very sweetly, "Do you want to learn the lesson with the fan?"

"No, we don't," Noël interrupted, just barely over his breath. I swallowed a taste of blind rage and continued.

Then Queen Elizabeth, now the Queen Mother, asked for "Michigan."

I was running rapidly through a good chunk of the repertoire and fancied it might be time to depart, not wishing to outstay my welcome. But no. King George wanted to hear one of his old favorites, "Rotten to the Core."

The essential prop was a brandy glass. Could I have

321

one, please? The whispers ran around the room. A glass. She needs a glass. Get her a glass. Finally, a footman obliged, and I was on again in the final number.

> ... I said, "Maud, you're full of maggots, and you know it.
> Your soul's a bed where worms queue up to breed.
> You don't know what life's for, Maud,
> You're rotten to the core, Maud."
> And Maud agreed.

Afterward, I said I really had to be off, with permission, to do my cabaret show. The Queen said, "Please come and eat first." I said I really couldn't, Ma'am, because you see— The Queen said, "That's too bad. We really must do it another time." I dropped a swift curtsy and a "Charmed, Ma'am." Then the King showed me out to the anteroom and foyer, carrying all my props and kissing me out the door to a Royal limousine which whisked me to my cabaret.

It had got to be so late that I sang for the second show that night without any supper, walking straight out on to the floor of the Café de Paris, while Sidney Simone's orchestra played my introduction.

It has been said that royalty needs comfortable shoes and a good memory. Certainly King George, no matter who the royal shoemaker was, had a memory that on one occasion put mine to shame. We spoke for the first time after the war at a garden party at Buckingham Palace, where scarcely anyone talks to anybody beyond a brief how-do-you-do and *no-*

body speaks to The Royals unless spoken to first.

He came through the crowd beside his equerry, with everyone stepping briskly aside to make way for im. "Bea," he said. "I haven't seen you since you were in Tunis."

"Thats right, Sir," I said, bobbing a curtsy.

"Did you get a touch of Gyppy tummy over there? I know I had it."

"So did I, Sir," I said, wincing as I remembered.

"Tell me, what did you take for it?"

I did my best to explain about the seven pills every four hours. The conversation lasted for four or five minutes, devoted to strictly medical matters. When he had smiled good-by and moved on to chat with another guest, some friends in the throng swarmed around, itching to know what had kept him so long with me. "What did he say? What did you talk about?"

I gave them a truthful answer. *"Diarrhea."* They didn't believe me. I was being as funny on as off again, so they thought. Oh, la-de-bloody-dah!

But let's hurry back to the U.S. and the post-Broadway run in Boston of *Inside U.S.A.* In January 1949, when something else happened that produced a lot of ripples on the pool of my life—so many, in fact, over so many years that it hasn't stopped rippling yet.

One of the performers in the show was a tall, husky, good-looking former United States Marine, a lieutenant who'd been wounded in battle on Okinawa on a day in 1945 which may have been significant—May 29, my birthday. Oh, I'm not all that superstitious, but . . . all these coincidences *do* impress; profoundly.

John Philip Huck, who thereafter has used the first two of his names for theatrical and profound purposes, had joined the company as understudy to the singing lead, while he had solo spots of his own. Being strong in the arm, he was assigned to keep an eye on me when I was immobilized in my mermaid costume and keep trouble away in general. He became increasingly useful throughout the two national tours of the show and was still a loyal companion some two years later when I started out on what was originally intended to be a three-week tour of the straw-hat circuit, which stretched into nine weeks of the summer and finally kept me busy for the better part of four years.

We'd run into trouble in finding a title for the show before we opened on a July night as hot as Grandma's oven on baking day at the Falmouth Playhouse in Coonamessett (love that name!) on Cape Cod. Perspiration sluiced every dab of make-up from our faces and sent it dripping off our chins.

The managing director of the playhouse was Richard Aldrich—Gertie now was Mrs. A. He kept after me for a title, until at last in desperation I said, "Oh, just call it *An Evening With Beatrice Lillie,* and let it go at that." Hardly a Charlot title, but my own, forsooth.

Mr. A. asked, "But what will you call the matinees?"

I said, "*An Evening With Beatrice Lillie,*" and that was that.

We enjoyed what in the trade is known as "an opening night triumph." Every house record was smashed to smithereens. The Joshua Logans were there. So was our old friend Jules Glaenzer of Cartier's, whom you met in 1924. Gertie sat in the audience with Helen Hayes, who had flown up from New York to see us. "Call it what you like," said Helen, too late for the christening, "but it's Bea's triumph and it must go to Broadway."

Our cast of thousands numbered exactly five. Besides Lady *Evening* with herself, there was Reggie Gardiner, more brilliant than ever in your humble's opinion; Xenia Bank; Florence Bray; and John Philip, impassioned in a gold-lined opera cloak, singing "Come Into the Garden, Maud." He also helped out Edward Duryea Dowling, as assistant producer, assistant director and general factotum.

As the audiences raved and gold continued to fill the till wherever we traveled, it became obvious that we must head for Broadway. By the time we opened at the Booth Theatre on October 2, 1952, I was working for vitually nothing, since I had hired myself for 80 per cent of the gross and took only nominal weekly expense money. Having spent all my salary on new dresses, I saw no need to replace my one mink coat, though it was thrown down on the stage and crawled over on hands and knees at each performance.

Lest any reader should feel an impulse to take up a collection at this point, I should explain that, having put up most of all the backing necessary for a Broadway production, I really did own most of the show. Every dollar and later every shilling coming into the box office provided a pretty penny for the bank account—and, as always, for the tax collectors in New York and London. It compensated rather comfortably for what had happened at Drayton Manor, where Britain's Labour Government had taken all my coal under their nationalization scheme—"expropriated for a ridiculously small sum," in the words of my solicitor, whose political sentiments you *may* be able to detect.

We had another very plushy first night, with Ethel

Barrymore, Cole Porter, Richard Rodgers and Lord knows who else in the audience, for which I apparently could do no wrong. The critics lubricated their typewriters. Brooks Atkinson of the New York *Times* led off with a "funniest woman in the world" bit. Louis Kronenberger in *Time* talked about "elegance punctuated with epilepsy." Walter Winchell called it a "Lillie-palooza" and detected "a dimple in every blush"; Walter Kerr, who wrote for the *Herald Tribune* then, went for "exercises in the magnificently irrelevant." *Collier's* (remember that one?) came up with "irrepressible mistress of caricature," and I didn't even know any gentleman of that name. *Look* put in a new ribbon and claimed that "drunken fairies tapped Bea Lillie on the head with a golden hammer"—as if I ever went to *that* kind of party.

The reason we scored so highly, I'd say, was that we all had a lot of fun, and I'd have hated myself if we hadn't enjoyed ourselves on stage. I did "Rotten to the Core," "Fairies at the Bottom of Our Garden," and even "Wind Round My Heart" again, now that enough time had gone by. There was a special version of "Please Be Kind" ("This is my fifth affair, so please be quick"), lots of other numbers, and a wonderful sketch with Reggie playing a bumbling Englishman explaining the Facts of Life to his son; me in pants again—short pants this time.

"It's time I told you about certain things. . . . You mustn't think of it as a vice. In a way, it's rather nice."

"I see . . . I see . . . Does *Mother* know?"

One face, fond and familiar, was missing from the Broadway opening night. We were still on our way to Broadway, playing at the little summer theatre in Olney, Maryland, not far from Washington, D.C., when, early one Saturday morning, the theatre manager telephoned John Philip and told him that one of my oldest and dearest friends had died of cancer in New York the day before. Would John be good enough to break the news to me after breakfast?

He refused. I could not be told, he said, until after the final performance of the week, that evening. Now this was a rather special day. Word had already filtered through to us backstage that in our matinee audience we'd have President Truman, his wife, Bess, and daughter, Margaret.

John had a problem. He didn't want my performances that afternoon and evening to be spoiled by tragic news, yet how could he keep the news from me for a whole day? On top of it all, there was the presidential visit to contend with. He decided to call together everybody but me and tell them the facts. He had a property man cut the cord of my dressingroom radio. All newspapers were barred from the theatre. A gang of stagehands was instructed to cordon me off without my knowing it, to keep strangers away.

We all gave our best during the first act that afternoon, hoping to please Mr. President and his family. Then at the intermission, Eddie was told that President Truman, Bess and Margaret wanted to come to my dressing room and pay their respects. John and Eddie felt sure someone would mention the death to me, so they hadn't any time to lose.

Outside my dressing-room door, the request was made. "Mr. President, I must ask you a favor. . . . We've kept the news from Miss Lillie all day so that it would be easier for her to get through two shows today. Would you please not mention it?"

Mr. Truman shook hands. "Of course," he said. "I understand."

327

Which is how our *Evening* that afternoon and night went so smoothly, until Eddie, John and Reggie, after the second show, told me of the death of Gertrude Lawrence.

Those *Evenings* added up to thousands. After nearly a year at the Booth, I had a two-month summer break in London, returning to open in Boston and tour and tour *and* tour. Then we took the whole kit and caboodle to England with three new numbers that Noël had written. We found a new leading man in Leslie Bricusse, who I am happy to report has since resorted to writing and composing and doing extremely well.

He made his first professional appearance in *Evening* at the age of twenty-three. He was so good when we opened at the Globe in London that as the final curtain fell, I grabbed him and we started waltzing around the stage together. After nearly a year in London—the provinces of England, Scotland, then all Ireland, north and south, we toured and toured and toured some more. I thought that we all stood up to it rather well, including my poor mink coat.

I kept the coat, but I lost my maid, Margaret, who had come to me from Winston Churchill himself. In London, I like to go shopping at that finest educational establishment in all England, Harrod's. I was asked there one day to an autographing party involving some recordings of the show which I'd made. When I found I'd forgotten my spectacles, I telephoned Margaret to bring them over from Park Lane.

The poor thing came over and stood in line behind Steve Cochran, whose name Hollywood conjures with, to reach the head of the queue. Spotting her but pretending not to, I scribbled a signature and handed her a record for her collection, and the autograph of "Johnny Ray."

After the session was over, I went nosing around the store into the pet department, run by a gentleman in a morning coat in keeping with Harrod's style. To-day's special was in live baby alligators, some fifteen inches long. I took rather a liking to one of them.

"Shall I send it to the Park Lane address, Lady Peel?"

"No, have it delivered by air to Noël Coward in Jamaica. It's for his birthday."

The card that accompanied went unsighed. It said simply, "So what else is new?"

I gather that Noël's reaction was a rare blend of curiosity and pique. He didn't know where the little monster had come from until several months later— on the evening that he brought the Duchess of Kent backstage and Leslie Bricusse fell downstairs to be presented.

But some correspondence that developed with Harrod's (to alligator, £6; to airfreight, £25) led my maid to jump to some wrong conclusions. She quit and left a note which said, "Madam, I must leave you. I will not work where there are alligators. I would have mentioned this, but I did not think it would come up." Poor dear. I hadn't the heart to tell her. Actually, she'd decided to try working in America.

To prove that everything comes to she who waits, even if it takes close to forty years, we must press on now to the *Ziegfeld Follies*, Golden Jubilee Edition, in which I was perhaps too easily persuaded to appear.

Flo himself, of course, was no longer with us, and the producers of the first *Follies* since 1943 were a Cincinnati businessman and his colleague, a talent agent. Nice enough chaps, and keen. Period. The headliners in 1943 had been Milton Berle, Illona Massey and Arthur Treacher. In 1956, Tallulah had been the star in a tryout tour, but she'd retreated from the scene when the production petered out before reaching Broadway. I was doing a long summer tour with another show of mine, *Beasop's Fables,* when John Shubert journeyed out to Ivoryton, Connecticut, to persuade me to have a fling in the *Follies.*

I eventually said Yes, headstrong as I was, but we still needed a leading man. That autumn, John Philip, who had produced and directed the record-breaking summer tour, found him appearing at the Café de Paris, which had long since been restored and reopened after the wartime disaster. (Yes, of course it's in *London,* but we were back there again after a tour of four months with *Beasop's Fables* and—well, I just felt like going home once in a while.)

Billy De Wolfe, who began as an acrobat and dancer in vaudeville, had just completed a long and successful period in films, and I'd heard all kinds of good things about his abilities. I asked John to take a look at Billy's act from the upstairs balcony to see whether Billy was the boy for the *Follies* and me. He was, without a doubt, and "Mis-ter Dee" and I have been pals ever since.

He had only one reservation when the *Follies* idea was put up to him: could he take a look at the scripts of the sketches in which he would appear? That struck me as a very good question, since I'd seen nothing of that nature as yet, and I'd made the same request earlier. We were constantly being reassured that, with millions available to back the show, the finest writers in the world would be engaged to produce the words and music. As things turned out, we had to dig into our drawers to find our own bits and pieces (bung ho!) because the magical new sketches never came to light. Our Cincinnati financier was much interested in sitting in the orchestra pit at rehearsals, giving the drums a whack. How reassuring!

The *Follies* had loads of publicity, interminable production numbers, baton twirlers and a generous serving of deep-chested show girls tall enough to keep a sandwich in their hairdos, if nowhere else. One of these beauties became a Mrs. Tommy Manville and another, later to be known on TV as Barbara Feldon, won "The $64,000 Question." What the show lacked was more than an ounce or two of originality.

One of those ounces was taken up by a sketch concerning an airline hostess given to singing, "I've Got a Feeling I'm Falling," and drawing her passengers' attention to the fact that the dishes are made of plastic so that "if there's a crash, the company feels it won't be a total loss."

Another ounce went into a sketch in which Billy and I played a pair of middle-aged shoppers, never knowing how it would end, because we ad-libbed it every night, keeping musicians in the orchestra craning their necks to watch us and see whether we'd round off tonight's venture with an Irish jig or a Spanish tango.

A little craning was also performed by your tireless correspondent, who was sent off on another moon ride. The garters distributed at each performance now numbered six. They were made of black lace, perfumed, trimmed with pink and blue, bearing a picture of Lady Folly herself and a slogan, "Welcome

Aboard, Ziegfeld Follies, 1957." The only thing that bothered me about the act was that if the stagehands swung the moon too low, some customers grabbed my shoes for souvenirs, and that ran into money.

We had our debut on Broadway in early March and were free in time for the fall season. Billy went off to open a restaurant on Cape Cod. Carol Lawrence, who had been one of us, went straight into *West Side Story*. John Philip, who played the singing lead, and gave sterling support acting in the sketches, continued as my personal representative. I noticed a Walter Winchell item that said John and I were "compatible." I enjoyed a certain amount of compatibility abroad and in New York until the time came around to do *Auntie Mame*, when I had to become incompatible and get back to work.

Several authors have claimed that they had me in mind when they picked up their pencils. P. L. Travers has said that *Mary Poppins* was written for and about me ("You *are* Mary Poppins" says her inscription on a fly leaf), and I thought Julie Andrews played the part beautifully. According to Noël Coward, Madame Arcati, in *Blithe Spirit*, who rides about the English countryside on her bicycle vanquishing poltergeists, was based on present company, though I couldn't play in the London première because I was engaged in World War II. Patrick Dennis (née Tanner), by his account, was thinking about his own aunt, played by me, when he wrote his novel, *Auntie Mame*.

As a matter of fact, I thought much the same as he did, and I tried to get theatrical rights to his book, but Rosalind Russell arrived fustest with the mostest, while I was occupied on stage in London. But as I was saying, everything comes to she who waits. . . .

The idea was that I'd play *Mame* on Broadway for a month before carrying her off to England for her first appearance in Europe. Roz Russell had left after a year and a half and had already made the movie, not yet released. I fancied I'd take a brief holiday first, so I took off for Capri to stay with Gracie Fields, a lady of indiscernible years like me and a friend for many of those.

I like to check up on Gracie once in a while because I am continually being mistaken for her, and each of us naturally thinks that she's the better-looking. The last official presentation made to me in Toronto of all places, the native heath itself, was a beautiful bouquet of flowers presented by a local matron with a nice little speech about that wonderful number, "The Biggest Aspidistra in the World," which only Gracie sings. Well, I mean to say. *Honi soit* can make a tree.

Business had been slowing down considerably for Broadway's *Auntie Mame* when Auntie Bea walked in. I'm rather happy to report that it picked up decidedly briskly, to the sellout point where the management would have liked me to linger on through the summer before leaving for London, but they'd already sold the scenery in advance for a touring company in California. Brilliant, eh?

Roz Russell, soon after my first night, was kind enough to telephone Robert Fryer the producer, to ask "What the hell was I doing in it for eighteen months?" That was the day after Brooks Atkinson, in a Sunday New York *Times* piece, was in a flattering mood about the new Mame, "Her impact goes deeper than clowning," he said. "It discovers a tender relationship between the comic beldame and her little nephew. By the time you read this, Miss Lillie will have made *Mame* her own."

Years later, for those kind words, I asked him around to tea in my New York apartment. My Irish maid had prepared beautiful English-style tea—paper-thin sandwiches, scones, cakes, toast and biscuits (okay, if you must—*cookies*).

"Would you care for some tea?" I asked the guest of honor in my best tea-for-two manner as this scintillating repast was served on, in and about the Peel silver.

"Tea?" he said. "No thank you ever so much. I think I'd prefer scotch." That was another maid who handed in her apron. Really, one doesn't know what girls are coming to these days.

It was Not Without Trepidation that I appeared as Mame in London. We had twenty-seven changes of scene, mostly carried out during stage blackouts, when I had to make eighteen costume changes. In the two and a half hours running time, Mame is off stage for barely twenty-five minutes. To keep me out of trouble, a strapping young bodyguard was provided to snatch me up and carry me out of harm's way while the stagehands galloped through their work.

In the wings, a crew of wardrobe hands simply hung clothes on my willing frame. Not so long after we started playing at the Adelphi Theatre, London, and in direct violation of a firm agreement *not* to do so, the Warner Brothers' movie opened in competition. "See the *live* Auntie Mame," screamed our advertisements. Some nights, I wasn't quite sure they meant me.

The stage version won hands down. The film lasted only three short weeks. In London, Mame was *us*, and I'm delighted that I never missed a performance in over a year as Auntie Mame, in Britain.

Some of the critics didn't care much for the show (others raved), but audiences jammed the theatre for the best part of a year. In all that time, I don't think they noticed that, in the hubbub of changing sets and my clothes, I occasionally appeared in a beard.

CHAPTER FIFTEEN

SOME FACTS AND FANCIES, TOLD LIKE IT IS

You don't think we should pause for a moment and dip into a dish of ice cream? Ah, well, I suppose not. I used to fear that ice cream would be the ruin of me, but I gave up giving it up a long time ago. "Not in the middle of the day," I tell myself now, but I don't listen very hard. If I'm to be ruined at my time of life, it may as well be on a diet of pistachio, chocolate or strawberry, with bits of nuts and syrup. The refrigerator at "Peel Fold" is kept stocked for every impulse.

"Peel Fold" is the name I gave the house I bought at Henley-on-Thames, England, just after the war ended. It was the name of the original Peel family farm back in the fifteenth century. Soon after we moved in, the rains came, floodwater crept across the mellow old brick of one of the terraces, under the french doors, over the long drawing-room floor, and I immediately revised the address to Henley-*under*-Thames. Luckily the river stays 'way from my floor these days, though that particular torrent cost me the lavender hedge I used to have, as well as many fine triple-lilac bushes.

I came upon the place quite by chance one Saturday afternoon when I was indulging in another modest pleasure, driving idly round the Oxfordshire countryside. The house, which is really three converted Queen Anne cottages, was known then as "Weir Cottage," the home of a Swiss match king's widow, Mrs. Florence Lowenadler, who had just died a month or so earlier. There are those of us who fancy we've since seen her moving about the house and peeping in the windows on occasion, keeping tabs on things, I guess. Ah, well, I believe in keeping open house, even for these highest of spirits.

A sign along the Reading Road just outside Henley said, AUCTION TODAY, so we climbed out of the car and beetled around for a while. I intended at first to buy only a vessel, moored in the thatched boathouse, that impressed me as being every bit as elegant as Cleopatra's barge and more practical in times when slaves are hard to come by. It was an *electric* canoe, propelled by thirty-six gigantic rechargeable batteries. I could picture myself and attendants gliding sedately downstream to London, sixty-five miles away by river, or upstream, past green lawns, willow trees and moor hens to Oxford.

Then it struck me that I'd have nowhere to keep my pleasure craft, so I made up my mind to put in a bid for the house and estate, too, complete with enormous Queen Anne rose gardens, lawn tennis court, croquet lawn and a pale pink marble Italian fountain that sings to itself as the water plays. My solicitor *naturally* was opposed to the purchase. First he curled his lip at the idea, then finished on his knees. "I beg you to reconsider; *waterfront* property. Even worse, *riverfront* property! The risks! The floods!" But fiddle-dee. Not wee Bea . . . Oh, no, John—no, John—*NO!*

News that the whole place was mine came when I was in a London hospital, in bed after a mite of minor surgery. Mary Gordon was visiting the bedside one afternoon when Bob Goldstein, still of Twentieth Century-Fox, arrived in his Rolls. I bore him no grudge for trying to marry me off to Clark Gable, so I told him all about the house I had just acquired.

Warming to the subject, I was out of bed in a flash—or was it a flush?—and off we Rolls-ed to Henley. Problem. No key. We contented ourselves briefly by creeping furtively around the terraces, peeking in through the windows, but temptation overcame me. I pried a loose brick from one of the terraces, took careful aim and smashed a pane of glass in the kitchen door.

Guilt and panic seized me. I ran to hide in the shrubbery. "We'd better tell the police that we broke a window, or they'll think there's been a burglar around, said Bob.

I had visions of being arrested. "No, no! *Please!*" I cried.

"But it's *your* house," said Mary.

It took a moment for that thought to sink in. "Well, in that case," I said doubtfully, "if you think it's all right—"

Inside, we got an impression of gloom, dampness, bilious yellow paint and Chinese lanterns. "*Weird* Cottage," said I, with a hollow laugh, and not even Mrs. Lowenadler laughed with me. But it was mine, and it could be made wonderful. So we went back to the Rolls, had high tea in Henley, and I returned to London, hospital and bed.

Days, months, a few years pass. It is 1950. Now there is John Philip laboring away to put the establishment in shape, with the help of a built-in married couple, Mary and Cecil. Sister Muriel, in country tweeds, clomps over the bare parquet floors, shoveling coal into the ancient iron furnace, staggering under the weight of the household electrical batteries as she and John carry them one by one into one of the labyrinth of service rooms, in the old mill house, where there is an antique dynamo, started by hand.

Imagine. How quaint! Making your own electricity in twentieth-century England, and 110 volts A/C current at that! It wasn't long before that was changed back to that scintillating native vintage, 220 D/C.

When "Peel Fold" had been made ready, Mumsie came to spend her last years there. Even in her eighties, she was a strong personality, active and sure of herself. In the attic one day, she was certain she had found a painting by Thomas Gainsborough. A famous London auction house concluded later while it was a very fair canvas, it was only a copy. "In New York," they said, "it would probably be rated genuine." Thanks pal, for them kind words. Pity! I've always wanted a *"Thos."*

Mumsie died in the Ivy Room at "Peel Fold," sitting in an armchair from which she could see the river flowing gently by and hear the murmur of water racing over the weir. Only a few days earlier she'd been singing *The Holy City* much as she'd done in Cooke's Presbyterian a lifetime ago. Muriel wanted the same song sung at the funeral, but we settled on *I Know That My Redeemer Liveth*. Mother lies buried in St. Margaret's of Antioch churchyard, in the ancient manoral hamlet of Harpsden, near Peel Fold.

Soon after her death, for no reason to be thought of,

I remembered that when I was a little girl, I once ran away from home and spent the night in tears because I wondered who, when I grew up, would make my dresses like my mother did, and what should I ever do without her.

One thing I do without her is to paint, as she did, and her father before her. In my experience anyone can paint if he doesn't have to. I've seen it happen to friends. They say, "But, Bea, I couldn't draw a straight line."

I say, "Then you're a natural. Who wants a straight line? That's not *painting*."

I started during the war—the *second* one, please— when I needed some painted china doorknobs, which were unobtainable in England. So I bought a doorknob, a plain wooden doorknob, painted it white, then when it was dry added some little flowers. It struck me as a beautiful job, if I do say so myself (and I do). What's more, I found that painting Took My Mind Off Things.

During my apprentice days I felt encouraged by the advice of Winston Churchill, who used to say, "Don't be afraid of the canvas." I have now reached the point where the canvas is afraid of me. I usually begin a painting by growling at the canvas, whether it's going to be a landscape, flowers, a Pekingese, or a Pekingese that looks like a flower.

I can paint just as well on all fours as standing up, and with brush, hands, fingers, fists. I can work away with the brushes for four or five hours at a time, then blot everything out in a minute and try again. I have a rule, never kept, that *nobody* may see a painting until it's finished, because I'm terribly, awfully, easily hurt. I am the originator of the "Don't Touch It" Society!

Some of my better works are exhibited under the Bechstein grand piano in the living room at "Peel Fold," since the light is dimmer there. I used to paint under the name of "Beatrice van Gone," but, in fact, a painting or two has been sold at quite a pretty penny with no signature at all.

I have also been buying paintings now and again ever since I contracted the habit one weekend as a guest of Helen Hayes in her fascinating, sugar-coated Victorian House in Nyack, New York. The walls were hung with the works of artists whose names even I could recognize, including Renoir, Lautrec and Picasso. But a lot of the talk between the other guests had to do with a painter I'd never heard of. Since the other guests were Vincent Price, then appearing with Helen in *Victoria Regina*, who certainly knows his paintings from his pumpkins, and Reggie Gardiner, by no means a Sunday painter himself, I listened respectfully.

"You really should see it," murmured Vincent. "A beautiful thing, a Modigliani." He mentioned the name of the Fifty-seventh Street gallery where it could be seen.

A few days later, I was on my way not to any gallery but to Hattie Carnegie's, as often was my habit. As I frequently do, I paid off the taxi a block away so that I could walk for a bit. Half a dozen steps, and I saw the place Vincent had mentioned. I fancied I'd take a look inside and went in, muttering to myself, "Now let's get that name right. It's Modigliani. Mo-di-glia-ni."

"Good morning, Miss Lillie," said a rather magnificent gentleman. "Are you interested in any particular painter or period? What would you care to see?"

"Mo-di-glia-ni," I said carefully and rather shyly, with a furtive look over my shoulder.

He seemed surprised, probably figuring me for a Landseer kink or a rooter for Gilbert Stuart. In a dark, velvet-walled room, he flicked on the lights. There on an easel stood the Modigliani, a large painting of a young lad, a rather special friend of the artist, I heard later, with a neck that struck me as perhaps becoming to a giraffe. A real life shocker! "That," I said aloud to myself, "is the worst-looking thing you've seen in all your born days."

"True. True," said my enraptured counselor and guide absently. "A wonderful, wonderful painting. You show such excellent taste, if I may say."

"Uh—huh."

"Oh, you really must have it, Miss Lillie. It's really quite superb."

"Well, I—*really* I'm not—"

"Don't you love the line of the throat and that delicious color of his shirt? And his hands? So unusual. You can't possibly go wrong."

Can't I though? "Er, well, how much—"

"For you, let us say $8500."

Ah, hah, hah! "Couldn't we say $7000?"

My gentleman smiled wanly. "Oh, Miss Lillie, you're just as funny off the stage as you are on it. The frame alone is worth $2000."

We laughed it up to $8500 again, then laughed it down to $8000. But, eventually, I didn't buy it. I hadn't that kind of money to throw away, I thought, and I really disliked the painting. The following Sunday, a column in the New York *Times* caught my eye, though it proved not to be too painful. The subject was Amedeo Modigliani in person, born July 1884, died of tuberculosis January 1920, followed a day later by his mistress, Jeanne Hebuterne, who was bearing his child when she opted out and did herself in.

The gentleman at the gallery kept writing me to buy the painting, whose name was beginning to haunt me—*Young Boy in Culottes.* In the end I gave in and bought it for $6500, including city sales tax and the splendid Renaissance frame.

Opinion among my friends was decidedly divided. Simon Elwes, who had painted my portrait, dismissed it: "I just don't care for that kind of thing." Noël offered me $10,000 as soon as he saw it. Rolf Gérard (a word about him in a momento) knelt down in front of it and crossed himself.

Perhaps that's what tempted me to keep it, or maybe I was beginning to warm up to the little boy. Anyway, I took it to London with me, and when the war came, put it in Sotheby's vaults for safekeeping. It goes back there when I'm out of England, but when I'm there, out it comes, so that I can hang it again, and watch, and wonder. Just what *did* Amedeo have in mind?

According to Sotheby's last valuation a few years ago, *Young Boy in Culottes* may now be conservatively figured as worth something in the vicinity of $250,-000. I take back everything I said. I like it! I *like* it! If it goes to a million, I shall definitely sell.

Not all my shopping expeditions have been so successful, though any list of personal pleasures would have to include trotting round the stores or to a favorite beauty parlor—Liz Arden's is always a nice place to go if you have nothing else to do; just for a slap and a tickle.

My good friend Mary Martin tapped me on the shoulder just before one Eastertime, when she was out on Fifth Avenue looking for new gloves and I was out just looking, thanks. Since the doors of Saks yawned before us, I suggested that we might go in together. The store was packed with last-minute shoppers, and no salesgirl would so much as nod to us.

After five foot-tapping minutes, I went behind the counter and pulled out a box or two of gloves for Mary to try on, each of us talking and taking our time about it. There was a salesgirl on each side of us, but they still weren't in the least interested. When Mary found a pair she liked, she paid me for them, I handed over the cash to one of the engrossed young assistants, and we took our leave.

"What I couldn't understand," Mary said later, "was how *no one* could be aware of a lady in a pillbox hat and a very long fur coat, selling gloves behind a counter at Saks." Neither, to tell the truth, could I.

Department stores and I have our ups and downs (excluding, of course, Britain's finest educational establishment). I was shopping for a bird cage for my parakeets in Macy's one day and thought the transaction was complete when the saleslady asked me to identify myself. I pointed out that the checkbook had my name printed on it. That wouldn't do. I presented my Actors' Equity membership card, bankbook, driver's license, a photograph or two and my fingerprints.

The custodian of Mr. Macy's treasures stared me straight in the eye and said coldly, "I don't know you." Another shopper, a fan, overhearing this, came over and assured the young lady that I was *myself* indeed. That did it. The saleslady went off to find the manager and a set of handcuffs, and I made a fast getaway, without the bird cage.

Next morning, with my friend Gladys Lacey, I set

out bird-cage hunting once more. A vengeful mood took me this time to Mr. Macy's deadliest rival. Mr. Gimbel recognized me instantly and picked out a lovely large cage. He was so happy, as a matter of fact, that he climbed inside and gave an audition for me, singing plaintively "If I Had the Wings of An Angel." However, he didn't get the part, because he couldn't balance himself on the swing. His excuse was that he didn't have his sneakers on.

"Think nothing of it," I said.

"Oh, I won't," he replied, handing over the cage with a beautiful smile. Then Gladys, chattering away like a magpie, climbed in, and I carried her home. Gladys is a "shocker"; an original Australian bird girl. (Her *Kokkaburra* is exquisite.) In truth, she keeps open mouth!

I like to take long walks, though not alone, since I am apt to get lost without a compass. I take up knitting from time to time as a relaxation, but I always put it down again before going out to buy a rocking chair. I enjoy gardens much more than garden*ing*, possibly as the result of an afternoon's attempt to help my Henley neighbor, Gladys Cooper, water her roses; I let them have it with a hose to such effect that they were washed out of the ground into the river. Dame Gladys has loved me to this day for it, bless her.

I am fond of striking up conversations with small children anywhere in the world and find that some of the best talks I've ever had have been with one-year-olds and younger. I like to watch little babies in the flesh, on television or anywhere.

Occasionally, wanderlust overcomes me, and we start packing again. I was once overcome and came to in Hawaii, with John Philip, Gladys, and husband

Franklin Lacey, who is a writer and a bit of a kook in his own right! Part of the time we stayed, rather suitably, on a ranch devoted to growing nuts, the macadamia breed.

Quite early during our stay, we took part in a demonstration of the value of a good Sunday-school upbringing. We were taking a drive on the main island, Oahu, when Franklin, who was the helmsman, bumped us along what began as a very rough road and finished as a desert of sand and rocky rubble, at the deserted northwest tip of the island, in which we rapidly sank to the hubcaps. Not a living soul within miles, and not one of us with more than a rough idea where to look for help.

We pushed and pulled and spun the wheels, achieving nothing except to dig the car in deeper. "Friends," I muttered silently, "we have had it."

There was only one more thing left to try. Gaily I raised my voice in the hymn they sang when the *Luistania* went down, and my fellow castaways joined in. To the strains of "Nearer My God to Thee" we miraculously inched the car back onto firmer ground and made our merry way homeward to Laie via hymn number twenty-seven.

I found Hawaii more beautiful than I expected and the people even nicer, so I kept busy with the paint brushes. I also found the island a bit like Prospero's, slightly mysterious, with one or two things I couldn't understand. Like the Mynah bird at a restaurant called "Pat's at Punaluu," owned by two nice people, Iris and Pat O'Halloran, where we went most nights for dinner and to listen and talk to the birds.

One evening I went up to one of the little creatures and said, in a phrase that was a catchword in the old-time British music hall, "How's your father?"

The mynah blinked its yellow eyes and answered loud and clear, "Fine." The O'Hallorans looked surprised. The bird had never said *that* before and though each of us tried him out again for weeks, he never repeated the act.

We received word somehow that Mary Martin was going to stop very briefly in Honolulu on her way to Vietnam to do *Hello, Dolly!* there. I've sometimes been able to produce at least a greenstick fracture of Mary's funny bone ever since, at an Elsa Maxwell party in Monte Carlo, Mary accused me of not having seen her in *Sound of Music*. Holding two pieces of Melba toast to my cheeks as a wimple, I managed to prove her wrong by going through her whole performance as Maria, adding a little advice of my own, "*Don't* get into the habit."

Mary wrote her account of what happened in Honolulu. "A very strange-looking woman dressed in a green muumuu, a huge hat covering her face, huge leis draped on shoulders and arms, slowly approached the plane. As I came down the steps, she knelt at my feet mumbling some mumbo-jumbo. I thought, How sweet of this native woman to welcome me to her island.

"As I started to give my grateful thanks, off came the straw hat—it was Bea. She had heard that our plane would touch down for thirty minutes and had driven for two hours to say welcome on my first sight of Hawaii."

There was something else I couldn't understand about the islands: the contrast between beauty and pain. This was August 1965 and I went to the Tripler Hospital to visit wounded men just back from Vietnam. One of them was barely twenty years old. Memories returned as I stood by his bed making with the

347

chitchat, breaking my heart to see him.

Shopping, knitting, travel—they may fill the days of a lady of leisure, but, alas and alack, I've never been one (and I've no intention of trying to change now). I hardly know what to do with myself when I'm not working. After *Auntie Mame* and the summer show we called *Beasop's Fables,* the TV tube took up more of my time, either to sit watching it or appearing on it, in New York, Hollywood and London; sometimes with the name in lights, sometimes as a guest on the talk shows.

Doing television is fun for me only if there's an audience. After all this time in the theatre, the old need to hear the magical, inspiring first laugh is as strong as when I was a little bit of a thing being booked by Harry Rich. Without an audience in the studio, TV is just summer stock in an iron lung.

Those cool young men like puckish Johnny Carson, boyish "Merv" Griffin and Ivy League Dick Cavett, who run the late-night shows so calmly that you know the world could come to an end without their skipping a commercial, always tell you, "You were great—just wonderful."

But someone like me—may the good Lord preserve her!—who is never satisfied with herself says more in hope than conviction, "Well, I wasn't so bad, considering."

Your friends, wherever they may be, say, "Darling, you looked ten years younger."

And you say to yourself, "That's all very well, but I wanted to look *fifteen* years younger."

If you're anything like me—the fabulous, legendary, so-called funniest woman alive—who works mostly from memory and without a script, you haven't the least idea what you're going to do as a guest on a TV talk show. So you decide to go for a long walk, hoping that something will occur to you.

The class may therefore safely conclude that it was a pleasure to write in a peacetime diary, which I was struggling to keep for a while, a day's entry that said, "Slept very well. My face is covered with *wax*. It says on the jar, 'For hands,' so I'm trying it elsewhere. Good news. Noël Coward called. Wants me to do his new musical, *High Spirits*. To play Madame Arcati. It sounds very interesting."

"Interesting" was a meager word for it. A year, all but a day or so, passed before scribble in the diary noted, "Well, tonight's the night for *High Spirits*. I have said my little prayer and asked, 'To help me give of my best, dear Lord.'" And the next entry, written in a rather calmer hand, reports, "Well, my prayers were answered. My thanks to everyone, including, of course, U-NO-HU up there, who answered my prayers."

High Spirits was based quite firmly on the play *Blithe Spirit*, which Noël wrote in 1940 and wanted me for, so he said, but, as I've said, a war and a previous engagement rather thoughtlessly interfered with that arrangement. Mildred Natwick played the first Madame Arcati on Broadway, and Margaret Rutherford originated the role in London and also did the movie. I counted myself fortunate, when my turn came, that I hadn't seen either one of their performances. It always has been much easier for me to create my own characterization in everything I've done.

The new musical credited music, lyrics and book to two others, Hugh Martin (of "Trolley Song" fame) and Timothy Gray, but the old master himself insisted on directing it, until the tribulation we encountered on the way caused the butterflies to flutter in his stomach so faithfully that the Philadelphia doctors diagnosed an ulcer, and it seemed that Gower Champion would step into the role, however unsung his contribution.

But back to the beginning. A quick look at the script, when it became available, and I was busily confiding to the diary that "I must have four or five more numbers." That was probably greedy, but I knew I had to have time on stage to work with, or else I'd be wasted in the part.

Every day we rehearsed and rehearsed. "I'm full of ideas," I boasted to the little green leather-covered book, which I mostly forgot to keep up to date; "some not bad."

Perhaps you will understand that most of the ideas had to do with improving the odds for Madame Arcati, and thus the show as a whole. She was the happy medium, who ran a beatnik coffeehouse by day and communed whenever possible with the "other side," after checking out the telephone numbers on her ouija board. Gradually, with a nudge here and a prod there, her importance grew. She expanded her costume with bicycle clips attached to her baggy trousers. She picked up an outlandish hat and more beads than you'd find in a bagnio in the Casbah. Even the bicycle on which she made her entrance acquired a rearview mirror. Then, later, there was added to the hat a stuffed canary and to the bicycle's rear end, if you'll pardon the expression, a little teddy bear.

I became a trifle supersititious about that bicycle after it did its best to polish me off one night in Boston during the pre-Broadway run. I rode it to and fro in front of a scrim, doing one of my numbers called, not inappropriately, "The Bicycle Song." Some little thing inside my skull prompted me on this occasion to dismount in mid-song, contrary to all stage-management directions.

There was I, trilling happily, when the bike took off and went flying toward the ceiling, rear end caught in the hard edge of the backdrop curtain, which was accidentally hoisting itself skyward. If Madame Arcati had been in the saddle, she would have been flung headlong into the orchestra pit some seven feet below and impaled on a cello. (Quick, Maud, the ouija board!)

The plot in which we were professionally engaged has to do, if you recall, with some odd goings on in a house on Hampstead Heath, where our happy medium brings back to earth a widower's first wife, to haunt him and his second, living spouse. Tammy Grimes was cast as Elvira, the first Mrs. Condomine, and I venture to say at this moment in the game that I thought she flew brilliantly in the part, though the merest mention of her name used to drive John Philip up the wall during the days when we were getting *High Spirits* into playable shape.

John took very personally any move to reduce the scope of Madame Arcati; and he felt that Tammy was overly ambitious. Too true, if truth must be known. It was John's idea to introduce Arcati's serenade to her ouija board, performed in a sleeping cap, nightie, and long-eared bunny slippers, which consistently brought the audience to its feet, yelling with delight.

In the course of fattening up the madame's role, a few words were exchanged between John and Noël, enough on John's side, in fact, to fill the pages of Webster's latest dictionary, if that's the one with all *those* words in it. Noël's wicked witticisms can sometimes be taken amiss, like his celebrated comment on hearing the British national anthem—"Isn't that one of the tunes from *Cavalcade?*" John favors the broadsword over the rapier—"You're old enough to be my mother, and should know better," was one fragrant phrase I remember from the on-stage battle that broke out after one evening performance during the second week in Boston, prior to Broadway.

Noël and I had always enjoyed a screaming fight or two together. He had directed me twice before. After one previous ordeal, he was sitting in a box on opening night, while on stage I felt I was doing awfully well, receiving all kinds of applause and thinking, "Noël's going to be so happy, too, that the show's going so great."

How wrong can you be? At the first interval, he stormed into my dressing room, not with encouragement, which always helps, but to rage, "Beattie, what's wrong with you? Have you been drinking? You are absolutely terrible." Drinking? Me? I swear I've never had a drink before or during a performance, ever, in all my years. I simply couldn't work that way.

Noël sat in front of the mirror and nervously picked up my powder puff to touch his face.

"Give that back to me!" I screamed. "You know I haven't been drinking, and you can have your bloody awful show." The fur began to fly. Insecurities were rampant.

It continued flying at the opening-night party that Ernie Byfield gave in the Ambassador Hotel. I was in no mood to drink anything that would be served there, so I imported my own beer. I left the party early, so upset that I sat in a little foyer off the corridor, carrying what was left of my then favorite beverage, waiting for the longest time for an elevator without even noticing that this wasn't the place where elevators ran. It was anger, not beer, that confused me.

At six o'clock the following morning, my telephone rang. Noël again, with his riposte—at last! "Because of you, it is a bloody awful show." He didn't actually say "bloody," but one of those words you didn't find in any dictionary in those days. It was all irrelevant in any case, since when the press was in, it was all raves.

Our *High Spirits* high jinks in Boston developed over the old argument that I refuse to take directions, which just isn't true. It depends on who is directing me and whether he understands that my idea of timing is usually utterly different from anybody else's.

One evening after the show, Noël was invited to dinner at the Harvard *Lampoon,* where he unburdened himself of a thought or two about me. Some of the group of students who had gathered to meet the old master were a bit taken aback by what he said, since they apparently thought I was pretty damn good as Arcati. One or two of them felt so badly that they in writing reported what Noël had been saying concerning my ability to memorize a script.

Such pleasantries, they said, as, "I'll be delighted if she can remember a line by the time we get to New York." "Her memory is going." "The other actors spend the entire evening feeding her her lines." All not true, I can assure. This resulted in perhaps the biggest battle of Noël's battle-studded career.

After our performance two nights later, when news of the *Lampoon* dinner conversation had spread, Noël Coward, author, actor and genius, was accosted and tongue-lashed by John Philip Huck, baritone and former U. S. Marine Lieutenant, who pursued Noël about the darkened stage for almost half an hour. The public address system was still operating, so that the din of battle could be heard by one and all in their dressing rooms, and as far away as Bunker Hill.

What especially irked John was the fact that on the *very morning* of the *Lampoon* dinner date, Noël had told him, "Johnny, you've been a great help. Beattie has never been better, never known her lines so well or been so well-oriented in such little time." Both John and I, great admirers of Noëly, were delighted.

So back and forth across the Colonial Theatre stage they dueled that night like Romeo and Tybalt. I didn't see it myself, but Noël retired to his hotel, and was scarcely seen for the next several weeks. He really was ill, and I couldn't help feeling sorry for him though he *had* asked for it. We had been through a lot together, and *I* understood him, even if John didn't at this point.

The show, restaged in Philadelphia with some new direction, became ready now for the Broadway première, though in my humble opinion it could have been made even better if Noël hadn't cut short his contribution.

On opening night on Broadway, I sent him a telegram: QUITE FOR NO REASON MY POOR FEET ARE FREEZIN' SO PLEASE SAY A PRAYER. I think he did. Counting our tour, *High Spirits* ran for over a year, until I'd fulfilled my contract, and Walter Kerr, on the first Sunday after our debut at the Alvin, wrote this:

". . . Who has ever hired Miss Lillie to do what a playwright put down on paper, of all things? Who has ever supposed that the progressive events of an evening could be in any way related to, or supported by, or kept in coherence with, the tentative one-foot jig the star would probably be doing the moment everyone's back—but not the audience's—was turned? One does not ask Miss Lillie to go where a show is going. One asks her to keep it from getting there. That is her specialty: total distraction from what everyone should be paying the strictest attention to. She is the road-block that refreshes the pause in the day's occupation that is known as the adults' hour. Children can do things in orderly fashion, a step at a time, if they care to; grown-ups know that nothing works out that way. Miss Lillie is grown-up. And gone, real gone, if I may put it that way. If she does not always say 'Shoo!' to the plot right out loud as she comes up, it's only because that is no longer necessary; plots have heard of her, and hide."

At the final performance of *High Spirits* in New York, the audience said hello with what is known as a "standing ovation." It made me nervous when I saw them all get to their feet. I didn't know what was going on. I felt like rushing out amongst them and embracing *them*.

As for Noël, I *do* love him, and I choose to believe he loves me. We kissed and made up without any trouble, when he wrote this *billet-doux* about *An Evening With,* in which he detected "one of the greatest stars of light entertainment that the world has ever known":

> Birds of love Divine lie bleeding at her feet, fairies dance with the heaviness of dragons at the bottom of her garden, moaning ladies shorn of their lovers descend into the utmost depths of bathos, all because Miss Lillie decided to turn on them the piercing, lethal beam of her dreadful irreverence and her implacable humor.

Amidst this holocaust of destruction, it is apparent to the least perceptive eye that she has subtlety, delicacy, wit and whether you like it or not, absolute truth. She is as incapable of a false note, in her performance as her clear, fresh voice is incapable of singing out of tune.

It may be gathered from all this hyperbole that I am an admirer of Beatrice Lillie, which is very true. I am also one of her oldest friends, which doesn't prejudice me in the least. If I loathed her with every quivering fibre of my being (which at certain dress rehearsals I have), I should still have to admit that an evening with Beatrice Lillie is one of the most enchanting things that could ever happen to anybody.*

Quite for a reason, thank you for those kind words, Noëly, and for all the others, too. Lovingly yours, *Lillie Bea-dle-dy.*

Noël must be counted as one of the most important men in my life, though I've felt no temptation to propose marriage to him. The desire to be married again to anyone has cropped up only once and then not proved very strong. The vows one makes privately are more binding than any ceremony or even a Shubert contract.

I have loved as a friend and kind of brother (never had one), Doc McGonigle. In the secret language I've shared and invented with a handful of friends, he is "Bane" and I am "Trink." With John Philip, whose idea it was, I have visited him in the Abbey of Gethsemani, Kentucky, where he worked for years

* Reprinted by permission of Noël Coward.

with Thomas Merton. "Doc" is a Trappist *lay* brother, and that's *that*.

In much the same way, with slight variations, I have loved Rolf Gérard, a young German doctor who escaped from Heidelberg to England with Prince Bernhard of the Netherlands, one jump ahead of the Nazis in the Second World War. Because he lacked a license to practice in England, he worked at first as a postal clerk in London while the war lasted, scribbling notes and sketches to St. John's Wood, assorted London theatres and Park Lane on post office forms and other scrap paper.

With Bob Goldstein's help, it was possible to obtain an early visa for him to the United States soon after the war ended. There Dr. Gérard transformed himself into a brilliant artist and set designer, with *An Evening With* among his credits, which also include a brilliant new *Carmen,* and other operas, for the Met.

In a totally different way, I love my son, and think so very often about the happy times with him. In order to press on with life, I feel that one must focus thoughts on the good memories and keep steadfast faith in an ultimate reunion in spirit somewhere, somehow.

Over the years, there have been lesser loves. Nothing promiscuous, mark you, but a small, select company of admirers from the ranks of motion-picture actors, concert artists, composers, statesmen and, on gala occasions, even royalty. The clergy and I share a mutual attraction for each other—platonic, of course. They're among my biggest fans, the non-feathered though upon occasion, airborne kind.

For twenty-three years, I have enjoyed the love and devotion of John Philip, which I think has been good for both of us. He has helped fill the void left by the loss of my father, my husband and my son, adding a unique *caring* quality of his own.

Have I now bared my soul and Told All? Ah, no! There's one thing more. So far in this tale, we haven't heard a single dog bark, have we? It should be recorded that dogs—to be specific, Pekingese—are important to my life. I've been keeping company with little Oriental gentlemen and their families for a number of years now, on and off.

The course of this long-term romance has been made difficult for a transatlantic commuter like me by the severity of British quarantine laws, which at this writing ban the importation of all dogs, without a six-month quarantine and two rabies shots, for fear of rabies. Now I doubt if there's anyone more terrified than I at the thought of a mad dog roaming the streets, but I must confess I think that quarantine, which keeps dogs in cages for six months when they are imported, *is not the answer*. Nowadays, supervised inoculation, medical examination and certification prove practically everywhere outside Britain that rabies *can* be controlled and prevented. I can only hope that my efforts to convince the British Ministry of Agriculture of this may one day result in dogs owned *by tax-paying residents of the British Isles* being allowed in to live there with them after a sensible period of, let us say, two weeks' quarantine and observation, plus an up-to-date rabies inoculation and a thorough medical examination at the port of entry. The dog would, of course, be non-transferable and his whereabouts subject to permanent investigation. It makes sense and I hope that this further step is soon taken.

In New York, there lives a tiny aristocrat of such rare breeding that only seventeen of his kind were recently known in the record books. He is completely black from snub nose to feathery stern, except for minute dabs of white by his front toenails.

I was boarding a plane at London Airport to fly to New York for my return as Arcati in *High Spirits*, after a Christmas-week holiday at home, when some friends, seeing me off, pushed a flight bag on to me. It went unopened until the seatbelt sign was off and we were somewhere over Windsor Castle, with "Peel Fold" barely visible on its bend of the Thames, off to the right front of the jet.

Inside the flight bag, quiet as a mouse and not much bigger, lay a black bundle of curls. I was furious. I knew all about British quarantine laws, which at the time meant six months in kennels before a dog could be imported.

Although thrilled with the babe in swaddlings, I was smitten by a sharp thought that this was virtually a one-way ride to the New World for him. I regret to say I became very cross at not having said, "Take him away; I don't want him; how *dare* you do this to him, and me?" All this because of an unnecessary law.

Every passenger wanted to fondle the mighty mouse. We fed him sips of milk and scraps of meat, and by the time we reached Kennedy Airport, I'd felt the anger disappear. Photographers were waiting, so they snapped our picture, as we clutched each other.

"What's his name?" asked one of them.

I hadn't the least idea. I said the first thing that entered my head. "Lord Button, of Henley-on-Thames." Which is the name he's had ever since, and he's lived up to it. Now for a flight of fancy . . . Read-*y*?

In Henley there once upon a time lived five of these

noblemen; now there is one, the palest beige and extremely hospitable. In a far corner, near the trickling stream where pike and chub swim, lies Mr. Lee of my dreams, who died in the night of a heart attack. His widow, Lady Pearl, was growing a trifle hard of hearing, but until recently she had their son, Hi-Fi, for company—of a completely proper kind—in her golden years.

Mr. Lee was my first American Pekingese. He was named for a Chinese laundry man in Las Vegas, though Mr. Lee was born in Virginia. I used to say—and meant it—that if I had to give up every personal possession but one, I would have chosen Mr. Lee. (Lee Shubert always thought that Mr. Lee was named for him. I hadn't the heart to disillusion him.)

He was the rarest of the rare not because of his color, a golden honey, but because he could talk. My friends considered his vocabulary to be somewhat limited, but they testified without prompting that he could say quite distinctly, "I want the ball" and "I love you," as well as "Up yours," and a couple of other choice bits.

He was an addicted partygoer, and he could ice skate with some proficiency, specializing in figure eights. I used to *dream* how he might go through one great adventure in life, though I would know nothing of it until he had crossed the great divide and been smuggled into England from Paris. Impossible, of course.

In my dream, I was having a hard time adjusting to the fact that I should have to bid him good-by when I left for Henley. Taking him to Europe and into France from the United States would present no problem, since there is no quarantine law in France, or in 95 per cent of the rest of the world. So I dreamed that a couple of friends of mine would volunteer to smuggle him in without letting me know about it.

Their first thought would be to charter a plane and fly him, like a spy or a case of cognac, into some Oxfordshire meadow by black of night. Then, as soon as I'd made my lonesome way home to Park Lane, they would hit on a better idea, though Mr. Lee might not have agreed with them if he'd foreseen what was going to happen to him.

They'd book two adjoining compartments in the boat train from Folkestone to London. Aboard the Channel steamer, in preparation for his exploit, they'd pour a teaspoonful of water and some Dewar's White Label into Mr. Lee until he was speechless. When his eyes began to roll, they'd serve him a few more doubles until he was dead drunk. Then they would insert him into a little carrying bag, which one of them could take off the boat and into his railroad compartment ready for customs inspection on the way to London.

When the inspector entered the first compartment, it was the second smuggler who'd hold the bag. When the inspector left, and before he had time to go into the adjoining compartment, Mr. Lee and bag could be passed quick as a wink from the second smuggler to the first, whose baggage had now been examined.

Then the impossible dream grew dramatic. In the taxi to my apartment, the two conspirators, checking the contents of the portmanteau, are afraid for a moment that Mr. Lee, in a torpor, has passed away rather than out. But they pinch his cheeks, and his bleary-eyed response assures them that all is well, when they pass Mr. Lee into welcoming arms.

They tell me nothing about how they'd managed it.

I am overjoyed by the reunion, and I ask no questions, concluding that he is sleeping so soundly because he is tired of his travels. I would become alarmed only hours later, when he staggers out of bed to cock a leg, teeters for a moment, then falls pie-eyed to the floor.

A rapid telephone call brings the vet hurrying on an emergency call. He pats and pricks Mr. Lee in a complete physical. His expert diagnosis calms my panic. "There is only one thing wrong with your dog, Lady Peel. He is stoned out of his mind."

In my fantasy, it was three days before he recovered from the hangover and felt quite himself again. Poor little wee Lee. But all this was ridiculous fantasy, wasn't it? A filmscript could result. I shall title it "Peke-A-Boo-Boo; My Flight of Fancy, by Mr. Lee."

My first London Peke, Ming-Ki Poo, once was with me in a taxi on our way to the Savoy when I sensed that something was happening on one of my gloves and saw a little trickle on the leather seat. The driver must have seen what had happened, too. Looking back as the doorman helped me out at the revolving doors of the hotel, he jumped out of the cab.

"Now, then. What do you mean by letting your dog mess in my taxi?" he demanded.

I turned to him, *every* inch a lady and at least six feet tall. I pressed a handsome tip into his grimy hand. "*I* did it," I said, and swept into the lobby.

I have been toying with the idea of concluding these pages with a touch of philosophy, if only I had one. All that comes to mind is a favorite motto, which I have believed in sincerely as long as I can remember. More than ever I believe it today, when there is so much past to think about or put aside, depending on the frame of mind one is in.

That motto is: *En Avant!* It's better farther on. Have faith in the good in life, and *don't* brood on the bad. Always *look* for the best. But perhaps these thoughts are too solemn for you or me. Let's just say, then, what was said to the cabdriver: "*I* did it." And I'm proud of it.

Well, now, I must be getting along. Is there anyone for Venice? Till we meet again, God bless one and all. Happy landings.

In other words: *Mizpah!*

*Three months on the
nation's bestseller lists!*

GEORGE S. KAUFMAN

by Howard Teichmann

George S. Kaufman—wit, playwright, stage director, newspaperman, ladies' man, card player, performer—shaped and dominated comedy in the American theater for forty years. In that realm, no man was his peer and few women refused him. Two wives, one daughter, an unknown number of mistresses, sixteen known collaborators, forty-five plays, twenty-six hits, two Pulitzer Prizes—small wonder that *Variety* credited Kaufman with the greatest track record in the history of the American theater. "What the Midas touch was worth in gold, the Kaufman touch was worth in laughter. . . . Genius is the only appropriate term to apply to him," wrote John Mason Brown. John Steinbeck called him "the greatest director of our time." James Thurber dubbed him "The Man Who Was Comedy."

"A dazzling book about a fascinating man. I loved it."

—Jean Kerr, author of *Please Don't Eat the Daisies*

"Readable, quotable and spicy enough to make it everyone's favorite reading for the months ahead." —Thomas Lask, *The New York Times*

A DELL BOOK $1.95

If you enjoyed *The Anderson Tapes*
this is your kind of book!

11 HARROWHOUSE

by GERALD A. BROWNE

Here is a novel in the Hitchcock tradition of
high adventure, romance, and suspense, a story
combining an ingenious *Rififi*-like theft with an
ensuing chase that moves across many of the
exotic faces of Europe. The place is 11 Harrow-
house, a dignified structure in London's posh
Mayfair district. The target is deep within its
subterranean vault—some thirteen billion dollars' worth of diamonds. J. Clyde Massey, a man
whose personal wealth runs into billions, com-
missions the heist not for love of money but
for the pleasure of revenge. For his operatives
he selects a most unlikely crew: Chesser, a diamond merchant, and his sensuously beautiful
mistress, Maren.

A DELL BOOK $1.50

If you cannot obtain copies of this title at your local bookseller, just send
the price (plus 15c per copy for handling and postage) to Dell Books, Post
Office Box 1000, Pinebrook, N. J. 07058.

If you enjoyed *The Forsyte Saga*
this is your kind of book!

THE ATHELSONS

by JOCELYN KETTLE

The Athelsons had ruled their vast estate in
Lancaster, England, for a thousand years. As the
novel opens they are fighting a desperate battle
against the changes brought by the dawning of
the twentieth century. To the isolated manor
house comes Justine, the beautiful young
daughter of a black sheep of the Athelsons.
Now her father is dead, and Justine is invited
to take her place as a member of the family. She
falls in love with the Athelsons and the land
they rule and care for—and she falls in love, too,
with her handsome cousin, Athel. But her
grandfather, as head of the family, forbids a
marriage between the two cousins. Here is a
novel that brings to life a vanished time, a
vanished breed of human beings, a vanished
code of conduct and honor. "Passion and nos-
talgia . . . close to Delderfield."

—*Kirkus Service*

A DELL BOOK $1.50

If you cannot obtain copies of these titles at your local bookseller, just
send the price (plus 15c per copy for handling and postage) to Dell Books,
Post Office Box 1000, Pinebrook, N. J. 07058.

From the publisher who brought you
the 6 million copy bestseller
The Doctor's
Quick Weight Loss Diet

THE TRUTH ABOUT WEIGHT-CONTROL

by NEIL SOLOMON, M.D.

In this informative guide, a Johns Hopkins-trained specialist who has spent ten years treating the problems of obesity in more than 1000 patients tells how to lose excess pounds—and how to keep them off. Dr. Solomon covers such topics as fad diets, the health hazards of obesity, the reasons one overeats, and the dangers of diet clubs and diet pills. This is the first weight-control book to pass the rigorous standards of the Book-of-the-Month Club.

A DELL BOOK $1.50

If you cannot obtain copies of this title at your local bookseller, just send the price (plus 15c per copy for handling and postage) to Dell Books, Post Office Box 1000, Pinebrook, N. J. 07058.

HOW MANY OF THESE DELL BESTSELLERS HAVE YOU READ?